PATRICK YOUNG ALEXANDER

1867 - 1943

Patron and Pioneer of Aeronautics

A Biography by
Gordon Cullingham
C.Eng., M.I.C.E., A.R.I.C.S., M.R.T.P.I.

Designed and typeset by Thameslink Ltd.,
38a, Thames Street, Windsor. SL4 1PR
Telephone: Windsor (07535) 63356
Printed by Lucas Graphics Ltd., Bracknell, Berks.
Cover design by Mike Magee.
Cover cartoon by courtesy of the Library of Congress,
Washington, U.S.A.

By the same author:

'The Royal Windsor Tapestry Manufactory, 1876-1890'

Handlist of Tapestries woven at the Old Windsor works.

Published by the Royal Borough of Windsor & Maidenhead, 1979.

© Gordon G. Cullingham, 1984
ISBN No: 0-9509 196-0-8

First published MCMLXXXIV by:

Cross Manufacturing Co. (1938) Ltd.
Midford Road, Combe Down, Bath, England. BA2 5RR
Telephone: Combe Down (0225) 837000

ACKNOWLEDGMENTS

Harald Penrose and his book "British Aviation, the Pioneer Years" pointed me in the right direction for research, which originally was for an article for our local history journal, WINDLESORA. Early in my research, the Cross Manufacturing Co. Ltd. of Bath suggested that I should write a comprehensive biography, a proposal that I accepted most gladly. I have had valuable help not only from Messrs. Cross and Co. Ltd., but also from the Science Museum and Library, the Library of Congress, Washington D.C. and the University of Texas, U.S.A., the Maritime Memorial University of Newfoundland, the Battye Library, Perth, Western Australia, the Public Record Office, the National Maritime Museum, Greenwich, and the local history and reference sections of libraries in Bath, Dover, Farnborough, Maidstone, Portsmouth, Redruth, and Windsor, the Windsor Guildhall Exhibition, the Royal Aeronautical Society, the R.A.F. Museum, Colindale, the Royal Meteorological Society and the Meteorological Department at Bracknell, Imperial Service College Junior School at Windsor, Haileybury College, and the County Record Offices of Berkshire, Hereford and Worcester, Kent and South Yorkshire.

Many people who knew Patrick Alexander and his work have helped me to obtain a balanced picture of this remarkable man. I would like to thank the following individuals and organisations for help, information and guidance given during research. Alphabetical order seems to be the least invidious method but does not reflect the amount of invaluable assistance given:

R.C.B. Ashworth;
J. Baker;
L.F. Baker;
Selina Ballance;
E.A.S. Beckwith M.A.;
H.L. Burgess, Batheaston;
G. Camm;
Cathy Clements, Mount Lawley, Western Australia;

S. Cody;
A.E. Coles;
H.F. Cowley;
L.R. Day, Keeper of the Science Museum Library;
Ian Duff B.A., F.R.A.S.;
D. Eunson, Trinder Anderson & Co.;
J.I.M. Forsyth, Bath;
P.S. Gilson, Falmouth;
Mike Goodall;
J.A.S. Green M.A.
Horst Hassold, Augsburg;
A. Helme;
Cathy Henderson, University of Texas;
M.H.H. Hobart;
L.W. Hoskins;
Judith Hunter;
R. Iwaschkin, Divisional Library, Farnborough;
Mrs. Audrey Kemp, Easter Dalchreichart;
A. King;
V.J. Kite, Area Librarian, Bath;
E.M. Lewis, Combe Down;
P.J. Loobey;
C. Love;
Alec Lumsden;
Rev. P.R.L.L. Morgan, Haileybury Junior School;
Valerie Moyar, Texas;
K. Matthews, Maritime History Group, Memorial University of Newfoundland;
Bob Mainwood;
A.W.L. Naylor, Royal Aeronautical Society;
Osbourne Studios, Falmouth;
Harald J. Penrose O.B.E., C. Eng.;
T.E. Pugh;
R. Putnam;
Dr. E. Richards, Worcester;
Mrs. Imogen Thomas, Haileybury College;
H. Mary Wills, Bath;
M. Woods, Meteorological Archives, Bracknell;
The Department of Cultural Resources, Raleigh, North Carolina, U.S.A.;
The Royal Geographical Society;
The Royal Cornwall Polytechnic Society, Falmouth;
The Windsor, Slough & Eton Express.

I am indebted to K. Marson, Mrs. A. Spittle and G. McDermott for French, Italian and Russian translations respectively.

Most valuable help with research has been given by Barbara Bassil, also Fiona Hunter and Pam Marson, who helped with photographic work.

Patrick and Christopher Stamford spared time from their whirlwind tours of Europe to delve into records for me before returning to Sydney, New South Wales.

My thanks are due to Miss Penni Dymond who transformed a paper chase of draft manuscript into word processed discipline, and to my son, Roger, who relieved me of the problems of publication, also Mrs. June Rogers who diligently read and corrected the draft manuscript.

If time and trouble spent on my behalf determined precedence, the first place would go to Mollie, my wife, whose help throughout the period of research and preparing the manuscript included keeping me supplied with photocopies without which I would have taken even longer to finish the drafts.

Last but not least, the generous help and encouragement of the Cross Manufacturing Co. Ltd. of Combe Down, Bath who sponsored this work and whose interest in Patrick Alexander stems from the fact that R.C. Cross, the founder of the company, was himself closely concerned with aeronautics and as a boy knew Alexander during the period of his ballooning experiments in Bath.

I am most grateful, and offer apologies for any inadvertent omissions.

Gordon Cullingham,
54 Alma Road,
Windsor,
Berkshire.
June 1984

CONTENTS

FOREWORD

Patrick Y. Alexander was a big man, physically and mentally and with a sense of humour. His conversation was ahead of his times, and covered every field of scientific endeavour. He was always well informed, both from personal knowledge and from the world's press. Lamed at the age of 18 in an accident at sea, he turned to aeronautics and aviation.

Losing both his parents and his elder brother in his early twenties, he inherited some £60,000 in 1890, and this enabled him to give generously of his time and ability in an endeavour to keep Great Britain in the van of aeronautical scientific knowledge. It was his personal ambition to be the first to fly - an ambition he might well have achieved but for bad luck - and his often painful lameness. For all his wealth and ability, he was not a lucky man.

He found that the work of Victorian aeronautical inventors had sometimes been anticipated and previously patented and so, with his friend Griffith Brewer, he published a book in 1893 entitled *"Aeronautics 1815 – 1891"*. This contained practical as well as absurd inventions once intended to master the unsolved problem of aerial navigation. They added that . . . . "aerial navigation is not an *impossibility* but only a *difficulty,* which may be mastered by careful study and perseverance."

He was one of the first acronauts to own a private balloon, which he used at Bath, where he made and used a parachute. He took the lead in sondes meteorological balloon work in England, and represented his country in European meteorological research. Highly regarded abroad, especially in Germany, he was invited to join prestigious balloon ascents, met many of the European royalty and assisted in the first Zeppelin flight. He was the first to demonstrate that wireless could be used for the automatic remote control of flying machines.

He did not have the higher technical training of, say, Sir Roy Fedden, nor the Wright brothers single minded dedication, and he was overtaken by those whose training, resources and ability achieved what he was unable to achieve—aerial navigation. He certainly succeeded in becoming one of the first aeronautical and aviation archivists by reason of obtaining and keeping the world's press reports on progress in newspaper cuttings books. These amounted to over 120 books each of from 200 to 400 pages between 1892 and 1913. They are now highly valued archives in the Science Museum library, with the other scientific books he donated.

No dilettante, he travelled widely, was a frequent visitor to U.S.A. where he was a friend of Octave Chanute and the Wright brothers, but his reports of the latters' progress and achievements were not at first believed. He tried to be an eye witness at a time when objective reports were few, and reporting was largely by relatively ignorant reporters. An entrepreneur and a patriot, he was closer to British Army aeronautical work than a civilian could expect to be, and was at times regarded abroad as a British Government agent, by reason of the knowledge he acquired during his travels, and his many visits to U.S.A. from 1902 to 1916.

He enthusiastically supported and led the education of youth in aviation and science. He built and operated workshops, sponsored courses, and made donations to the Aeronautical Society which averted bankruptcy. To the United Services College he gave two fully equipped workshops for studying aviation. He built a full size glider in which, tethered in the blast from a wind machine, the boys could practice airmanship. The glider was towed into flight at Gosport. The school became the Imperial Service College, to which he made a gift of £10,000. He helped many needy inventors, a reputation that resulted in him being regarded as a "soft touch". For some reason he expected to die by the time he was 50, and by the time he was 55, he was in danger of bankruptcy, being rescued by his aeronautical friends and the Imperial Service College, Windsor. He died almost penniless in 1943, a proud man who resisted charity.

This is not a history of aviation—to set out the triumphs and failures of those days would take many volumes—but the biography of a man the value of whose work was not recognised in his lifetime.

Chapter 1

Aeronautics and Aviation in 1867

At the time of Patrick Alexander's birth, a number of technically minded men were giving increasing attention to aeronautics, (flight by lighter than air machines), and aviation, (flight by heavier than air machines). He was to live through, and participate in the period of the burgeoning of aviation.

He was born on March 28th, 1867, at Hern Villa, Belvedere, Erith, Kent, to Andrew Alexander and his wife, Harriotte Emma, formerly Young, from Tydd St. Mary, Cambridge. Andrew Alexander was a mechanical engineer from St. Andrews, Scotland. His family came from the Gorbals, Glasgow. The Alexanders had another son, John Edmond, three years older than Patrick.

A civil engineer of some standing, with an office in the City, Andrew Alexander was keenly interested in aeronautics and aviation and as a mechanical engineer he was able to combine his interests with practical knowledge. He became a founder member of the Aeronautical Society in 1866 and read a paper to the society in 1868, "Power in Relation to Weight in Aerial Navigation", which was published in the third annual report. Another paper by him, "Aerial Flight as Dependant on Man's Muscular Exertion", was included in the sixth annual report of the Society. The President of the new Aeronautical Society was the Duke of Argyll and members were men of science and foresight who were determined to solve the problems of mechanical flight. They began to pool and publish their knowledge and experimental results as never before.

Some technically trained men were known to Patrick's father. One such was Francis Herbert Wenham, (1824 – 1908), who read his important paper "Aerial Locomotion" to the Aeronautical Society in 1866. In 1874, Wenham's experiments impressed Octave Chanute, (1832 – 1910), then a 42 year old American railroad and bridge engineer visiting England. Chanute built the first great bridge over the Missouri river and gathered historical and contemporary information methodically from all over the world, eventually publishing the first scientific, definitive history of aviation, "Progress in Flying Machines", in 1894.

The history of aviation is littered with "solutions" to the problem of powered flight by man, which proved ineffective.

Wenham later conducted a fruitful correspondence with Octave Chanute.

1

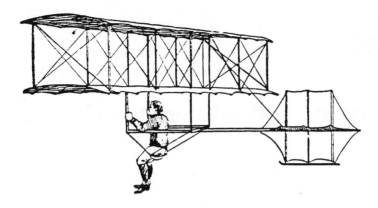

Octave Chanute's Hang Glider of 1894

Patrick Alexander was to be attracted by Chanute's 'hang glider' designs from 1894 and by those by the German Otto Lilienthal of 1895 as were many designers, including the Wright brothers. Patrick Alexander was to copy into a book of typescript manuscripts many of the papers read in the last few decades of the 19th century as well as illustrating them with drawings.

But this was in the future. In 1871, when Patrick was four, the Alexander family moved to 7, Lansdown Terrace, Worcester. It was a pleasant early Victorian house, one of a walled group on a steep hillside with views across the Severn Valley and the city of Worcester.

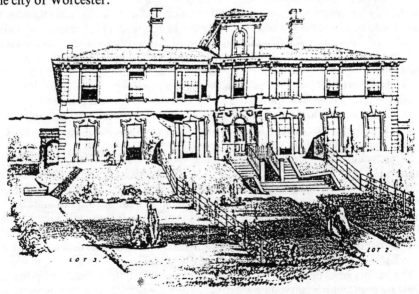

The Alexanders' Home In Worcester in 1871

From the time of the first successful Montgolfier hot air balloon ascents in 1783, it was realised that aerial navigation was possible, but the problems of mechanical flight and heavier than air machines appeared such that most of the scientific world could not be persuaded to take the idea seriously. There were "flappers", who tried to copy the flight of birds with their 'ornithopters' and tower jumpers who for centuries had tried to glide safely from the heights with contraptions fixed to their bodies, with monotonous lack of success.

The list of machines that failed to fly grew longer. 'Flappers' quickly flapped themselves to pieces, helicopters were impotent to raise their weight, but a few models did fly well, powered by elastic, steam, or clockwork. The hang glider appeared between 1891 and 1896, designed by Otto Lilienthal (1848 – 1896), the German pioneer. Patrick was to contact him, as he contacted everyone whose designs showed promise. Many he was to help financially. He was known for his unobtrusive generosity.

In 1875 his father went to see Moy's "Aerial Steamer" at the Crystal Palace. Driven by steam, this represented in tethered flight, the result of 10 years experimental work. It had two wings, a 3 h.p. engine driving twin fan type propellers, and lifted itself all of six inches off the ground. Unfortunately it was wrecked in a storm and had not impressed the doubters, but Andrew Alexander told his sons that we should all one day be travelling in aeroplanes, and not balloons, (nor presumably, airships).

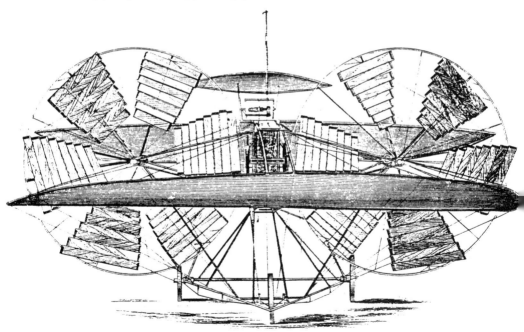

Moy's 'Aerial Steamer' tested at the Crystal Palace in 1875. The tandem wing, steam driven machine lifted just clear of its circular track.

3

4

About 1875, Andrew became manager of the Cyclops works of Charles Cammell & Company in Sheffield, 'Manufacturers of Rolled Iron Armour Plate to the Admiralty'. In 1881, when Patrick was 14, the family were living at Ivy House, 209, Western Bank, Leavy Greave, which now forms part of the site of Sheffield University. The 1881 Census shows that the Alexander household included a cook and a housemaid.

Andrew Alexander was one of a team that grappled with the problems of naval armour against shell fire which was becoming increasingly powerful. Previously, 'The Warrior' of 1860 had 4" iron armour with 18" of teak backing and half inch thick iron lining. This was not enough. The 'Bellerophon' of 1865 had 6" armour, the 'Hercules' of 1868 had 9" and the 'Devastation' of 1871 had 12" armour. By 1876 the 'Inflexible' had armour some 24" thick and it became obvious that iron alone was not sufficient. Cammell and Co. started to make a compound armour of iron with a steel face which was fitted to the battleships of the 1880's.

Later, solid steel armour and tempered armour of nickel steel enabled the thickness to be reduced, even though guns continued to increase in power. The 'Wilson Compound Plate', made by Cammell and Co. was not improved for many years.

The young Patrick went to school at Wesley College, one of the most popular and successful educational establishments in the district, on the Glossop Road, Sheffield. The College had a Royal Warrant constituting it a college of the University of London, with power to issue Certificates of Bachelor and Master of Arts and also Bachelor and Doctors of Law. He probably learned the basic French and German that would be so useful to him during his travels.

Patrick Alexander became interested in practical aeronautics at an early age, no doubt encouraged by his father. In 1878, he built his first elastic driven aeroplane, a "Penaud" type, which flew well.

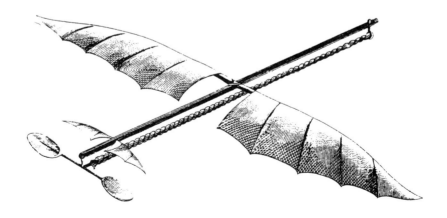

Penaud's 'Pusher' model monoplane, 1871

Alphonse Penaud, (1850 – 1880), would have followed his father, a French admiral, into the Navy had it not been for a hip disease, so he devoted much time to aeronautical design and his rubber driven models were to do much to foster airmindedness among youth. Patrick was delighted when his model flew. It had a wing span of 18″, a wing area of 76 sq. ins, with the wings bent up at the ends to provide a 'dihedral', or shallow 'V' as viewed from the front. The small diamond tailplane also had dihedral tips. The 8″ propeller was at the rear - it was a 'pusher-type' design.

Model aeroplane clubs became popular and by the Edwardian era, young men everywhere were given an opportunity to participate in the new sport. Patrick was growing up in the last decades of the Victorian era, when aeronautics were mainly for the well-off.

The relatively stable Penaud design, and similar aircraft were difficult for a pilot to control and manoeuvre and it was not until the 20th Century that the Wright brothers designed an unstable aeroplane that had its equilibrium in the air maintained by the actions of the pilot. None of this was previously understood.

Andrew Alexander considered that mechanical powered flight was possible and would come, but Patrick's thoughts turned to the design of devices for steering balloons. Some of these were to be patented but none were really successful.

During the school holidays of the late summer of 1878, Patrick was taken by his father to see the Paris Exhibition. There was the excitement of the long journey from Sheffield to London and then to Dover, where they boarded the new "Calais - Douvres" twin screw steamer from the Admiralty pier. This was followed by the train journey across the strange and not particularly interesting French countryside to Paris, where their luggage was examined. The wonders of the great Exhibition overwhelmed him.

The Trocadero, situated on a hill, formed the Grand Entrance. This was in the shape of a semi ellipse, the Grand Festival Hall forming the centre, and flanked with two towers that were ascended by lifts. The hill sloped down to the Seine, one feature being a cascade of water. The houses of Algeria, Egypt, Tunis, Persia, Monaco, China and Japan, to name a few, were on either side of the way down to the river, with many more curious details and exhibits. Near where the Seine was crossed by a bridge was a large head in bronze, about 30 feet high. This they found was to become part of a great symbolic figure designed by Frederic Auguste Bartholdi to be presented to the United States by the French people to be called the 'Statue of Liberty'. The head towered above the nearby buildings, and was a sight that Patrick would never forget, being reminded every time he sailed into New York, sometimes in great ships brilliantly lit, and sometimes in ships darkened to avoid unwelcome attention from U-boats.

Apart from the magnificent buildings and their contents, the attraction for Patrick and his father was the great balloon of the veteran Henry Giffard. This was capable of taking 52 passengers up at a time.

It was filled with nearly 900,000 cubic feet of hydrogen, which had taken 3 days to produce from 180 tons of sulphuric acid and 80 tons of iron turnings, and was held captive by a huge steam winch, which allowed it to ascend to over 1,600 feet, then hauled it down again. Passengers paid 20 francs a head, and while watching

The Statue of Liberty in Paris

the monster make an ascent, Patrick and his father waited for their turn. It was a fine weather amusement, and no advance upon the steam driven dirigible that Giffard had demonstrated 27 years earlier, but the excitement of the ascent deeply impressed the young Patrick Alexander.

There was much else to see, including the British Pavilion with its Prince of Wales Dining Room, brilliant with silver and glass, the walls hung with Royal Windsor tapestries depicting "The Merry Wives of Windsor" which flanked the tapestry portrait of Queen Victoria, as well as the Arts and Industrial products of many countries.

Obviously, there were many more sights to see and marvel at in the great Paris Exhibition than any one person could take in, let alone a small boy on his first visit to a foreign country, but Patrick Alexander left with a taste for travel as well as a keener interest than ever in aeronautics.

Before Patrick left school in 1884, the Tissandier brothers had demonstrated an electrically propelled elongated balloon at the Paris Exhibition of 1881.

On December 12th, 1881, Walter Powell, M.P. ascended from Bath gasworks, (using a balloon supply later to be used by Patrick), in the War Office balloon Saladin, on loan to the Meteorological Society. The head of the Army balloon factory at Aldershot, Captain Templer, and Lieutenant Agg-Gardner accompanied him. The latter took the place of Major Trollope, Grenadier Guards, whose train arrived late, so that he missed the flight. They went up through the winter cloud and snow taking meteorological readings, the wind apparently being northeast and taking them towards Cornwall. But on descending they were appalled to hear the sound of breakers—the wind had turned northerly and they were rapidly nearing the cliff edge near Bridport. Hastily discharging gas, they crash landed. Templer and Agg-Gardner, along with the ballast, were thrown clear but Walter Powell appeared to hesitate and the lightened balloon with him still in the basket shot up and out to sea, never to be seen again.

The accident was widely reported at the time and long remembered, especially in Bath and Malmesbury.

It was to Bath that the Alexanders moved from Sheffield when Andrew left the Cyclops works, but first Patrick was to enter the great iron and steel works learning the mysteries of plate rolling. It was not long before he decided he would prefer to go to sea as an apprentice Merchant Navy officer.

Chapter 2

1885: Patrick Y. Alexander goes to Sea

Patrick Alexander's Indentures for 4 years with J. R. Anderson of 4, St. Mary Axe, London, are dated 1st April 1885, just 3 days after his 18th birthday.

The firm was about to become Trinder and Anderson, later of Leadenhall Street, London, whose West Australian Line barques sailed between London and West Australia, calling at Fremantle. Some of the larger barques went to Sydney and Adelaide. It was on one of the smaller barques, the 'Minero' of 478 tons, bound for Fremantle with a general cargo, that Patrick was to sail the next day, Maundy Thursday, 2nd April, 1885.

Captain D. Davies, a Welshman from Cardigan, a man of 50 and the oldest man on board, seems likely to have had the reputation of driving his ship and his crew hard.

William Angus, an Able Seaman from Glasgow and a second apprentice, William Crowley of London, were the only members of the crew apart from the Captain who had sailed in her before. William Crowley had been apprenticed at the age of 11, and this was his third year at sea. The Minero's log gives Patrick's age as 16, but this is an error.

A crew of 14 was required by the Ship's Articles including six sailors, and eight 'Able Seamen' had signed on,—two as the ship was due to sail. William Johnson of Gothenburg, who signed on earlier failed to appear, so the ship sailed one man short. The First Mate was John Lord, 38, of London; the Second Mate Edward Richardson, 26, was from Lincoln. The ship's carpenter was Henry Lyddon, 43, from Bristol. With £5 per month, he was the third highest paid man on board, after the Captain and Mate. The other members of the crew included John Collins, the Cook and Steward from Axminster, Abdullah from Judah, Albert Ehlers of Hamburg, and James Noble of Belfast. Two others were to desert at Fremantle— Charles Jones of Witchford and the cabin boy, John Pitt. The last to sign was John Hardie, of "Stew Bedford".

The Articles specified the scale of provisions, commencing with the daily issue of lime and lemon juice "and other antiscorbutics required by 30th and 31st Victoria c.124, s.4;" 1lb. of bread daily, 1lb. 8 ozs. of beef on Sundays, Tuesdays, Thursdays and Saturdays, and 1lb. 4ozs. of pork on each of the other days of the week, plus half a pound of flour three times a week, and similarly one third pint of peas. There was a daily ration of one eighth of an ounce of tea, half an ounce of coffee, 2 ounces of sugar, and 3 quarts water. NO SPIRITS ALLOWED was stamped on each form. Some of the crew made an allotment from their wages, none of which exceeded £3 a month and that only after the first month - the deduction of the first month's wages was to cover the cost of their sea going clothes, or 'sea chest'.

The 'Minero' was built on the Clyde two years earlier, and owned by a Californian man. She was typical of the iron and steel barques built after 1875 towards the end of the era of sail. Some were to survive - mostly under the Finnish flag, until the second World War.

A typical barque of the 1880's

A barque was square rigged on the foremast and mainmast, this was ideal for sailing before the wind. The mizzen mast had 'fore and aft' rigging.

As an apprentice, Patrick had everything to learn, including noting the exact second that the Time Ball dropped at 1p.m. on the Greenwich Observatory roof, and checking the ship's chronometer for accuracy.

The scene as the Minero sailed was one of the usual apparent disorder with cargo to be checked for safety at sea, ropes coiled, stores stowed in the proper order for use as needed, and an unpractised crew to be licked into shape despite hang overs. It was a 'dry' ship, and the crew had enjoyed their last drinks for many weeks, some not wisely but too well. A steam tug pulled them clear of the crowded docks into clear water, sails were set, and they were off.

The temperature was falling—it was 7 degrees colder than the previous day, and the WSW wind was freshening. This helped them to clear the Thames estuary, and then they were sailing down channel with a brisk wind astern, as it had conveniently gone round to the NNE, there being an anticyclone over Ireland. Ahead was the Bay of Biscay—and a NE gale, as the Captain had learned. It was not long before Patrick Alexander was realising the full meaning of "Oh!" in the song "Bay of Biscay, Oh!" As the days passed, with the weather getting warmer, the first porpoises gambolled about their bows, the first flying fish appeared, a school of whales was sighted, and sea sickness abated at last. The sun was hot at midday, as they sailed south-west towards South America in the trade winds. A glimpse of the distant island of Madeira was followed two days later with a sight above the horizon of the Canary Island peaks.

When the wind failed, ships with engines left them behind, to wallow in the oily swell, until a breeze took them on their way.

Short handed as they were, it was hard work each and every day. Patrick learned that they were in the tropics and 200 miles west of Cape Blanco, the most westerly point of Africa and the Sahara desert. Three days later they were looking for a sight of the Cape Verde islands.

As they approached the equator, they enjoyed the easterly "trade winds" that blow westwards towards America, which had terrified the crew of Columbus and which seemed to preclude their ever being able to sail east again.

Entering the doldrums near the equator, the north-east wind dropped, and again they wallowed in the heat. At the equator, the crew made the traditional sport of those crossing for the first time. Patrick was subjected to the usual horseplay by Neptune, his Barber and their retinue, being lathered, shaved and half drowned, before it was decided he had been duly initiated. They had already been a month at sea, and now they were in mid-Atlantic, and at last came into the constant south-east winds that blow south of the equator. A week later they sighted the tiny isle of Trinidada and the Martin Vas Rocks—the last land they were to see before Australia. They had sailed over 4,500 miles and there were over 8,000 miles to go.

For another two weeks they sailed southwards, and it grew cooler then colder every day. At last some 7,000 miles out, they entered the westerly winds that blow almost continuously in the South Temperate Zone. These winds would take them all the way to Australia. But now it was mid-winter and they encountered the gales which Neptune threw at them, with every sort of foul weather that these southern latitudes can produce, especially in the winter. First they had to pass the meridian of the Cape of Good Hope. The southern tip of Africa was far to the north, and out of sight. Now there were many sea birds to be seen of many different kinds, due to the abundance of fish in the area.

The course so far had been a great arc, and far longer than the direct route followed by steamers, but sailors had learned that by following the prevailing winds, the longer voyage could be completed in less time. The fastest clipper to Australia might take only 70 days, but the Minero would be fortunate to take less than 80 days, no matter how hard Captain Davies drove his ship, and the crew. Then came calamity for Patrick. While aloft helping with the sails, he lost his grip in the cold wind and fell, breaking his leg as he hit the deck. It was 2nd June, they were 60 days out from London, hundreds of miles from anywhere, and it would be 3 weeks before they reached port in Australia. The second mate, Edward Richardson, did his best telling Patrick "My brother is a doctor, so I know what to do". But it was no joke having a broken limb, to be without expert skilled attention, and to be thrown about as the Minero rolled and plunged interminably through the heavy seas. Patrick was strapped into a bunk for the break to join up as best it might. The other members of the crew had to work harder and longer to make up for his absence. They were now two men short, and a crew of twelve instead of the fourteen required by the ship's Articles. No longer could Patrick try to use the sextant to fix the ship's position as instructed by the Mate, nor take a turn at the wheel, nor turn out to alter sail as conditions changed.

They had sailed nearly 9,000 miles in 60 days, and Cape Town to Fremantle is 4,708 miles. This distance they covered in about 20 days with the aid of the westerly winds, sometimes at gale force, with icebergs to look out for ahead.

11

At last came the cry, "Land ahead". Soon the dark outline of Rottnest Island—which was a prison for Aborigines—could be distinguished on the horizon, and they sailed towards the port of Fremantle.

With Arthur Head on the starboard and Eleanor Rocks and Entrance Rocks to port, they entered the wide Swan River and dropped anchor in Gage Roads. Captain Davies deposited the ship's Articles at the Fremantle customs on 22nd June 1885. They would be collected on 29th July when they had unloaded their cargo and planned to depart for Champion Bay, Cossack, and England via St Helena. But their departure was to be delayed, as was unloading, by bad weather.

They found the usual congested conditions at Fremantle, and George Shenton (he was Sir George Shenton in England but not in the colony), their local shipping agent, told Captain Davies that it would be a few days before they would be able to tie up to the jetty. It was possible that one of the lighters that the colonial government were providing shortly to alleviate the problem would arrive, but he was not optimistic. Complaints were terse about the delays in carrying out the official plans for improvement of what was the chief port of the colony.

They were followed in by the schooner 'Mary Smith' from Cossack, 1,000 miles north of Fremantle, whose cargo was 40 bullocks for the Fremantle butchers. These were driven bellowing over the side of the schooner to swim ashore as best they could, to where the butchers' drovers waited.

Due to rough weather it was to be 16 days before the Minero could commence unloading the cargo she carried for Fremantle, and then could only proceed intermittently.

There was much to see; at the jetty was the brig 'Laughing Wave' loading horses for Guam, and the steam ship 'Natal' preparing to leave for Singapore via some of the northern Western Australian ports. She carried passengers as well as cargo. The coastal schooner 'Minnie' entered the river and dropped anchor, as did the barque 'C. Paulsen' from London. The cutter 'Maud' was being fitted out for pearling in the northern waters.

Patrick Alexander learned that the pearling industry was carried on by naked aborigines who were employed to collect the oysters at low tide and to leave them on the shore in the sun to rot, and then boiled down in 'pogie' pots after which they cleaned the shell and bagged it for export, while collecting any pearls left in the putrifying flesh. When an easterly wind was blowing, the stench of the pogie pots could be smelt 10 miles off shore. When Patrick Alexander was in Western Australia pearling was in its heyday, and pearl buttons were made by the ton. The aborigines were reputed to swallow some pearls for trading after a voyage.

Although it was winter in Western Australia, Fremantle and Perth 12 miles upstream, were pleasant areas with farms and orchards, saw mills and boat building—both were developing fast. Fremantle was the first and last port of call for European mail carrying ships, with more cargoes to handle than the facilities could cope with.

In 1885 there were rumours of gold being found in the desert that extended for hundreds of miles east of the Darling range which bounded the coastal strip of Western Australia. It was the year of the first gold rush to a place called Hall's Creek. The great gold rushes to Kilgarn and Coolgardie were of the 1890's. Desertions were already common, and within a week of dropping anchor, Captain Davies had to report to the Water Police Station that Charles Jones, A.B. and John Pitt, cabin boy had deserted. Sailors and competent workmen were scarce, and the Water Police assisted the masters of vessels by rounding up reluctant seamen from the many licensed premises. It was the custom for masters to pay £1 into the Court at Fremantle for this service, and the money would be passed on to the police. Prison sentences passed on seamen for misdemeanours were couched in terms of so many days or weeks, or "until the vessel sails, whichever comes first". From time to time the police did actively seek out deserters, but once they had gone beyond the settled areas they were not usually pursued. The police would note any known deserters said to be up river or around a particular station as the farms were called. Unless a person of authority was likely to collect the men if the police went out and brought the deserters back, such cases were apt to be seen as "unwarranted for action" and the men would remain at large in the colony. Charles Jones and John Pitt were not heard of again in connection with the Minero. Perhaps they decided to "Go for Gold."

The Minero was now 3 crew members short, 4 counting the virtually incapacitated Alexander, and Captain Davies tried to get replacements. On 29th July he managed to get one A.B. to sign on at the Water Police Station, where the Captain recovered the ship's articles, and paid the sums due. Between then and 10th August the Minero was reported to be at Fremantle or Champion Bay, and may have made voyages back and forth. She finally was reported as sailing from Fremantle at 3.30 p.m. with "original cargo" being piloted to the north of Rottnest Island on 7th August, and arriving at Champion Bay on 10th August "with English Mail". This was another unlucky day for Patrick Alexander.

In the North West Division of Western Australia, Cossack and Port Walcott are some 1,000 miles north from Fremantle, including 180 miles through the Dampier Archipelago. With a population of under 200, plus uncounted aboriginals, Cossack was hot, dry and uncomfortable, being 500 miles into the tropics. But there were goldfields inland in the West Pilbarra, and cargoes of wool and pearlshell for small ships like the Minero. At that time the maps of Western Australia implied that half the area of nearly 1,000,000 square miles consisted of goldfields. Some huge fortunes were made in the area, but many staked their all, and lost.

Great storms sweep in from the Indian Ocean, and violent typhoons wreck the coastal and pearling fleets. In some areas the temperature greatly exceeds 100 degrees fahrenheit day after day.

The climate of the "Nor West of Australia" - once known as the Never Never - is violent and unpredictable, and very few people of European descent can acclimatise to live there permanently. What had been a wilderness was in process of being made a great wasteland. Sheep and cattle stations could raise water by windpumps, and the water used to grow feed for cattle and sheep.

The first settlers with their small flocks stayed near permanent surface water, then by artifical watering great areas of pasture could be stocked, and left unguarded until the time came for shearing. When the water level fell, and the pasture was overgrazed the tough merino sheep first cleared the more palatable grasses, then the coarser species, and when drought persisted, they ate the ring bark of trees and grubbed in the sand for roots before dying of hunger and thirst. The native plants lost their capacity to recuperate and when rains did come, the structure of the soil broke down, making vast deserts. The West Australian wool bonanza came and went. It was for this that the Cutty Sark was transferred to the Australian wool trade when the Suez Canal opened in 1869.

Then there were the gold strikes. The Western Australians had dreamed of rich alluvial fields being discovered to match the miracles of 1850 and 1851 in New South Wales and Victoria. Then in 1885—when Patrick Alexander was there—Charles Hall and James Slattery found alluvial gold at Hall's Creek, 200 miles inland from Wyndham, the tiny port of the Kimberley country. Within a few months hundreds of men had set out to trek to Hall's Creek, some with little more than a pack, a pick and a shovel. Many died from thirst and heat exhaustion, or were drowned in flash floods. Those that survived risked dysentry and typhoid.

Small sailing ships and barques like the Minero brought in supplies, and carried away the bales of wool and bags of pearl shell from the little ports of Cossack, Port Walcott, De Grey landing, Carnarvon and Onslow, Broome and Roebourne. The Minero was the first wool ship to negotiate Condon Creek and to load there. Thousands of "get rich quick" immigrants were attracted to the area, and found that the aboriginal tribes were more warlike than those of the south. The casualty rate was high, and conditions were most unlikely to have attracted Patrick Alexander. A raconteur in later years, not one of his tales apparently mentioned the Minero or Western Australia, only that when going round the Cape he broke his leg and hence his lameness.

With the shortage of crew, Patrick Alexander had to help to the limit of his capacity. He was getting about with the aid of a crutch. Then came another mishap, as the Captain related in his log which he entered up on 29th November 1885, the day after leaving Port Walcott and Cossack for England:

"Patrick Alexander left the ship Monday 10th August at Champion Bay. Having broken his leg on June 2nd, getting on well but this day his crutch slipped he fell and broke the same leg in the same place... was taken to Hospital. To join the ship at Cossack November 26th...his effects forwarded to Champion Bay...Patrick to come home by Helena Mean.

On 10th August the Minero was approaching the anchorage at Champion Bay in rough weather. The deck was wet and slippery when Patrick Alexander slipped and fell heavily—he was a big young man. He was lucky to be near the only hospital for hundreds of miles, especially as the weather was getting worse.

He was taken to the Victoria Hospital at Geraldton, the township that adjoins Champion Bay, both are on the Greenough River. With a population of under 2,000, Geraldton was the port for loading lead ore which was useful for the purpose of 'stiffening the ship' for the long voyage home round Cape Horn. It was also the port for the Murchison Goldfield, 280 miles inland.

The Minero was expected to sail from Champion Bay for Cossack and the Nor' West on Saturday 15th August, but the weather became worse, until it developed

Victoria Hospital, Geraldton Hospital, Western Australia, 1885 Photo. 2306B, courtesy of the Battye Library, Perth, W.A.

into what was recorded as "unprecedented heavy gales." With both anchors out, the Minero had to ride it out and wait for better weather, but instead it got worse and worse, and on Tuesday night, 18th August, first one cable parted, then the other anchor started to drag, and the barque was in danger of being wrecked on a lea shore.

Captain Davies managed to get a message to the shore for another anchor to be brought out and the "Daylight" was chartered for this perilous undertaking. She made a brave attempt, but was driven ashore without reaching the Minero. Fortunately the gales at last abated, and the Minero sailed for Cossack on the Thursday morning, 20th August. She reached Cossack on 30th August, and called at the De Grey river landing for loading wool from local stations. She returned to Cossack on 26th November and departed from there fully loaded for London via St. Helena on 28th November without Patrick Alexander. There is no record of his being a passenger on the Helena Mena, and he may have returned as a passenger on another sailing.

His name does not appear on the crew lists of the returning Minero nor of the Helena Mena. The Helena Mena, a composite barque of 673 tons was built at Sunderland in 1876 and named Helena after the eldest daughter of one partner in the ship, Mr. J.T. Monger, and Mena after the eldest daughter of the other partner, Sir George Shenton. Monger and Shenton were the Western Australian agents for Trinder, Anderson and Company since 1880. She would arrive from London about September and aim to sail for London as soon as the cargo of great bales of wool and bags of pearl shell could be stuffed into the hold, with Jarrah wood and lead ore as "stiffening".

The Minero arrived back in London on 27th March 1886, after a voyage of nearly 18 weeks from Port Walcott. All the barques came back "Round the Horn", a voyage of nearly 15,000 miles consisting of over 6,370 miles eastwards Fremantle to Cape Horn, then north eastwards across the South and North Atlantic to London.

When the crew of the Minero were paid off on arrival in London, no one received any extra pay for sailing short-handed, and the shipping company saved having to pay anything in respect of the two deserters.

As the Helena Mena was bigger, with a crew of 18, she might be able to make a faster voyage home than the Minero, especially as the latter now had a crew of only 11.

Leaving Fremantle on 14th January 1886, the Helena Mena arrived in London on 19th April after a voyage of 96 days, nearly 14 weeks.

Patrick Alexander's indentures were cancelled nearly 4 months later on 11th August 1886. Despite treatment in England, it was clear that he would be lame for life.

The 'Helena Mena'

Chapter 3

And so to Ballooning at Bath

Patrick's father had retired, and the family now lived in Lansdowne, Bath in a large terrace town house, 8, Portland Place, with a fine view over the city. The convalescent Patrick Alexander resumed his interest in aeronautics, in which he had faith at a time when few people had even seen a balloon drift across the sky, with aeronauts in its flimsy basket peering down at the earth below.

It took even greater faith in science to believe in heavier than air flying machines, but his father was one of those who was convinced it could be done. Sir George Caley had come near the secret with his designs of 1809/1810, published in his classic triple paper on aviation, and with the glider he built in 1853. This had been launched on the first man carrying flight, bearing his coachman as ballast.

Attempts to propel airships were bedevilled by the inadequate power and excessive weight of the motors available. The designs of William Henson in 1843 for an "Aerial Steam Carriage" had been taken up and their virtues and capabilities overstated so that they fell into disrepute. Henson's friend John Stringfellow of Chard had made an improved model which Patrick and his father knew about, and in 1905 Patrick was to salvage and have repaired the relics of Stringfellow's machines for presentation to the Victoria and Albert Museum, as examples of Aeronautical Archaeology.

While he had been at sea there had been the Second Aeronautical Exhibition at the Alexandra Palace, and there was increasing interest among some scientists about flight. Bristol University now had a wind tunnel with a fan for aerodynamic experiments. Patrick Alexander became increasingly interested in propellers, astronomy, parachutes, meteorology and balloons, and he started to study the specifications for aeronautical patents applied for by previous experimenters.

About 1888 he was occupied with experiments on syntonic (untuned) wireless telegraphy and had some contact with Oliver Lodge, Professor of Physics at Liverpool University College. Oliver Lodge was knighted in 1902. Patrick Alexander is reputed to have personally developed a coherer - an indispensable piece of apparatus in those days for wireless telegraphy.

This knowledge was to develop into his wireless controlled "Indian Mail" (as the French termed it) experiments over the Pas de Calais. Charles Dolfus, who knew Patrick Alexander well, wrote that he was a "Pioneer of Space", and confirmed that he was the first to have the idea that wireless could be used for automatic direction of airships and aeroplanes. Dolfus described the paper that Alexander wrote on the subject as "extraordinary". The "Pas de Calais" experiments were recalled in a French report in 1908 when a Mr. Branly claimed to have discovered the means of guiding torpedoes by means of radio waves. The report included a reference to the schemes of the Hungarian engineer Telsa—who also put forward the possibility of applying electrical waves as a guiding force in the air—mentioning Patrick Alexander's earlier work. Patrick Alexander gave talks upon his work, and retained an interest in radio for many years, including Cody's experiments for the Navy with aerial carrying kites.

He may not have received much encouragement from Sir Oliver Lodge, who published "The Work of Hertz and his Successors" in 1894. Lodge was the scientist whose studies were the inspiration for the initial invention of radio and on 1st June 1894 he demonstrated the essential features of a system of wireless telegraphy at the Royal Institution. He also described a coherer, then a tube of iron filings. Oliver Lodge said he could see no practical use at all for wireless telegraphy, and saw his work only as an extension of knowledge of the physical laws of electromagnetic radiation. But in Italy young Marconi saw it as a practical means of communication, and he had come to England in 1896.

Cartoon by Sir Leslie Ward of Oliver Lodge, Professor of Physics, who was knighted in 1902.

Between 1885 and 1890 Patrick Alexander suffered a series of bereavements. His elder brother John Edmond had died in May 1886, aged 22, apparently while Patrick was in, or en route from, Western Australia, then his mother Harriotte Emma died on 8th May 1887, age 46. The death of his father, Andrew, on 3rd July, 1890, aged 62 left him quite alone at the age of 23. He followed sadly their funeral processions to Lansdowne cemetary. His father had left him everything—the total amounted to £58,670, a large sum for those days, enough for a gentleman to live in considerable comfort. He decided to leave the big house in Portland Place, and went to live at the Lansdowne Grove Hotel, Bath, and then at nearby De Montalt Wood, Summer Lane, Combe Down, Bath. This house was not quite so large, and had a small factory in its extensive grounds, with a tall chimney that stood stark above the pleasant fields and hills of the area. The factory had been used to make bank note paper, and then as a furniture factory until 1905.

Patrick Alexander turned increasingly to aeronautics and meteorology in particular and science in general. Aeronautics became his almost fanatical occupation, with a fortune in the bank, and no one to say nay, he both bought and built balloons, equipped his workshops with the latest tools and machinery, and employed two or three skilled men. A public electricity supply in Bath became available in 1890, and Patrick Alexander would be keen to take a supply to power electric motors in his city workshops, but in 1902 he was still using oil engines for power at Batheaston. His engineer was the burly Mr. Carter who appears in several photographs. Another casual employee was little Charlie Poole, of London, with a history of sea-going and gas distribution work. A skilled gasman was a useful assistant for a balloonist, and he can be seen in some of the later (1902) photographs, usually wearing a wide brimmed hat, and Victorian cycling clothes.

Mr. Carter was a member of the Aeronautical Institute and Club, and in May 1902 gave talks to the members in London about Patrick Alexander's pioneer meteorological balloon experiments at Batheaston.

Patrick Alexander's first fully equipped workshop may have been the old paper mill at De Montalt Wood. The shell of another of his workshops survives and is conserved in Combe Down quarry, two miles from Bath city centre in the complex

Patrick Alexander's Balloon Workshop
(Inset: The plaque above the entrance)

19

of industrial buildings of the Cross Manufacturing Company who have placed a commemorative plaque above the entrance door.

Another workshop was in his occupation in 1894 at 24, Ballance Street, Bath, (adjoining Portland Place, where he lived before 1891). It no longer exists, nor does the prestigious one he erected later at The Mount, Batheaston, which he bought in 1900. These were his "Experimental Works, Bath" as he had printed on his letterheadings.

In 1893 these included an engraving of his meteorological station, complete with a thermometer screen with dry bulb and wet bulb vertical thermometers to calculate dew point, humidity and vapour pressure as well as maximum and minimum temperatures, a rain gauge, anemometer, and, floating up into the sky, a weather balloon or sonde. On the right hand side of the engraving is a small telescope or theodolite.

In 1891, Patrick Alexander ordered an 8″ refractor astronomical telescope with a focal ratio of F:12 made by Sir Howard Grubb of Dublin. This was erected in Bath, its subsequent history is recounted later. He needed to track pilot balloons released before starting a balloon ascent, so as to ascertain wind directions at different heights—with the tragic end of Walter Powell M.P. in mind. Bath is not far from the coast, and an ascent that carried a balloon over the sea could end in disaster.

In May 1891, there was to be a free (i.e. not captive) balloon ascent at the Naval Exhibition at Chelsea. Patrick Alexander exchanged correspondence with Griffith Brewer, a patent agent of Leeds, about the event.

"Sunday, 31st May, 1891
　　　　　　　　　　　　　　　　　　　　　　De Montalt,
　　　　　　　　　　　　　　　　　　　　　　Monkton Combe,
　　　　　　　　　　　　　　　　　　　　　　Somerset.

　　Tuesday the 9th June will suit me very well. I shall leave this about 8 in the morning and be at Chelsea at 11 where I presume the start is to be made. Thank you very much for the Photos I wanted to keep but sent them back as I thought they might be the only set. May I ask if you have any objection to my taking with me a few Thermometers and Hygrometers for observation of Dew Point. I am writing Spencer by this post.

　　　　　　　　　　　　I remain yours truly,
　　　　　　　　　　　　Patrick Y. Alexander."

His letter to Percival Spencer was to book his £5 seat on the 11 a.m. ascent from the Naval Exhibition at Chelsea.

The photographs he mentions were probably some taken from a balloon by Griffith Brewer who became a competent aerial photographer, using both manual and automatic cameras. Brewer's first balloon ascent had been a month before on 9th May 1891, when he booked a seat with C.G. Spencer and Sons for the first ascent of the season at the Naval Exhibition, Chelsea. The cost, £5, was a sum that Brewer could not afford to repeat, but he wanted to learn ballooning, so he offered to go to the Exhibition every Saturday and help prepare the balloon. If there were not enough paying passengers at £5 a head, he would pay £1 and to this arrangement

Percival Spencer, the balloon manufacturer, agreed. Whenever there were no passengers—perhaps when the weather was rough—Brewer would go up with Spencer and thus, by the end of the season, he was sufficiently skilled to take charge of a balloon as an amateur pilot. There were virtually no private balloons and hardly any private ballooning. Amateurs either hired a balloon or paid for their seats in a balloon that went up at an Exhibition. Not until 1902, with the formation of the Aeronautical Club of Great Britain—which acquired some balloons—did several members have their own private balloons.

The aeronaut on Griffith Brewer's first flight at the Naval Exhibition, Chelsea, on May 9th, 1891 was Percival Spencer. Brewer wrote of this flight in his book, 'Fifty Years of Flying':-

> "It was a windy day with low clouds. The car of the balloon filled with bags of sand and held by the ground crew was rolling about in a manner to delight the crowd. Spencer told the three passengers to get in the car. They rolled about with the ballast, bags of which were then removed until the balloon was found to lift. More bags were taken out to ensure a good lift, the order "Let's go" was given and the balloon "literally shot up into the air" . . . "We were part of the show, and nothing impressed the crowd so much as a quick ascent." In less than a minute the balloon entered the clouds and the crowd must have wondered what would become of the balloonists who enjoyed the adventure and novelty of being in the clouds followed by the surprise and delight of coming out into brilliant sunshine, with the sea of clouds rolling away into the distance."

When Griffith Brewer got home that night, he found that his father had also been at the Exhibition and told how he had seen some men get into the car of the balloon and that the balloon had rolled about in a terrible way. When it had been released it had shot up into the air and disappeared into the clouds. He did not know what had happened, but he thought they must all have been lost. Griffith Brewer told his father that he had been one of the passengers, adding that the danger "which seems apparent to everyone on the ground, is largely imaginary and is seldom experienced by those who actually go up in balloons."

When Patrick Alexander and Griffith Brewer made their ascent on 9th June, 1891, the aeronaut was Spencer's son-in-law, a Frenchman by the name of Auguste Gaudron. The four were to strike up a close friendship that continued for many years. Patrick made several ascents with Gaudron from the Crystal Palace as well as Bath and later invited him to make the Centenary Ascent from Sydney Gardens, Bath, on 8th September, 1902. This was the centenary of Andre-Jacques Garnerin's ascent from the same site in Bath in 1802. Garnerin (1769 – 1823) made the first parachute descent in England on September 21st. 1802. Gaudron made hundreds of ascents and parachute descents and also designed an airship which flew in 1897, but could not be navigated due to lack of engine power - a common fault in those days.

Patrick Alexander was one of the few with balloons of his own. He ordered from Spencer a "three-man", (some reports say "five-man") balloon which he named "Queen of the West". By mid summer 1892 he had made several trips, one of which was made with a friend of his, Philip Braham, and reported by the Bath Argus on the 14th May, 1892:-

DAY UNTO DAY

"1p.m. 3,000 feet over Weston, Philip Braham and Alexander". Such was the message on a post-card which yesterday was "dropped" us, as it were, in the most literal sense, from the clouds. Rather, I should say, it was dropped by the two gentlemen named, who were essaying an aerial trip, and picked up and posted to our address by an obliging Westonian. This morning I called round at Mr. Braham's, in George Street, and found both him and his comrade looking remarkably merry after their adventure. It appears they started from the Gas Works shortly before one o'clock, and descended at twenty minutes past two at Chewstoke, having travelled something over seventeen miles.

For upwards of an hour, Braham says, they were above the clouds and quite out of sight of land. Cloudland he describes as something making a most magnificent picture, the fleecy masses resembling as much as possible a multitude of icebergs, and combining in a lovely array of tints of every conceivable colour, while above was a deep blue sky - an Italian-like sky, quite different to anything which we see from below. Only a slight sensation of motion is perceptible when out of sight of everything but the clouds, and so rarified is the air that one can close his eyes and imagine he is not moving at all.

It is the idea of Mr. Alexander, who has made trips of this kind before, to construct some instrument which will denote speed and direction above the clouds, and other journeys are contemplated by the two gentlemen. The greatest altitude attained yesterday was 8,500 feet, and at the height of a mile a carrier pigeon was despatched, the bird shooting down like a rocket until it reached a denser atmosphere. The descent was safely accomplished on a hillside, and the aeronauts and their trappings came back from Pensford. On the last occasion Mr. Alexander covered fifteen miles in just as many minutes. Mr. Braham rather enjoyed his unique experience. "It was a most agreeable trip," he added, "and we didn't meet many people on the way!"

Editorial, Bath Argus, May 14th, 1892:-

THE BALLOON ASCENT IN BATH
Experience of the Aeronauts

"A few particulars regarding the balloon ascent made by Messrs. Alexander and Philip Braham, from Bath, yesterday, will prove interesting to many of our readers, and it was with this object that we approached these gentlemen on the subject this morning. It appears that this is only the second ascent of the balloon, which was built for Mr. Alexander by Messrs. Spencer and Sons, of London, balloon manufacturers to the Government, and the car is capable of holding five persons. It has been named the "Queen of the West," and the height from the car to the top of the balloon is 65 feet. The balloon holds 35,000 cubic feet of gas and on its first trial went at the tremendous speed of 15 miles in 15 minutes. Its motion is described as being most easy, and Mr. Braham, stated that a person blindfolded would be unable to detect any motion when sailing through the air. Yesterday the atmosphere was beautifully clear when the balloon left the mother earth shortly before one o'clock. On reaching a height of 3,000 feet postcards were thrown from the car (which contained Mr. Alexander and Mr. Braham), one of which was received at its destination. The highest altitude which the aeronauts reached was 8,500 feet, but on going up a pigeon was sent out about a mile from the earth. It dropped for a considerable distance owing to the light atmosphere in which it was liberated being unable to sustain it. The balloon, with its living occupants, got into a current which was apparently taking them towards the Forest of Dean, but after travelling amongst the clouds for about an hour and

22

a half a successful descent was made at Chewstoke, about 17 miles from Bath. While above the clouds a magnificent prospect was unfolded to the balloonists; the shadow of the clouds formed a halo around the car, which was distinctly glorious, while the colour of the firmament above was perfectly blue and brighter than Italian skies. The temperature did not drop to any great extent during the journey, which proved profitable and enjoyable to the two aerial travellers, whose primary motives in making these ascents are for purposes of meteorological observation as well as for experiments which have yet to be developed.''

Less than a month later, on the 28th June 1892, the two of them made another ascent, again reported by the Bath Herald and the Bath Argus:-

"The balloon, containing Messrs. Alexander and P. Braham, to whose ascent allusion was made in this column yesterday, was carried by a current of air in the direction of Keynsham, and then by varying currents the direction was south-west, north-west, and almost due north. Passing over the city on the first change of current the atmosphere was beautifully clear, and the view of the city was very fine, but near Malmesbury the aeronauts got into a rain-cloud and this so increased the weight of the balloon that it was deemed advisable to descend, especially as there was a wood looming near. The balloon went to a height of 6,000 feet, and several electrical observations were taken as well as attempted photographs of the earth.''

Bath Herald, 29th June, 1892:-

Our intrepid citizens, Messrs. Braham and Alexander made another visit to cloudland yesterday. Starting shortly after one o'clock their balloon steered for the direction of Keynsham, then doubled back, and the aerial voyageurs ultimately found themselves at Marshfield, where they were stranded in consequence of the inclemency of the weather, after having been aloft for just over an hour. Strawberries were enjoyed at an altitude of six thousand feet, but on coming down their cargo of the luscious fruit got hopelessly entangled with the contents of the sand bags, as the car gave a bump on reaching Mother Earth again, but this did not deter a number of Marshfield youngsters who were attracted by the unexpected visitors, from having a feast. The voyage, in spite of the rain, was an enjoyable one, and Mr. Braham, besides taking two photographs en route, made several interesting experiments in connection with the rain band, his apparatus for testing which is likely to turn out exceedingly useful. A number of facetious post cards were distributed, one addressed to the editor of a local Conservative contemporary, reading "A message from heaven. Vote for Baptie and Ayde.'' The only discomforting feature of the afternoon's trip was that the cloud clippers were to rattle back home from Marshfield on a springless cart, the contrast between that and the steady and almost unconscious motion of the balloon being decidedly in favour of the latter.''

On Saturday the 16th, July 1892, Patrick made an ascent with a 'friend from Leeds', no doubt Griffith Brewer. This time a note of scepticism crept into the Bath Journal report dated 23rd July:-

"When I saw Mr. Alexander and his friend step into the small car of a balloon on Saturday morning and give the order to "let go", I began to speculate whether the nerves of the voyagers would be equal to their daring. As the balloon was being inflated it was swayed to and fro by the wind which came as a presage of the thunderstorm. For a little time after leaving terra firma the car was tilted a little, though it appeared to right itself after it had reached a considerable altitude. At the time of the ascent it was obvious that a thunderstorm was imminent, though probably not even Mr. Clayton, the local weather prophet, anticipated that it would be of such long duration. Under these circumstances the wisdom of going up to meet the storm may well be doubted. Happily, the venturesome aeronauts reached the earth again in safety, having been up less than an hour. They saw the vivid flashes of lightning piercing the whirling inky cloud masses, and were able to gather some idea of the intensity of the storm. The grandeur of the scene doubtless left an impression which will not easily be effaced, but was it worth so hazardous a journey to obtain it? An open gas bag in a thunderstorm is not the safest vehicle in the world, and those trusting themselves to it last week might easily have paid a tragic penalty for thus voluntarily running into danger. It is difficult to see in what way the cause of science can be served by ascents under such risky conditions. I am free to admit that we have much to learn in what has been termed "the science of aerial navigation," but thunderstorms are not calculated to assist a solution of the problems."

Bath Weekly Journal - 23rd July 1892:-

"When the storm broke over the city many persons thought of the aeronauts, Mr. Alexander, of Bath, and a friend from Leeds, who made an ascent from the Gas Works at half-past twelve. It appears that they reached a considerable altitude and watched the lightning playing in different directions, but descended before the storm actually reached them, landing safely near Thornbury at twenty minutes past one. They had scarcely time to pack up their traps ere the rain descended in torrents."

"It is pleasing to note that the occupants of the balloon which ascended on Saturday from a field adjoining the Gas Works, for whom so many inquiries were made during the heavy thunderstorm which subsequently prevailed, are none the worse for their trip. Mr. Alexander was accompanied by a gentleman from Leeds, and the balloon, immediately on starting about one o'clock, soared away to a considerable altitude in the direction of Gloucester. They appear to have landed, however, before the storm was at its height, the descent being made at Alveston, near Thornbury, shortly before half-past one. The aeronauts had no sooner got again on terra firma than, as one of their friends remarked, "down came the rain," and no little inconvenience was experienced in sheltering their traps from the watery visitation."

The above newspaper cuttings come from another of Patrick Alexander's great interests—a series of Press cuttings on aeronautics and aviation dating from May 31st, 1892 to 20th September, 1913, eventually amounting to over 120 volumes, each with 200 to 400 pages. The cost was considerable, but this was not a problem for the wealthy young man to worry about.

Patrick Alexander and Griffith Brewer made a number of ascents together, sometimes from the Crystal Palace or Battersea Park, and sometimes from Bath, where a special pipe had been laid from the Bath gasworks into a field. The Bath facilities were used by balloonists as an alternative to the inflation facilities at Battersea Park, (subsequently the site of a great electrical generation station) and at Crystal Palace. At The Mount, Batheaston, he had the gas supply brought into the garden and a balloon inflation valve installed which was only removed in 1970, when a gas leak recalled its existence.

Griffith Brewer was as enthusiastic as Patrick about aeronautical matters. He had a cheerful, rounded face, with a snub nose, was stocky in build but a trifle overweight. Patrick Alexander was a big, tall man, with a bad limp and a resonant voice. He was a good singer, according to Charles Dolfus.

The Crystal Palace included an important centre for engineering and aeronautics. The great aeronautical engineer Geoffrey de Havilland (1882-1965) attended the Engineering School there from 1900 to 1903. His autobiography records memories of the work and fun and games there, and mentions such events as the 1900 Automobile Club 1,000 mile Motor Car Trial which ended at the palace. One car, a Panhard, was driven by the Hon. C.S. Rolls (1877-1910) who won a gold medal for the best performance of the 65 drivers. For relaxation Rolls was attracted to ballooning sometimes at tthe Crystal Palace, where there were ballooning facilities including a school. Patrick Alexander was among those who made ascents from the Crystal Palace, but the palace ballooning records appear to have been destroyed.

The great cricketer Dr. W.G. Grace lived near, and would assist at ascents, being photographed upon occasion. The heyday of ballooning lasted from about 1901 until around 1910.

Griffith Brewer - a painting during his period as President of the Royal Aeronautical Society, 1940-42

Photographed by his automatic camera suspended from the balloon net, August 1907. In the basket, Eustace short and Griffith Brewer. In the hoop, Oswald Short and the Hon. Claud Brabazon.

Chapter 4

The Collaborators publish "Aeronautics"

In 1893, Patrick Alexander and Griffith Brewer, the two aeronautical enthusiasts, collaborated in the publication of "AERONAUTICS", an abridgement of Aeronautical specifications for patents published by the Patent Office dating from 1815 and 1891. This book, recently reprinted in The Netherlands, contains some fascinating drawings.

The preparation of this book required a great deal of research by both Griffith Brewer and Patrick Alexander. Griffith Brewer, with his Patent Office contacts, probably did much of the extraction of specifications, while Patrick Alexander's research, based on his "Experimental Works" facilities, evaluated the designs. This is the preface of their book:-

PREFACE

Owing to the large number of specifications which have been filed at the Patent Office, it is extremely difficult for inventors of the present day to ascertain if their inventions have been anticipated.

It is hoped that those interested in the subject of Aeronautics will find this work of benefit to them in their researches, though it must not be expected that all the information contained in the specifications is comprised in so small a volume.

In the yearly indexes published by H.M. Patent Office, many inventions are included under the heading "Aeronautics" which do not particularly refer to the subject. This error in the official indexes is partly the fault of inventors who wish to cover an enormous ground under one Patent. Say, for example, an inventor patents a new motor, and states in his specification that the said motor may be employed for driving locomotives, traction-engines, ships, balloons etc. The Government would probably place that invention under each of the separate titles, comprising the apparatus to which the motor could be applied. No doubt this is the best way to evade unnecessary responsibility in compiling such indexes; but in a work of this condensed description it would be impracticable to follow their example, as the reader searching for improvements in aerial machines would hardly appreciate a light sprinkling of traction-engines or ironclad war-ships.

Many of the specifications describe inventions which are no doubt impracticable; some are even ridiculously absurd and are probably the result of dreams. All these, however, are equally included with the ingenious inventions, as in weeding them from the remainder we should make the work incomplete and therefore of little value. Besides, many practical suggestions may be gleaned from the most absurd inventions; and is it not premature to criticize a question which is still unsolved?

It has to be hoped that so many failures will not deter inventors from still striving to master the great problem of aerial navigation; for it should be remembered that aerial navigation is not an *impossibility* but only a *difficulty,* which may be mastered by careful study and perseverance.

Griffith Brewer
Patrick Y. Alexander

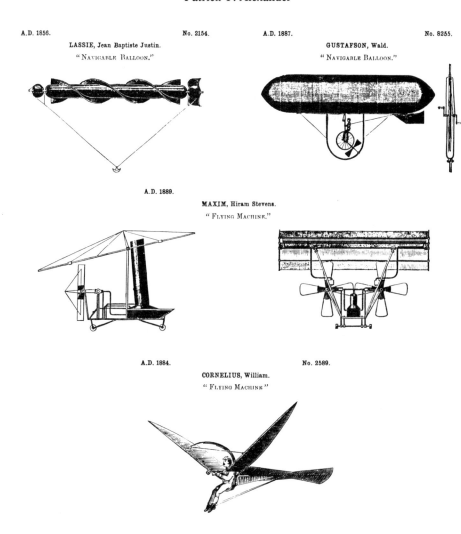

A.D. 1856.   No. 2154.

LASSIE, Jean Baptiste Justin.
" NAVIGABLE BALLOON."

A.D. 1887.   No. 8255.

GUSTAFSON, Wald.
" NAVIGABLE BALLOON."

A.D. 1889.

MAXIM, Hiram Stevens.
" FLYING MACHINE."

A.D. 1884.   No. 2589.

CORNELIUS, William.
" FLYING MACHINE "

Engravings from "Aeronautics"

27

"Industries and Iron," 29th September 1893 reviewed "Aeronautics" favourably:-

AERONAUTICS. By Griffith Brewer and P.Y. Alexander. London: Taylor and Francis. 160p.p. Crown 8vo. 6s.

"The question of air-flight is at present occupying considerable attention. It has a fascination for the chimerical worker, while the hard-headed man of business and the engineer sees in it a field in which it is self-evident there is much to be done, and rich rewards awaiting the successful designer of a practical air-ship. In reviewing such a work as the present we have little concern with the pros and cons of aeronavigation or the vexed question of planes v. lifting wheels. Likewise, we do not need to stop to consider the question of navigable balloons as compared with the vessels carrying their own ascensional machinery. It is to those who are engaged in discussing these questions that this book appeals. In itself it is nothing more than a series of carefully-compiled abridgements of the patent specifications which have been lodged with Her Majesty's Patent Office between the years 1815 and 1891, for such appliances as fall under the head of "Aeronautics," and which, when tested by common sense, do really come within such a designation. The work is well got up, is furnished with copious references and sufficient illustrations to render the text intelligible, and is printed in an excellent manner. As a guide to future workers in this field it might be recommended as an elementary text-book, largely of what to avoid. Read in connection with the articles which are appearing in our own columns from the pen of Mr F.W. Brearey, the book should prove of perhaps greater value than by itself. The weekly papers of a lighter kind have repeatedly called into requisition the services of aerial fleets, and serious-minded monthly magazines have also popularised the belief that such triumphs of engineering could, and most likely would, prove mighty engines of destruction.

In this way the call for such a book as the one before us has arisen, and in our opinion the want has been ably met by Messrs. Brewer and Alexander in the present work."

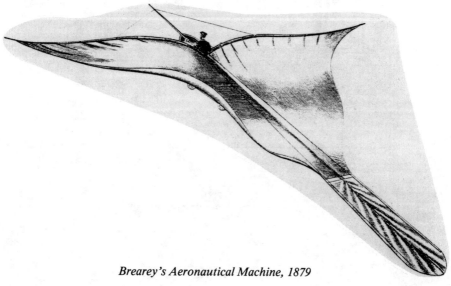

Brearey's Aeronautical Machine, 1879

Mr. F.W. Brearey was the first Hon. Secretary of the Aeronautical Society. He contacted everyone interested in aeronautics and gave lectures at which he exhibited model aircraft which flew well enough to show that mechanical flight was feasible.

On Wednesday, 7th June, 1893, Patrick Alexander wrote again to Griffith Brewer.

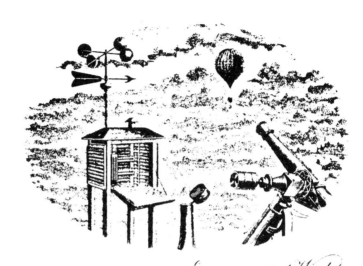

Experimental Works.
Bath England.

G . Brewer Esq.

    30 East Parade

        Leeds

Wednesday June/7/93

Dear Sir,

    G. Brewer Esq.,
     30 East Parade,
      Leeds.

                        Wednesday June/7/93

"Dear Sir,
I have to thank you very much for your letter of yesterday's date. For the past few months I have been busier that ever in experimenting with propellors in air. I have tried various shapes of varying dimensions and have settled to try a pair of reciprocating propellers (somewhat resembling the action of a fishes tail) on the balloon. I have constructed a rough model with a surface 8' long and 1' 6" broad made of fabric and wire and this was vibrated about 200 times a minute and kept pulling on a spring ballance to the amount of 35 lbs. I fancy if I can get the balloon ballanced I can work up and down without losing gas or ballast. I am going to use

two propellers working against one another and I expect a pull of between 60 and 80 lbs. the apparatus is actuated by my feet. Within the next fortnight I hope to try it. I have signed the article on balloon bursting and I think it very good. In July I think I shall go to London for a week or ten day's holiday as I am beginning to feel rather knocked up I have not been away for a regular holiday for three years,

Hoping you are quite well,
I remain,
Your truly
Patrick Y. Alexander."

(Author's note: Spellings left as the original).

Patrick Alexander was busy experimenting with improvements to balloons with the object of making them less subject to the direction of the wind. On July 7th, 1893 he applied to the Patents Office for a 'Provisional Patent Improvement In or Connected with Balloons', (No. 13264).

Etienne Montgolfier and his brother launched the first hot air balloon at Annonay on 4th June, 1783, and the former soon realised that their balloons must be navigable like boats (or "dirigible" to use the contemporary adjective since Anglicised into the noun for airships and zeppelins) and he thought that a little windmill or "moulinette" might be mounted in the gondola and turned by a crank. He also considered oars, but was persuaded that no such contrivance could win a mechanical advantage sufficient to compensate for its weight. Other inventors in France including Blanchard dreamed of making a navigable balloon. The latter claimed that waggling a sail and rudder had enabled him to tack against the wind. Perhaps Patrick Alexander believed the claim. He was convinced that the problem could be solved, just as later he was to dream of levitation, and spent much time and money on apparatus that was ineffective.

George III was interested in the French experiments, and despite discouragement by Sir Joseph Banks, President of the Royal Society, the King invited the Prussian scientist and collaborator with the Montgolfier brothers, Professor Ami Argand, to come to Windsor Castle.

On November 26th, 1783, the Royal Family were amused by a 30' balloon which Argand filled with hydrogen and then tied the neck. He handed the string to the King, and the balloon floated up to where the Queen and princesses watched from an upper window of the Castle. The King allowed the balloon to rise up to them, then pulled it down again, repeating this until eventually he released the string and Windsor's first balloon silently soared away. The problem of aerial flight was solved, but the difficulty of aerial navigation remained.

The patent no. 13,264 "to control balloons in altitude and propelled as required" was intended to fill a long felt want.

No. 13,264 A.D. 1893
Date of Application, 7th July, 1893
Complete Specification Left, 7th Apr., 1894 - Accepted, 9th June, 1894
PROVISIONAL SPECIFICATION
IMPROVEMENTS IN OR CONNECTED WITH BALLOONS

I, PATRICK YOUNG ALEXANDER, of The Experimental Works, Bath, in the County of Somerset, Gentlemen, do hereby declare the nature of this invention to be as follows:-

The object of my invention is to construct balloons in such a manner that they shall be more efficient than heretofore, while at the same time such balloons may be controlled in altitude and propelled as required.

According to my invention I fulcrum the inner ends of two oars to the hoop or other suitable part of the balloon, and a cord running through the net is attached to the outer end of such oars for the purpose of supporting their weight. Hooped irons are attached to the upper sides of the oars and cords are connected to the ends of such hoop irons from whence they pass to the car over pulleys or other suitable runners. There are thus four cords descending to the car, and a pair of stirrups are attached to the said cords in such a manner that on the stirrups being raised and lowered alternately the oars brought backwards and forwards simultaneously at an angle to the wind, and thus raise or lower the balloon as required. By lowering the supporting ropes so as to allow the propelling oars to act at an angle, the balloon may be propelled in a horizontal direction, and by elevating the supporting cords the propelling oars may be raised up beside the net and thus be out of the way when a descent is being made. Additional cords may be attached to the propellers for the purpose of raising same to the net when required.

The altitude may be varied at will by altering the temperature of the gas within the balloon. This I accomplish by means of a steam pipe which may be constructed of any suitable material, though I have found varnished silk to answer the purpose well. The said steam pipe may be situated within the balloon in any suitable way or shape, and steam is admitted to the said pipe from a generator situated in the car. It will thus be seen that by altering the supply of steam, or cutting it off entirely, the temperature within the balloon may be varied, and thus any required expansion or contraction of the gas is obtained.

Instead of the ordinary valve hitherto used I employ a long vertical tube stiffened by a spring or other suitable means, the said tube communicating with a hole in the upper part of the balloon. When it is required to allow an escape of gas, the lower part of the tube is raised by means of a cord, when the gas is free to pass through same.

I mix a blue or white pigment with the varnish employed in coating the balloon and thus render same opaque thereby preventing the rays of the sun passing through the gas.

By coating one half of the balloon with a non-transparent material and leaving the other half of a transparent nature the altitude may be varied, as by turning the opaque and transparent sides respectively towards the sun, the temperature of the gas is altered as required.

By sliding a weight or sand bag down to a knot situated on the grapnel rope the jerks imparted by the grapnel to the car may be minimised.

A suitable valve for the top of the balloon may be constructed of steel or other spring in conjunction with some textile fabric, which when in its normal position maintains a twist-like form. By pulling a cord in connection with the said valve, the twist is opened and a free passage for gas is thus made.

Dated this 7th day of July 1893.

BREWER & SON,
London and Leeds, Agents for Applicant.

No. 13,264 A.D. 1893
Alexander's Improvements in or connected with Balloons
COMPLETE SPECIFICATION.
Improvements in or connected with Balloons.
I, PATRICK YOUNG ALEXANDER, of Experimental Works, Bath, in the County of Somerset, Gentlemen, do hereby declare the nature of this invention and in what manner the same is to be performed to be particularly described and ascertained in and by the following statement:-

My invention refers to Improvements in, or connected with Balloons, as hereafter described, whereby I am enabled to vary the altitude, and effect motion in a horizontal direction, by the employment of oars operated by improved means, to further regulate the degree of altitude by variation of the expansion or contraction of gas within the balloon through variation of heat, either by rendering the balloon more or less impervious to external heat, or by imparting heat to the interior by suitably arranged steam pipes, whereby I am also enabled by an arrangement of such pipes or chambers, to stiffen the structure, and cause the balloon in case of injury by shot or the like, to form a parachute. I provide means whereby I am enabled to minimise the jerks imparted by the grapnel to the car of the balloon by the employment of a counterweight, and I also provide means whereby the grapnel may be turned over or reversed in position as required all as described.

In order that my invention may be clearly understood, I will proceed to describe same with reference to the accompanying drawings.

Figures 1 and 2 show respectively in side elevation, and plan as arrangement of oars for propelling or regulating a balloon in altitude as required. According to my invention I fulcrum or suitably pivot, the inner ends of two oars AA to a triangular frame B, which is attached to the hoop C of a balloon. Cords DD, as shown at Figure 1, are attached to the outer ends of such oars AA for the purpose of supporting their weight, whilst at the same time they are enabled to swing backwards and forwards. Hooped irons E are attached to the upper sides of the oars, and cords FF, GG are attached to the ends of such hoop irons, from whence they pass to the car over pulleys or other suitable runners. There are thus two pairs of cords descending to the car, and a pair of stirrups are attached to or formed by the said cords, in such a manner that on the stirrups FF and GG, being raised and lowered alternately, the oars AA are brought backwards and forwards simultaneously at an angle to the air; now a balloon when free is stationary in the air somewhat the same as a boat drifting in a stream is stationary in relation to the water, so that when the oars AA are suspended horizontally, and rocked backwards and forwards, they act after the manner of a scull in the stern of a dinghey, being feathered at each stroke, and thus the balloon is or may be raised or lowered as required.

By lowering the supporting ropes DD, so as to allow the oars AA to act at an angle, the balloon may be propelled in a horizontal direction, and by elevating the supporting cords, the propelling oars may be raised up beside the net, and thus be out of the way when a descent is being made. Additional cords may be attached to the propellers for the purpose of raising same to the net, when required.

In Figures 3 and 4 I have shown two arrangements whereby these oars AA may

32

be swung backwards and forwards by other powers. Fig. 3 shows the application of a steam piston the oars AA, the reciprocating action of the piston rod H, causing the oars AA, to be brought backwards and forwards, turning on their pivots A¹A¹. Figure 4 shows an oar A reciprocated by the impact of a series of jets J, discharged alternately from each side of the oar.

Owing to the expansion and contraction of gas in the balloon, caused by the varying temperatures, it follows that the altitude of the balloon may be regulated by raising or lowering the temperature of the gas within the balloon. This I accomplish by means of a steam pipe K, or chamber (Fig. 5) which may be constructed of any suitable material, though I have found varnished silk to answer the purpose well. The said steam pipe may be constructed as shown at Figure 5 by making a portion of the balloon itself form part of the pipe K, or the pipe K may be supplied with steam through the pipe K¹ (Fig. 5) being provided from an apparatus in the car or from any other suitable supply; and when held out by sufficient pressure, the pipe K acts as a framework within the balloon, and in the event of the balloon bursting, would ensure it being converted into a parachute. This will prove especially advantageous for ballooons employed in war purposes, as when pierced with shot, a violent descent is prevented. It will be readily seen that by altering the supply of steam, or cutting it off entirely, the temperature within the balloon may be varied to any required extent, and thus any required expansion or contraction of the balloon is obtained.

I may mix a blue or white pigment with the varnish employed in coating the balloon, and thus render same opaque, thereby preventing the rays of the sun passing through the gas. By coating one half of the balloon with a non-transparent material, and leaving the other half of a transparent nature as shown at Figure 8, the altitude may be varied, as by turning the transparent or opaque side to the sun, the temperature may be raised or lowered as required.

Instead of the ordinary valve hitherto used, I employ a long tube L, as shown at Figure 9, connected to the upper part of the balloon, and communicating with the atmosphere by an opening; this tube is made capable of being contracted lengthwise and is held out and its shape normally retained by, say a spiral spring, or by rings L¹ placed at suitable distances apart. L² is a cord running over pulleys L³ and is employed for contracting the tube to the position shown at Fig. 10, when the gas in the balloon is enabled to escape.

Another form of valve for the top of the balloon, may be constructed of steel or other springs in conjunction with some textile fabric, which when in its normal position maintains a twist like form. By pulling a cord in connection with the said valve, the twist is opened, and a free passage for the gas is thus made.

In order to minimise the jerks imparted by the grapnel to the car of the balloon, I slide a weight, such as a sand bag M (Fig. 11) down the grapnel rope N, to a knot or stop N¹ on same, and the weight of the said sand bag takes up most of the shock by causing the grapnel rope to act as a spring. The grapnel P may be lowered down the rope N by a cord R, in such a manner, that it comes on the ground in an inverted position, and thus the flukes do not engage with the ground until the cord R (Fig. 10) is released, when the grapnel P turns round or is reversed and effectually stops the balloon.

At Figures 12, 13 and 14 I have shown modifications of my improved arrangement of grapnel rope. At Fig 12 the grapnel is shown being dragged, in an inverted position, by means of the trailing line R, whilst the grapnel rope is looped up and held by the liberator S. When it is required to cause the grapnel; P to engage with the ground, for the purpose of stopping the balloon, the trailing line R is slackened, as

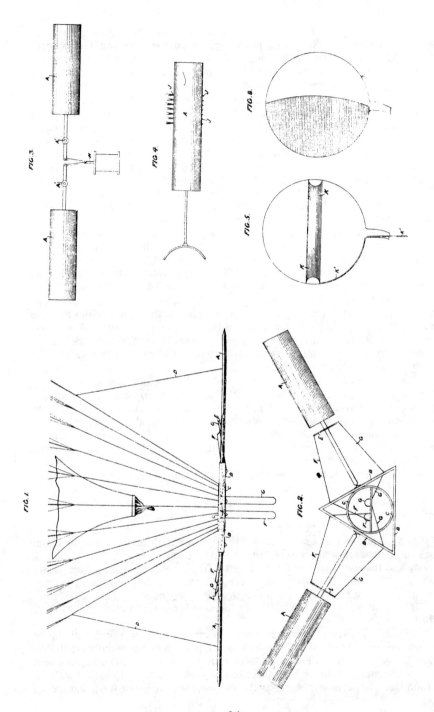

Patrick Alexander's Specification Drawings, No. 13,264, July 6th, 1893

seen at Fig. 13, and the grapnel P is immediately turned over and holds the balloon. Should the place of descent be considered unfavourable, the liberator S is disengaged, and the grapnel P immediately becomes reversed as shewn at Figure 14, leaving the balloon once more free.

Having now particularly described and ascertained the nature of my said invention and in what manner the same is to be performed, I declare that what I claim is:-

1. The two oars, so constructed, arranged and operated, that they are made to strike the air at an angle, all substantially as shown and described.
2. The particular arrangement shown at Figures 1, 2, 3 and 4, for propelling and regulating balloons, substantially as described.
3. A steam pipe situated in a balloon for altering the temperature of the gas, substantially as described.
4. A steam pipe is situated in a balloon for forming a rigid framework, substantially as described.
5. A steam pipe or chamber located within a balloon so arranged or constructed as to form a rigid framework therefore and to serve for varying the temperature of the contained gas substantially as described.
6. The particular arrangement of parts as shown at Figs. 5, 6 and 7 substantially as and for the purposes set forth.
8. The employment of a tubular valve, substantially as shown at Fig. 9 and 10 of the accompanying drawings.
9. The method of preventing the shocks of the grapnel being imparted to the balloon, in combination or not with the grapnel releasing devices substantially as described and illustrated with reference to Figs. 11, 12, 13 and 14 of the accompanying drawings.
10. The general arrangement, construction and combination of the various parts forming my improvements in or connected with balloons, substantially as and for the purposes set forth.

Dated this 7th day of April 1894.

BREWER & SON,
London and Leeds, Agents for Applicant.

Four days later, on 11th July, 1893 came Patent No. 13455 'Adjustable screw propeller or fan' (Alexander, P.Y., The Experimental Works, Bath).

Patrick Alexander decided that the people to meet were those engaged in aeronautics not only in England, but in Europe also. There was Colonel Templer who had survived the crash landing of the Saladin balloon from Bath in December 1881 when the unfortunate Walter Powell M.P. was lost at sea. The Colonel's experiments with balloons using goldbeater's skin and hydrogen were becoming well known.

The balloon section of the British Army had developed from the enthusiasm of Colonel James L.B. Templer, who since 1878 had spent his own money developing the section at Chatham. He was never really thanked for his work, but the War Office made him Instructor in Ballooning.

Lieut. Col. John Capper had been given command of the Balloon section of the

13,455. July 11, 1893. **Adjustable screw propeller or fan.** ALEXANDER, P. Y., The Experimental Works, Bath.

Figs. 1 and 2 are end and side elevations respectively of the screw propeller or fan composed of a Z frame A, B with the ends connected by a stay C, and having the spaces E between the frame and the stay filled with flexible material to form the blades. The frame A, B may be composed of two telescopic tubes A^1, A^2, Fig. 3, of which A^2 slides within the other and is clamped by the piece H. This joint permits the pitch of the blades to be altered and the length of the framework adjusted. In a modified arrangement a bottle nut-joint is used.

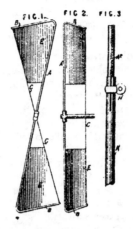

Royal Engineers at Aldershot which had been transferred there from Chatham. Capper became a great friend of Patrick Alexander, and they discussed flying machines at every opportunity. Alexander needed experience and knowledge of the experimental work going on in Germany, where Otto and Gustav Lilienthal were reputed to be making great advances in aeronautics. Alexander was to spend much of his time during the next few years meeting Lilienthal, and the British experimenters Maxim, Moy, Wenham, F.H. Phillips and Percy Pilcher. Later in America he was to meet Octave Chanute, Professor Langley, Orville and Wilbur Wright.

But first he visited Otto and Gustav, near Berlin, where he was to become friendly with several important figures in German aeronautics.

Chapter 5

The First Successful Piloted Gliders

Early in the 1890's, possibly 1891, Patrick Alexander went to Germany to contact Otto Lilienthal (1846 - 1896), the key figure in piloted glider design and flight. Lilienthal was one of the greatest men in the history of aviation. He was the first man to launch himself successfully into the air with what we now call a "hang-glider", and fly. He built a number of machines, and early in 1893 he built his glider Number 6, with which he made many successful glides. For light breezes he built Number 7, and then Number 8, a few replicas of which he sold.

Lilienthal had published in 1889 his classic "Der Vogel flug als Grundlage der Fliegekunst" (Bird Flight as the Basis of the Flying Art), and as a result, Patrick Alexander did some bird watching on his own account, and recorded his findings in a pencil sketch of one that particularly took his attention because, when taking off from a pole, "the bird never once flapped his wings." He added on his drawing of bird flight in orbit "the bird always had the head turned towards the centre of the orb" . . . "the wings placed at an angle" (like a kite) "so that the wind picks or pushes it up into the air."

Otto Lilienthal and his younger brother Gustav did not attempt to imitate the flapping movements of a bird's wing, but concentrated upon the soaring and gliding of some of them with outstretched and apparently rigid wings. Patrick watched how seagulls took off from a post and soared without flapping their wings when the wind was favourable, and how they could return effortlessly to the starting point.

Percy Pilcher (1866-1899) also built gliders and went to see Lilienthal and took his advice on what they jokingly called 'aerial tobogganing' - a term that became misused subsequently with powered flights by the Wright brothers.

Patrick Alexander obtained copies of illustrated articles in the journal "Nature" (Vol.xlix, p.157 and vol.lixii p.177 etc) dated October and Decmber 1891. These graphically describe how Otto Lilienthal, the civil engineer of Gross-Lichterfelde, near Berlin, appeared to have come close to solving the problem of human flight in a heavier than air machine. At that time the apparatus was stated to consist of a steel wire frame covered with canvas, and capable of opening and shutting for easy transport like a huge umbrella. Later, willow was used.

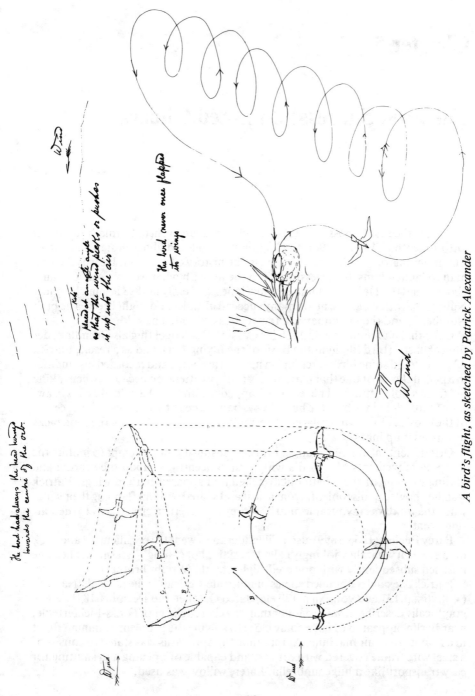

The bird had always the head hung towards the centre of the arc.

The bird held an eye right so that the wind peels or pushes it up into the air.

The bird can use flappa the wings

Wind

Wind

Wind

A bird's flight, as sketched by Patrick Alexander

Lilienthal's Flying Machine

The two main wings of the machine were spread out in flight on either side of Lilienthal, with a third rudder and tail plane wing behind him, which was stated to act like a bird's tail, enabling the aviator to change direction and to slacken speed when he wished to alight. Crowds would assemble whenever Lilienthal was known to be about to "take the air." He would take a short, quick run, which caused the great wings to flap, then he would leap into space, against the wind, from high ground. Using his body to preserve his balance, he would glide in a great curve and land, not unlike a modern "hang glider." Lilienthal was working in 1891 on a carbonic acid motor - he and his brother Gustav had a factory making small steam engines in Berlin.

He flew from the windward side of the hills and escarpements of Steglitz and around Berlin. Reports and photographs of his successful flights in the world's press ignored the bumps, bruises, sprains and other injuries he suffered. On July 25th, 1894, when flying an especially successful machine with which he soared to about 200 feet after being launched from a tower 20 feet high, the wings collapsed and he fell to the ground. His fall was broken somewhat, but he was badly injured. Later, on August 9th, 1896, his career ended after a fatal crash from a stall - the sort of risk he had repeatedly warned others about.

In a press cutting he kept of 1897, an obituary for Lilienthal was heavily underlined by Patrick Alexander:

> *"Lilienthal's sad fate has not damped the ardour nor crippled the ingenuity of the inventors of airships. Their faith in the possibility of aerial locomotion remains unshaken, their bodies likewise, and so on until a trial trip is undertaken."*

Everyone who was interested in aviation wanted to see Maxim's great machine at Bexley, Kent. Griffith Brewer just happened to sail a balloon supervised by

Percival Spencer into Kent, with Mrs. Crayle as passenger. Percival Spencer sat in the hoop under that gas bag above the basket that contained Brewer and Mrs. Crayle, merely to issue advice, and not to control the balloon. Mrs. Crayle's vivid account of her first balloon flight published in "The World" dated 26th August, 1891 relates how she paid her £5 for the flight from the Naval Exhibition Chelsea in a "shabby, rickety battered misshapen clothes-basket below a balloon with little bits of sticking plaster to patch up holes, and a long rent neatly mended . . . " After many adventures Mr. Spencer consulted a map, pulled the string that let out the gas, and they landed more or less normally. They received hospitality from an American, whose two daughters gave them tea, and took them and their balloon to the railway station - after they had been shown the huge contraption that turned out to be the Maxim Flying Machine in its shed. The American was Mr. House, the engineer of Sir Hiram S. Maxim, and the house was Baldwyns Park, Bexley. Griffith Brewer related the story to Patrick Alexander, who commented upon their navigation - and luck.

Maxim was one of the great experimenters at this time (1891/4). His articles about "Experiments in Aeronautics" had been published, and his great steam driven machine at Bexley received considerable attention. He demonstrated that he had enough power to get the machine off the ground though he prudently restrained it by rails. The press was getting tired of repeated claims and failures. Some sarcastic person said that the only novel thing about a flying machine was that it would not fly. But machines had been made that flew, if only models. Hargrave of New South Wales was regarded as one of the most successful experimenters and Herr Kress exhibited his "Dynamic Flying Machine" at the German Naturalists' Society meeting. It did fly, but was regarded as not much improvement on Hargrave's devices.

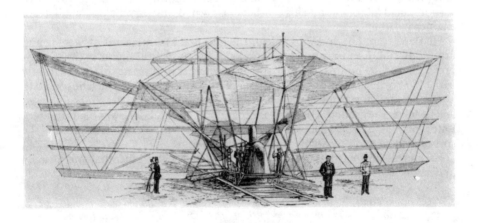

Maxim's Flying Machine

In 1896, the eminent scientist Lord Kelvin said "I have not the smallest molecule of faith in aerial flight other than ballooning". This was the year that Sir Hiram Maxim came near to solving the problem of "mechanical flight" with his flying machine with its steam engine and 18ft. diameter propellers, which briefly lifted off the track before crashing.

One mechanical engineering press report read:

"He has produced a very curious and interesting machine, but he is not one step nearer to flying than any of his predecessors. It is quite true that he might get his flying machine up into the air, and that being there he might guide it to a certain extent, but there is no evidence available that the machine being up could be brought to the earth again, without risking its total destruction and the lives of those on board. The fact that by the aid of a screw a body could be made to fly has been known for many years. Mr. Maxim has further proved that it is possible to make a steam engine which can raise itself and several persons off the ground by the aid of a screw; but this is about all. As we have already said, Mr. Maxim has made a flying machine which does not know how to fly. In teaching it, c'est la premier pas qui coute, and the cost will be so great, that it is unlikely that any second step will be taken."

Chapter 6

The World Fair - Chicago 1893

Patrick Alexander collected the programme and report of the Aerial Navigation Conference at Chicago World Fair, 1893. This had two sections, Aviation and Ballooning, a total of 29 papers being submitted, fifteen from American scientists, five from England, three from France, and others from Australia, Algeria, and Egypt. The English contributors were Crosland Taylor F.R.G.S. 'Observations of Birds' and 'Theories of Soaring and Sailing', also 'Gliding or Soaring Devices'.

F.H. Wenham submitted 'Suggestions and Experiments', and General W. Hutchinson, British Army, 'Design of Navigable Balloons' - this was evidence of his advocacy of airships, both for Army use, and as a saving in cost to the taxpayer. It would be ten years before England produced a reliable airship, whereas the French had built several.

The American group included Professor A.F. Zahm, aerodynamicist, who Patrick Alexander later visited. Subsequently, he was able to provide the British Army Observer, Col. Capper, with letters of introduction to Zahm and other aeronautical Americans, at the time of the St. Louis Exhibition in 1904.

An important contributor from New South Wales was Lawrence Hargreave, of Sydney, with his 'Experiments in Flying Machines, Motors and Cellular Kites'. A few years later (1899) his toy box kites were to be found in every toy shop. In the same year, Hargreave met Pilcher, who incorporated the Australian's ideas in a triplane glider, but was fatally injured before he could test Hargreave's theories. Santos-Dumont built an aeroplane in 1905 based on the Hargreave's design and "Colonel" S.F. Cody developed the Hargreave's kite design. Cody was to fly one of his kites at Patrick Alexander's 1902 Garnerin balloon ascent centenary celebrations at Bath. Hargreave's papers, which he read to the Aeronautical Society in 1897 and 1899, were received with great interest.

Octave Chanute, at the opening of the of the 1893 Chicago Conference, set out the difficulties to be surmounted. The problems related to the motor, the propelling instrument, the form, extent, texture and construction of the sustaining surfaces, to the methods of getting under way, or steering the apparatus in the air and of alighting safely. He reviewed calculations as to the weight that could be sustained in the air by each horse power. He said that Professor Langley had shown that 200 pounds could be supported with one horse power, adding that "Mr. Phillips of England had shown that 72 pounds per horse power could be sustained. Driving balloons at low velocities - a maximum of 14 miles per hour - was insufficient to stem a wind on any but rare occasions. Some said speeds of 26 miles an hour are practicable, but this has yet to be proved."

It was to be ten years before the Wright brothers showed how the problems were to be solved. Meanwhile, Patrick Alexander studied the reports, filed them with his newspaper cuttings, and experimented at his Bath Experimental Works.

Other cuttings referred to the disappearance of Solomon Andree's balloon in which he had set out in July 1897 to cross the North Pole, also "War Balloons" - "the turning of balloons into dynamite carrying airships, that could drop 400 or 500 pounds of dynamite into trenches" . . . Mr Reed of Hot Springs, Arkansas, U.S.A. boasted that he could build an airship in 30 days that would carry enough dynamite to reduce the city of Havana to ruins within an hour. This was at the time of the Cuban insurrection against the Spanish. Meanwhile, the Royal Engineers - then the Army's air section - were experimenting at Lydd with dropping shells from balloons. The report in Alexander's file reads " . . the experiments showed that a bomb was as effective in destructiveness when dropped over a building as if hurled upon it."

By the end of 1897, the Aeronautical Society of Great Britain had been resuscitated after a moribund period following the death of the foundation secretary, F.W. Brearey. Captain Baden-Powell - brother of the Chief Scout - had, at 20, been the youngest member of the Society, and lived to be the oldest. He became Secretary in 1896, founded the Journal at his own expense, and was President from 1900 to 1907. He was a great friend of Patrick Alexander, and was the first to lift a man by kite (June 27th, 1894). He designed a famous variation for the launching of gliders, and had a water chute built at the Crystal Palace, down which he shot on the cascading water, with the expectation of taking off. He built an experimental laboratory in the country - at Gatton Park, Surrey where Patrick Alexander wrote to him (calling it Colman's Park - the Mustard magnate was the owner) asking "What on earth are you up to . . .?" This was after he had expressed interest in Baden-Powell's screw experiments. He later replied to an invitation from Baden-Powell to assist financially, "I do not consider it advisable . . . I think you might do good woik with your 8 h.p. motor, but there is so much being done now by other people with screw propellers and grater (sic) powers than 8 h.p. that I am inclined to mark time for a little as far as screw propulsion is concerned."

The press tried to use aerial reporting, and in March 1893 the Daily Graphic attempted to cover the Oxford and Cambridge boat race from a balloon. The attempt was a failure as the winds were unco-operative. Patrick Alexander hoped that he could solve the problem of aerial navigation.

Patrick Alexander continued to collect the published reports of every aeronautical contrivance. In 1897, some headlines were becoming sarcastic, e.g. "This Machine is Interesting on Paper because it hasn't reached the Experimental Stage Yet". The unnamed imaginative inventor was already envisaging airships as common as trains. The reports of Octave Chanute's progress were restrained, he made no rash claims, nor wild forecasts.

"What was needed was a motor that would carry a man on a journey", he said. No suitable engine was available in 1902. "It will be used for exploration and war purposes - it will make rulers less anxious to go to war. The load it can carry will be light, and the expense heavy, but man will undoubtedly reach a speed of 100 miles an hour," said Chanute.

Patrick Alexander contacted others engaged in aeronautical experimental works. Horatio Phillips had been working on the problems of flying machines for many years - his first patent is dated 1875 - but there was no income from such experiments, successful or otherwise, and he eventually had to stop. His hydrofoil wings in a tandem arrangement looked promising, and were illustrated when such schemes were under consideration, but beyond a hop or two, none of his machines flew. He was interested in aerodynamic research, a subject that Patrick Alexander continued to develop. Phillips' large "Multiplane" model, which he built and tested at Harrow, successfully demonstrated that his ideas were right.

From Australia had come news of Lawrence Hargreaves, whose work in isolation was sufficiently advanced as to influence designers in Europe and America. He invented in 1893, and brought to London in 1899, his box kite design which was of help to the Wright brothers and Colonel Cody in England, as well as to Patrick Alexander when he first built gliders at Bath around 1901, also Farnborough in 1904, and later in 1910, at Windsor.

Lawrence Hargreave, from Wollahra Point, Sydney tried to design a light aeroplane where the engine preceded the 'plane on the principle of a boy and his kite. He was seeking to eliminate the need for the skill of the operator, whereas it was this skill that the Wright brothers were to demonstrate so successfully.

The front runner in U.S.A. appeared to be Professor S.P. Langley, whose models flew sufficiently well to attract an American Government grant, after which he was unsuccessful in getting his manlifting machine to become airborne. This failure was in 1903, by which time Patrick Alexander had paid him a visit.

Probably the most important contacts made by Patrick Alexander were with Octave Chanute in 1902, and guided by him, with the Wright brothers in America the same year.

i. F.H. Phillips

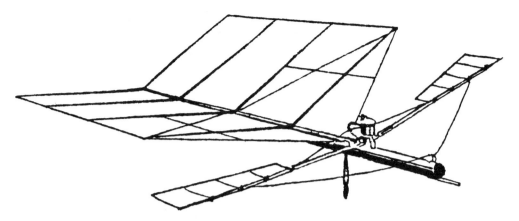

ii. Lawrence Hargreave

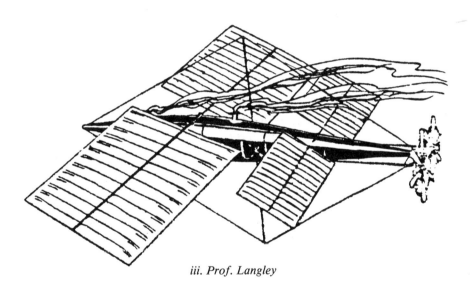

iii. Prof. Langley

Early Flying Machines

Alexander was aware of the development of the Otto four stroke engine which had been invented in 1876 and improved by Daimler in 1884 but no record has been traced of his having any interest in such engines - or in automobiles - until the lack of a reliable British aircraft engine led him to donate a prize of £1,000 for a satisfactory power unit for aeroplanes in 1909.

He found Dr. Graham Bell was working on what was to become the Tetrahedron design for kites, and on his Aerial Experiment Association.

45

Hargreave's Kite

There were not many matters connected with aeronautics in which Patrick Alexander was not interested, including industrial chemistry. For recreation he enjoyed ballooning, and travel, and is reputed to have gone on safari, but when is not known.

Anyone - including the British Government representatives - who wanted to know the current progress with aeronautics anywhere, approached Patrick Alexander in the first decade of the 20th century. When Colonel John Capper wanted to visit the Wright brothers, who else would he think of approaching but Patrick Alexander? Colonel Capper recorded that Patrick Alexander gave him every help, and reported, "Before leaving England I was given - through the courtesy of Mr P.Y. Alexander, a gentleman who is probably better acquainted personally with all interested in aeronautics in Europe and America than any other living individual - a number of letters of introduction to various gentlemen who are interested in aeronautics and who I might be able to see in St. Louis or might visit if they lived within reasonable distance of my route." The occasion was the St. Louis Exposition of 1904. The introductions included Octave Chanute, Wilbur and Orville Wright, Professor S. Langley, Marvin, Manley, Zahm and several others, all prominent in American aeronautics.

Chapter 7

Patrick Alexander's Biggest Balloon — The 'Majestic' and Scientific Ballooning

Patrick wrote a letter dated 24th August, 1893:

Griffith Brewer Esq.,   Experimental
                                                          Works,
    Leeds.   Bath, England.

    Thursday Aug/24/93

"Dear Sir,

    I have to thank you for yours of yesterday's date. I think you may like to hear that I have given the Spencer's an order for a 100,000 Cubic foot balloon, 60ft. diameter. to be used for high and long ascents. Mr. Percival Spencer thinks it will keep up in the air for a week it certainly will if I can get some good propeller to check her turning and have a good trail rope. Trusting you are well,

I remain,
Yours truly

Patrick Y. Alexander."

The largest balloon in C.G. Spencer and Sons advertisements at that time was 80,000 cubic feet capacity, which could carry 8 passengers, the cost being £250.

    The balloon was duly made, and its size and design excited much interest. As the following Sunday Chronicle article dated 17th June 1894 (from Patrick Alexander's collection) states it was one of the finest balloons ever made, and one of the largest then in existence:-

    "Stretched along the floor of part of the factory I saw the coat or skin of the largest balloon now in existence. It is known as the "Majestic" and was launched on February 21 from the Crystal Palace, having on board Messrs. Percival and Stanley Spencer, E. Brewer, and P.Y. Alexander; and after a successful trip it came down near Horsham. The circumference of the balloon when inflated is 180 feet, and its diameter rather more than 57 feet. Its capacity is 100,094 cubic feet, and its weight, without

47

passengers or cargo, one ton five hundredweight. No less than 10,000 superficial feet of the finest silk were used in the making of the balloon, and there are 120 gores, each of which is 18 inches wide in the material. The lifting power is very great; it can carry as many as twelve passengers under ordinary circumstances. The car, which weighs 510lbs, is a huge square basket, having seats, with lockers beneath them, in which provisions and other matters may be stowed away.

The "Majestic" was begun on August 12, and was completed on February 18, so that over six months were spent in its construction; and the total cost of the work was nearly £2,500. A balloon of this size, you see, is not a trivial investment. To fill the "Majestic" with coal-gas involves an expenditure of about £20; the cost of hydrogen gas to fill the same space would be at least 20 times as great, but hydrogen gas to raise the same weight as a full charge of coal gas could be used for ten times the cost, or say, £200. The lifting power of hydrogen is so much greater than that of coal gas that a relatively smaller quantity is able to do the same work; but considerations of cost and convenience make the coal gas much more practicable under ordinary circumstances.

The "Majestic" is now being used as a captive balloon at Woodhouse Park, Shepherds Bush, carrying a dozen passengers at a time. But it behaves exceedingly well on what we are known as right-away ascents, which are unrestricted ascents into space; and is, though not the largest, yet one of the finest balloons ever made, and certainly now the largest now in existence.''

Certificate of Balloon Ascent, 1909

49

In 1894 Patrick Alexander took his Majestic balloon to Germany for scientific ballooning. This had been started shortly after the first Mongolfier ascents in 1784 using barometers and thermometers, and several aeronauts made observations which aroused interest in scientific circles, but nothing noteworthy in a scientific sense had been done. The English scientific aeronaut Glaisher was the first to adopt really accurate methods, and he made twenty-eight ascents, most of them with Coxwell, for scientific purposes, and his work was specially noted in Germany, including temperature, dew points, barometric readings, electrical properties of the atmosphere, oxygen tests, magnetic variations, the height and constitution of clouds, their density and depth, wind directions at different heights, and acoustical observations. The Germans were very impressed with his work, and credit him with guiding their own scientific ballooning programme. Improvements in instrument design resulted, and several German scientists became friendly with Patrick Alexander, including Professor Assman, a meteorologist and President of the Berlin Balloon Club in 1890, Professors Berson and Suring, two meteorologists who worked with Patrick Alexander, and several military officers including Captain von Sigsfeld, Major von Tschudi, and Major Moedebeck. Anyone supporting aeronautical experimenting seems to have been sought after by Patrick Alexander, who met the youthful, arrogant Kaiser Wilhelm 11, German Emperor for almost 30 years until November 1918. The Kaiser personally made up the deficit on the cost of German scientific aeronautical work.

It was a change for Patrick Alexander compared with the relative lack of interest in high places in England. The Levant Herald printed the following report in the edition dated 10th September, 1894:

"Some extremely interesting experiments of a scientific character are to be made in Berlin in a few days in the German balloon Phoenix and the English balloon Majestic, the latter having been taken to Berlin by its owner for this purpose. Both balloons will ascend together from the neighbourhood of Berlin, in order to make hygrometrical observations and to test the uniformity of the temperature and electricity of the air at equal heights. The Phoenix belongs to the Meteorological Institute of Berlin, a society which enjoys the patronage of the Kaiser, who takes an immense interest in aeronautics, in view of the advantages that the army may derive from the balloon department. The two balloons will make their observations in their first ascent as far as possible at a constant distance apart, and the aeronauts going up in them hope to obtain information that has hitherto not been established concerning temperature, wind, and other interesting and important details. They will remain in the air about twenty four hours, and will devote some days afterwards to examining the results of their observations, which will be tested later in the second ascent that they contemplate making."

The German aeronaut, Captain A. Hildebrant, a Captain and Instructor in the Prussian Balloon Corps mentions Patrick Alexander also his Majestic balloon several times in his book originally published in German in 1908 as 'Airships Past and Present' and republished in English in 1973 under the title 'Balloons and Airships'.

Alexander is mentioned as being the only English meteorologist participating in European scientific ballooning. He became a member of the international organisation which culminated in a number of simultaneous ascents being made, the first on July 14th, 1893 from Berlin and Stockholm. On August 4th, 1894, ascents were made from Berlin, Goteberg, and St Petersburg (Leningrad) after which the organisation was joined by Lawrence Rotch, the director of the Blue Hills Observatory near Boston U.S.A., Besancon, de Fonvielle, Hermite, and Teisserenc de Bort of France, Colonel von Kowanko, Colonel Portzeff and General Rykatscheff of Russia, and Andree of Sweden, "together with Patrick Y. Alexander of England - who lent his balloon Majestic." There was no other support from England for several years but the greatly respected veteran English balloonist Glaisher was made an honorary member.

In 1896 there was an International Commision in Paris consisting of most of the above aeronauts and scientists including Professor Assman, who interested the Kaiser in his work. There was Professor Berson - who travelled from Berlin to Kiev in Russia - 930 miles - with Dr. Elias, for meteorological purposes, and Dr. Hergesell, director of the Meteorological Institute in Alsace and Lorraine - he was made President. By 1894 the experimental funds had run out, but the Kaiser gave money to enable the work to continue.

The balloon Majestic is mentioned in Dr. Assman's report "Zeitschrift fur Luftschiffahrt, 1895," as having 3,000 cubic metres capacity, and being the largest, and "private English property." A note adds "If London had taken part in these experiments, Assman would, of course, have adopted Greenwich time". (P.43, Vol 13). Instead, Paris time was used. The report contains tables of ascents, barometric readings, altitude and temperatures.

A great deal did not go according to programme, as certain thermometers did not register low enough, an unmanned balloon burst as did a two man Austrian balloon. Another was torn to pieces on landing by illiterate and hostile peasants.

"Scientific Ballooning" was also reported, such as in the Stanley Spencer's "Golden Penny" account of an ascent from the Crystal Palace on Thursday 15th September 1899 with Patrick Alexander's German friend Dr. Berson. They reached a record height of 27,200 feet in less than two hours in the balloon "Excelsior" which had previously been used as a captive balloon at the Earls Court Exhibition. For the special ascent it was inflated with hydrogen made from 48 carboys of acid (four tons), and three tons of iron filings, giving 32,000 cubic feet of gas, which was dried by passing over unslaked lime. The balloon had a capacity of 56,000 cubic feet, and therefore they set out with plenty of room for expansion. They reached 14,000 feet in 17 minutes, and Spencer noted that if asked what was the sensation, he could only say that there had been an entire absence of sensation, no cold, no motion, only absolute tranquility, and perfect rest, and the grandest view possible. By discharging 2 cwt. of ballast, they managed to reach 27,997 feet, where the cold was severe, and they inhaled oxygen through a rudimentary apparatus consisting of a rubber tube and glass mouthpiece. The only sound heard was that of a cannon being discharged. The open mouth of the gas bag was discharging hydrogen, they were soon nearing the North Sea, and so they decided to descend; they were dropping at a rate of 1,000 feet per minute. The discharge of lime ballast at first disappeared upwards, then repassing downwards as the descent slowed. All the ballast was discharged, they entered warm air near the ground, the trail rope touched, and they soon landed with a bump near Upminster, the emptying balloon having acted as a parachute. The usual crowd of amateur assistants arrived, the balloon was packed into the basket, and driven in a cart to the nearest station at Upminster. The Rev. Cooke who lived nearby, gave them tea, then drove them to the station.

Berson later ascended in Germany with Professor Suring to a record breaking height of 35,400 feet, having calculated beforehand that human life was impossible at 36,100 feet. They lost consciousness after releasing gas and awoke nearly an hour later down to about 18,000 feet. They breathed the oxygen through the rubber tube connected to a glass mouthpiece, which could drop out of the mouth, resulting in fatal accidents.

Because of the dangers of height, small unmanned balloon sondes were developed to carry recording instruments aloft, to be hopefully recovered after the balloon had burst at a preset maximum altitude, when the instruments parachuted back to earth, complete with instructions for return. Instruments cost £60 per set, so their return was a matter for concern. About 60% were recovered, but damage sometimes occured.

No-one was participating in such experimental work in England until Patrick Alexander planned a parachute descent using one of his own design and manufacture.

The idea of celebrating the centenary of the 1802 balloon ascent by Andre-Jacques Garnerin at Bath was being developed by Patrick Alexander, and associated with it was an interest in parachutes, possibly because Garnerin was making parachute descents from his balloon before coming to Bath. The reason why no such descent was made by Garnerin at Bath is not known, but the design of his parachute appears to have been far from satisfactory, and the unfortunate parachutist came down swinging violently, resulting in his being sick, which is as good a reason as any for limiting the number of parachute jumps. The Garnerin parachute was made of white canvas and was 23 feet in diameter. At the top was a round piece of wood, nearly a foot in diameter, with a hole in the centre. The

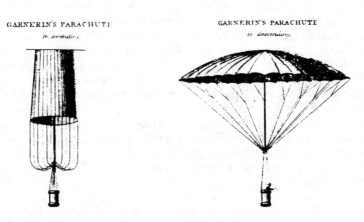

Garnerin's parachute, ascending and descending

circle of wood was joined to the canvas umbrella shaped parachute by 32 short tapes. There were 32 more similar tapes each about 23 feet in length which connected the edges of the umbrella to a small ring which carried the cords from which suspended the small dustbin shaped basket used by the parachutist during a descent. The ring was connected through the centre of wood circle to the netting around the balloon, which had no basket. When the balloon burst, by height or was released by Garnerin, the whole contraption came down and the parachute opened. Garnerin was hurt at least once on landing for his descent was over-rapid, but the idea of a parachute had been established.

Patrick Alexander's design for his parachute is not known. He may have followed the type used by Garnerin, or that used by his friend Auguste Gaudron. It is reputed to have taken him 10 years to develop, and concurrently he made several balloons in his workshops. Major C.C. Turner in his book "The Old Flying Days" states that by 1894 he had "run through" eight balloons. He possibly commenced with captive balloons in 1892, making ascents from Bath.

The story goes that one day between 1894 and 1896 - the records are contradictory as to the exact year - Patrick inflated a hot air balloon in Bath before a jeering crowd, climbed into the basket with his parachute, released the mooring ropes and gained height. Then to the horror of the crowd, he was seen to jump from the balloon basket. After a few minutes the queer umbrella contraption opened, and he landed safely, if painfully, because of his bad leg. The feat was hailed in Bath as the first parachute descent, which it was not. Garnerin had made the first parachute descent at Paris on 22nd October 1797, and his fifth, the first in England, on 21st September 1802.

Chapter 8

Patrick Alexander and W.G. Walker go to town with "The Helicopter Project"

Patrick Alexander had acquired an office at 47, Victoria Street, Westminster by 1897, the same address as his colleague William George Walker A.M.I.C.E., M.I.M.E., consultant engineer. They co-operated in experiments with aerial propellers, and these experiments were reported in detail in 'Engineering', dated February 16th, 1900. They were aided by a grant from the Royal Society, who issued a report upon the experiments. The design of propellers (or airscrews, or fans as some called them) had been neglected. Their first experiments evaluated propellers from 2 ft. to 5ft. in diameter, with tip speeds up to 15,000 ft. per minute.

The term 'propeller' only became synonymous with 'airscrew' from about 1845-1855, and prior to that it referred to any propelling device, writes Charles Gibbs-Smith. The term 'Screw-fan' was used by some writers up to the end of the 19th century, "propellers with a horizontal thrust" said some inventors to distinguish their proposals from helicopter screws. Design and efficiency of propellers differed greatly. Some favoured what looked like a pair of table tennis bats inclined at each end of a centre pivoted whirling rod.

George Louis Outram Davidson patented in 1889 (No. 13207) an "Aerial Machine". This consisted of "an elongated balloon attached above a 'body surface' to which the car is attached, and to which two wings and bow and stern rudders are pivoted." He added "the 'Power of the attraction of the earth' is employed as a means of propulsion." The leading edge of the wing was raised when the balloon ascended, and lowered when descending, so as to make progress.

Patrick Alexander included the above patent in "Aeronautics 1815-1891", and appears to have been impressed by the theory, as he mentioned similar basic specifications in later years. No illustration was included in "Aeronautics".

In August, 1898, William George Walker was employed by Mr. G.L.O. Davidson to make experiments with propellers required for an experimental flying machine that Davidson's "Air-car Construction Syndicate Ltd" would construct as soon as the necessary £9,000 was subscribed. This machine would, stated Mr Davidson, be able to go from London to the Riviera in one hour, from London to New York in 11 hours, and round the world in 80 hours . . . (There were many inventors who designed aircraft before the Wright brothers' success. Few of them even made a 'hop', and fewer had any degree of practicality). Shortly afterwards Alexander and Walker decided to carry out a series of experiments on propeller design, to ascertain the 'laws' that applied to thrust, speed, horse power, and blade angle.

Mr. Davidson persisted with his invention, and the Dundee Advertiser (7th November, 1910) reported:-

GYROSCOPIC FLYING MACHINE

"The gigantic flying machine under construction at Taplow in the valley of the Thames by Mr. G.L. Davidson, a native of Aberdeenshire, will be officially inspected tomorrow by a War Office expert who has been deputed to investigate the inventor's claim. The machine is built on the gyroscopic principle, the lifting power being obtained by means of two rotary wings each 27 feet in diameter. When completed the machine will weigh 7 tons, and the total cost will be little short of £12,000. The inventor calculates that it will be able to carry 25 passengers, in addition to a crew of three hands, at a rate of over 100 miles per hour. During the fourteen months it has been under construction Mr. Davidson has given continuous employment to twelve skilled workmen, and has incurred an expenditure of £7,000. The machine has recently been inspected by Lord Roberts, Vice Admiral Foote, President of the Ordnance Board, Rear Admiral Farquhar, and other eminent service men..."

In 1910, Patrick Alexander was living at the United Services College, Windsor, only 4 miles away, and would have been interested in the project which arose from the work of himself and W.G. Walker 11 years earlier.

Patrick Alexander appears to have kept in touch from Windsor with Mr. G.L.O. Davidson, who in 1913, while still living at Taplow, built a "gyrocopter" which was claimed to be capable of carrying twenty persons "and would supplant both aeroplanes and dirigibles" - if he could get the necessary further financial support. The Daily Sketch featured his flying machine in 1913, but there is no record of it being completed. Alexander was sufficiently interested as to collect these press reports, which mention visits of inspection by Government engineers, but these may relate to the 1910 visits.

Griffith Brewer, who became President of the Royal Aeronautical Society 1940-42, stated in his obituary for Patrick Alexander that the latter's scientific work at Bath had been the subject of discussion in scientific circles all over Europe, and his Experimental Works at Bath was one of the foremost places of aeronautical and meteorological experimentation in England.

They worked on the Helicopter project (or Vertical Screw Aerial Machine) at 47, Victoria Street, Westminster and at the Experimental Works, Bath between October 9th and 20th, 1899.

A paper read by Mr. W.G. Walker to the Aeronautical Society in October 1905 gives details of the "The Vertical Screw Aerial Machine, with Special Notes on the Lifting Propellers". Mr. Walker stated that "This machine was taken in hand in 1899 with the assistance of Mr. P.Y. Alexander. A staff of competent draughtsmen were employed in getting out fully detailed working drawings of different powers. The propellers are 30 feet in diameter, revolving in opposite directions mounted on separate shafts, one inside the other, by this means the necessary reactions for rotation is obtained. The steam engines are below; the engines in this particular design are of somewhat novel type; the bed plate cylinders are connected to one of the shafts, the outer one, and the crank shafts to the inner one, so that we have the engine bed cylinders revolving in one direction, and the crank shaft in the opposite direction. The engine was composed of two cylinders opposite to each other so as to effect a perfect balance. The cage containing the water tube boiler and place for the man is seen below. A machine was designed to give a lift of about 1,200 to 1,300 lbs. capable of carrying one man. The power of the engine being about 50 b.h.p., or a lifting thrust of about 24 lbs. per b.h.p., it was decided to use steam at a pressure of 150 lbs. per square inch. The machine was to be made of high grade steel. "The problem was to design a machine capable of lifting itself and a man off the ground. By numerous calculations and experiments I came to the conclusion that in the case of machines of this type a minimum of 50 b.h.p. would be necessary to lift a man off the ground."

"After a number of repeated sets of drawings had been got out I came to the conclusion that a machine of this kind could be constructed to weigh about 1,100 lbs., or about 1,300 lbs. with man and fuel, the water and fuel to last ten minutes. We knew exactly what the propellers would do, so that it was only a question of weight of machine for necessary power. The motive power proposed was steam, but taking into account the many little complications which were sure to crop up, and in consideration of the small margin of lifting power over calculated weight, it was decided not to make the machine, but the propellers were made and tested."

The account is of interest for the apparent division of responsibilties between Walker and Alexander. The financial assistance came from the latter, the propellers were made at the Experimental Works at Batheaston. The novel design of the engine, is in the context of "we", but the numerous calculations are in the first person singular, as is the conclusion about the total loaded and unladen weights. The propellers return to the "we" context, and the final decision not to make the machine was no doubt a joint one.

The Alexander and Walker report received considerable attention in European scientific and aeronautical circles. A typical article was printed in France by 'Les Inventions Nouvelles' dated 31st March, 1901 and this, when read by a modern designer of propellers, is stated to demonstrate the relatively elementary stage reached in design at that time. The French article deals with the ebbing of interest shown by the public because of repeated lack of success by aviation designers. It was obvious that inventors were repeating the same mistakes as those in previous failures; they failed to use the very considerable experience provide by contemporary experimental work, and in this context the work on propellers of Alexander and Walker is specifically mentioned. Because of the failures of inventors who worked by their own unproven theories, and did not use available proven data, the public had become apathetic and the press reports sarcastic. Where careful experimental work was demonstrated as in the work of Lilienthal, Chanute and similar designs - these carried weight, but the efforts of those whose designs failed to fly were ridiculed and then forgotten.

The object of the experiments was to ascertain the lifting powers of 30ft. diameter propellers, five of which were built and tried.

The room used, in a large shed on the Thames Embankment at Westminster, was 210ft. long, 68ft. wide and 60ft. high. The propeller shaft ran the length of the room with its axis 17 feet above the floor. The centre of the propellers was 30ft. from one end of the room, to give room for air circulation. The propellers had a swept area of 707 square feet, the sectional area of the room being 3,600 square feet. They regarded the area of 2,893 square feet for the return flow of air as adequate. Tests were made with both "narrow" and "wide" blades, using 2 or 4 at one time, at speeds from 20 to 60 revolutions per minute in stops of 5 r.p.m., the thrust in pounds, revolutions per minute of each propeller and the portable steam engine indicated and brake horse power steam pressure, with tip speeds up to 20,000 feet per minute. The blades were set at 12.5 degrees in six tests, and at 21 degrees in two tests. The blades are described as "four wide", "two wide", four narrow", and "skeleton", the overall swept diameter being 30 feet.

Calculations were subsequently made for 12 and 18 blades. In the case of 18 blades, it was calculated that a propeller 50 feet in diameter running at 30 revolutions per minute would produce a thrust of 3,700 pounds, with an indicated horse power of 190. The experiments were widely reported in France and Germany. Santos-Dumont refers to his propellers being based on these experiments in an account of one of his successful one-man airships, which he navigated in Paris around the Eiffel Tower.

In 1898 one propeller used by Santos-Dumont for his airships consisted of two approx 12″ squares of aluminium whirling in a circle of 32″ diameter.

The following laws were stated to be proved up to a tip speed of 15,000 feet per minute:-

1. The thrust varies as the square of the speed;
2. The thrust varies as the disc area of the propeller;
3. The horse power varies as the cube of the speed, and for small angles as the square of the pitch angle;

   The thrust divided by the horse power was found to vary inversely as the tip speed increased.

   In the case of the particular propellers tried, a thrust of 15lbs. per horse power was obtained at a tip speed of 15,000 ft. per minute which was regarded as equivalent to a thrust of 30lbs. per horse power at a tip speed of 7,000 ft. per minute.

   Blades were tried at different pitch angles varying from 5 to 35 degrees.

   At a tip speed of 15,000 feet per minute the efficiency of the propellers commenced to break down - a phenomenon also noticed, by Mr. Parsons on the first turbine ship, the Turbina, where the small screw propellers broke away from the water at high speeds, by cavitation.

The work of Alexander and Walker was referred to by Dr. Barton of Beckenham who was commissioned by the War Office to build an "aerostat which will carry five men." (Motoring Illustrated April 19th, 1902). Dr. Barton had been experimenting for nearly 20 years. His son Dudley appears to have been precocious - at the age of 11, in knickerbockers and a sailor suit, he "not only made and adjusted parts for his father's models, but also took his father's three and a half

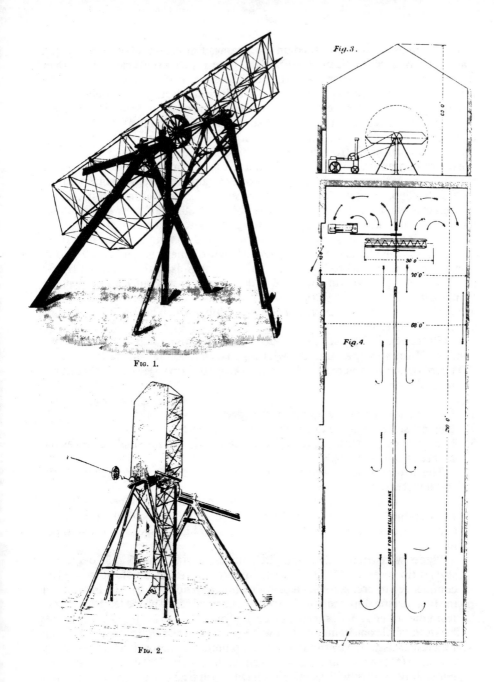

Fig. 3.

Fig. 4.

FIG. 1.

FIG. 2.

Propeller trials at Westminster in 1899 for the
Vertical Screw Aerial Machine

b.h.p. New Orleans car to pieces and put it together with perfectly satisfactory results."

'The Engineer' dated 18th February, 1902 described the story and design of Dr. Barton's airship in detail. Patrick Alexander was involved in the design of the propellers, adding that "Experiments recently carried out at Mr Alexander's Experimental Works at Bath show that a thrust of 25lbs per brake horse-power can be obtained without excessive weight. Each pair of fans will be driven by an oil motor, with electric ignition, each of the three motors exerting 45 brake horse power."

W.G. Walker read a paper about the experiment to the British Association meeting at Dover on September 21st, 1899.

"Flight" printed the following account some five years after the date of a lecture which is some indication of Patrick Alexander's reputation, as the lecture was originally given to a meeting of the Aeronautical Club at King's College in a date "towards the end of 1906", this was before "Flight" commenced publication in January 1909.

"Patrick Alexander's great forte", stated "Flight" October 28th, 1911, "is the making of experiments, and his lecture gained its charm from the practical demonstrations which he gave . . . by the aid of very simple apparatus . . ." The subject was "propellers and Spinning Models", and he showed that when a propeller is made to revolve in front of another propeller free to turn on the same shaft, the free mounted propeller is not only set revolving by the air driven by the first propeller, but it moves towards the latter in the teeth of the air impact.

He demonstrated the partial vacuum outside the perifery of a spinning propeller by a sheet of tin held near a pivoted motor and propeller, which followed the sheet when moved away, the motor and propeller swinging round on its pivot. The object was to show that shrouded propellers were inefficient. Similarly a propeller should be clear of the wings (or "decks" as he termed them). He also demonstrated the type of pivoted frames that would continue to spin in a current of air - these led to the rotary advertisement signs used to this day.

He then showed the "Aerial Tourbillon", which consists of a stick of semi circular section mounted on a spindle through the centre of its flat face. When set spinning with the convex side towards the draught, it came to rest, but if set spinning with flat side towards the draught, it continued to spin, and even to increase in speed. This is the theory of the spinning cricket ball, which can be made to swerve in the direction of spin.

He continued with demonstrations of certain falling bodies, commencing with a flat sheet, which refuses to fall edgewise, but swerves in a horizontal position, then zig-zags down. Variations of this were shown which might lead to a rotary parachute. A piece of paper in the shape of a "T" would fall stable if dropped tail first, but unstable if dropped head first.

A hollow triangular prism will rotate about its longitudinal axis while falling, and eventually descend with its axis horizontal.

In March 1907, Patrick Alexander followed up his lecture on propellers at King's College to the Aeronautical Club with a gift to that body of experimental apparatus which he had devised for the purpose of ascertaining the effects produced by

59

The Apparatus presented by Patrick Alexander to the Aero Club for observing the nature of air currents.

A motor driven propeller fixed to a pivoted beam, A, which is balanced on B, which is itself pivoted to the stand, C. The lower end of the rod is provided with balance weights B1.

The mechanism for observing the nature of air currents from propellers driven by the apparatus, left.

different forms of propellers.

The apparatus consisted of three items, one having an electric motor driving a propeller and mounted on a pivot beam and balanced on a vertical pillar, which in turn is pivoted on a stand, so that reactions can be counterbalanced by weights, these being adjusted to restore balance when propellers were being tested. A large steel cylinder about 5ft. long and 2ft. in diameter, mounted in a frame so that its height could be adjusted to that of the propeller under test, and the effect similarly measured by the use of weights to restore balance.

The talk given by Alexander in 1906 to the Aero Club printed by "Flight" in October 1911 had been previously printed in Automotor Journal in the edition dated December 29th 1906 and later criticised by Mr. S.L. Salzedo:-

"12.1.07

MR PATRICK ALEXANDER'S AVIATION
THEORIES

To the Editor of THE AUTOMOTOR JOURNAL

Sir. - Will you allow me to raise a doubt in respect to one of the interesting suggestions of Mr. Patrick Alexander regarding aeroplanes and propellers in your issue of December 29th.

I refer to the experiment in which a fixed propeller is made to revolve in front of another propeller mounted freely on a spindle, and in which it is shown that the free-mounted propeller, set rotating by the spirally moving air from the motor driven propeller, likewise moves towards the latter in the teeth of the air impact.

Mr Patrick Alexander concludes from this that a shaft lying fore and aft and driven by a propeller deriving its power from its own motion through the air, would be "worth its weight."

Does Mr. Alexander mean that this shaft should have a propeller both fore and aft? If not, I fail to see the parallelism. If he does, I suggest that with any length of shaft and an aeroplane in motion, it is highly questionable whether the air would retain its spiral velocity between the propellers. Even assuming that it did, I think Mr. Alexander has been led into some confusion of thought; the only result, as shown by the experiment—and this is the main point—would be to draw the propellers towards each other, which would obviously be without effect on the movement of translation of the aeroplanes. I venture with all defence to think that there is a generic resemblance between this suggestion and that of the gentleman who proposes to fit bellows on aeroplanes and balloons in order to blow them along by an air current directed upon the balloon or aeroplane!

Yours obediently,

S.L. SALZEDO."

Dalston, N.

Chapter 9

The Boer War 1899-1902
and Patrick Alexander makes a
Grand Tour of Europe's Aeronauts

Colonel Templer, the balloon expert of the British Army was ordered to South Africa in 1899 with the steam traction engine transport he had developed. Patrick Alexander wanted to go as a civilian observer to see how "War Balloons" were being used. There is a French note that he did get to South Africa, and visited the Transvall, but it is doubtful whether this is correct. In any case he would have been unable to make progress in the war zone, nor could he have got far from the supply base at Cape Town. The British Army first used balloons for observation purposes in the Bechuanaland expedition of 1884 and the Sudan which culminated in the Battle of Omdurman in 1898. Major Templer and Lieut. Trollope of the Grenadier Guards (both of whom were friends of Patrick Alexander) were sent out in command of a balloon corps which had some successes at first by reason of destroying the Boers' chances of fighting them by surprise and ambuscade. Newspaper accounts were illustrated with imaginative scenes of successful charges by speeding traction engines, but the artists were wide of the mark. The traction engines and the balloons were of limited value, but balloon observations and signalling were becoming useful. On his return, Baden-Powell gave a talk to the Aeronautical Society on 15th July, 1901 on the successful practical application of balloons during the South African campaign, including Ladysmith, Colenso, Frere and Spion Kop and on the march to Paardeberg.

Major Baden-Powell had been an excellent secretary of the Aeronautical Society, and when he was ordered to South Africa, Patrick Alexander promised to keep him informed regarding aeronautical matters, and sent the following letter dated June 11th, 1900:-

"Experimental Works,
Bath.
Monday June 11th, 1900

Dear Major Baden-Powell,
I promised to write and let you know how Zeppelin was going on.
I have just returned from a tour through Paris, Strasbourg, Friedrichshafen, Vienna, St Petersburg, Berlin, and Stuttgart.

Graf von Zeppelin is working away and I think the balloon will be ready very shortly he had bad luck with the gas holders, they got wet on the Railway and were seriously damaged, so much so, that fresh ones had to be made, however, he is very sanguine about getting a trial this summer.

At Strasbourg I saw Moedebeck he has just been transferred to Swinemunde on the Baltic. I do not know the reason but between you and I he is very disappointed or rather sore about it as he has been a long time in Strassbourg. Who knows but what the Germans are really going to make experiments with balloons at sea, this is only guesswork on my part, however, being an artillery man and a soldier, of course he has to go where he is ordered, privately I have heard he does not like the change.

Kress has finished his flying machine but is waiting for the engine he also hopes to get a trial this summer.

At St. Petersburg I had a long chat with Kowanko he tells me Danclivski's balloon is no good! however he seems to be absorbing the attention of the press and numerous illustrations and descriptions of his balloon have appeared in the home and foreign newspapers.

Berlin is going strong, their new Aeronautical Observatory is finished and they are now sending up kites and kite balloons with self registering balloons for sounding the upper atmosphere. They are also preparing a balloon of 300,000! cubic feet capacity to stay in the air for several days and nights together I have been asked to assist and there will be 3 others besides myself. I wonder where we shall travel to, we intend waiting for a westerly breeze and hope to come down somewhere in Asia, this is what Andree ought to have tried before the North Pole - The Exhibition from an aeronautical point of view is good and they have a splendid place at Vincennes for balloon ascents. I do sincerely hope you will be home in time to take part in the Aeronautical Congress September 15th to 20th. There will be several hundred people there and at present everything is looking promising I only hope the Parisiens will be quiet until it is all over.

We tried our big screws with good results and they have excited quite a flattering attention.

We are now experimenting how to turn them round either driven from their centres by engines or by small propellers placed at the tips.

I have never had the pleasure of meeting your brother but he has excited everybody's admiration at the splendid defence of Mafeking. I wonder if it is too much to hope if he will lend his support to getting the Government to notice the Aeronautical experiments now going on, the foreigners are receiving assistance from their respective governments.

Wishing you every success.
Believe me
Very sincerely yours

Patrick Y. Alexander"

There were many interesting aeronautical projects developing in Europe in 1900, when Patrick Alexander made his grand tour. He knew Count von Zeppelin who was busy at Lake Constance, Friedrichshafen with his first aerial ship, which he was building in a huge floating hangar. This was anchored so that it swung with the wind, so as to minimise stress and to facilitate bringing the great German balloon - as it was called at first - out of its shelter.

63

In Vienna, Wilhelm Kress had constructed a full size man carrying flying boat, similar in some ways to that of Professor Langley in America. At the time of Patrick Alexander's visit, it awaited its engine. The test flight commenced in October 1901, on the Tullnerbach Reservoir. While taxi-ing it was capsized and wrecked by too sharp a turn before it could try to take off, Kress was a Russian of German origin who became an Austrian.

Paris was the leading aeronautical country at that time, and the venue of the 1900 Conference of the Commission for Scientific Ballooning. When Patrick Alexander visited Paris, he would stay in first class hotels such as the Elysee Palace, in the Champs Elysees, or the Hotel Continental, in the Rue Castiglione. He had become an active member of the French Aeronautical Club, and supplied reports to the secretary, M. Emmanuel Aime. The French club made more ascents than any other club, no less than 500 in 1900/01 without an accident.

Patrick Alexander was elected one of the Pilotes de la Societe in 1902, the only Englishman, apart from the French speaking Maurice Farman.

At the second city mentioned by Patrick Alexander in his letter to Major Baden-Powell, Strasbourg, he met an old acquaintance, Major Moedebeck, the meteorologist and officer of the Prussian Balloon Corps. Moedebeck was interested in Patrick Alexander's invention of an "Aerosac" and he wrote an article, 'Der Aerosack von Patrick Y. Alexander', dated July 1903 for the "Illustrierte Aeronautische Mitteilungen".

> The Aerosac invented by Patrick Alexander. The Germans described it as "a pillow case, into the mouth of which a hoop has been inserted." Hoisted on a pole, it behaves the same way as the Japanese "May Carp" which is hoisted above a house on May 5th if a son has been born in the preceding year.

At St Petersburg, he had his long chat at the International Commission for Scientific Ballooning, with the Chief of the Russian Balloon Corps, Colonel von Kowanko. Alexander also knew two other Russian officers, Colonel Pormortzeff and General Ryjatscheff. In September 1889, Colonel Kowanko was making experiments with carrier pigeons for balloon messages and aerial photographs, and Patrick Alexander was to propose carrier pigeons be used in the giant balloon ascent from Berlin of September 1900.

The American press was to credit him with being attache to both the Russian and Japanese governments at the time of the Russo-Japanese war 1904/05. His books of cuttings include comtemporary papers from both these countries (and Korea) with no note as to how he acquired them. Sir Alexander Bannerman was British Attache to Japan at the time, and there may have been some confusion between the two "Alexanders". No records have come to light, but steamer passenger lists might solve the mystery.

The Russians took aerial photographs on films of collodion according to a wet process. The negatives were developed in a primitive dark room in the basket of the balloon; the collodion films were stripped from the glass and secured to the pigeons. The results were said to be a successful, but tedious and awkward, and another method was adopted whereby the undeveloped film was delivered by the bird to its home loft.

Illustrierte Aëronautische Mitteilungen.

| VII. Jahrgang. | Juli 1903. | 7. Heft. |

Der Aërosack von Patrick Y. Alexander.

Gegen Ende Februar hatte ich die Freude, in Neisse durch den Besuch von Mr. Alexander aus Bath beehrt zu werden, welcher mir seinen «Aëro-sack» vorstellen wollte.

Der Aërosack besteht aus einem zylinderförmigen Sack aus ungedichtetem Leinen oder Baumwollenstoff, welcher, horizontal liegend in der Luft gedacht, vorn eine durch Schnurre und Leine verstellbare Öffnung hat, während der entgegengesetzte hintere Teil ein verhältnismäßig nur kleines kreisrundes Loch besitzt.

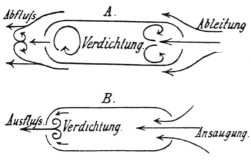

Mutmaßliche Bewegung der Luft im Aërosack.

Das Merkwürdige an diesem neuen Luftbau war das Verhalten des vorn auf denselben auftreffenden Luft-widerstandes unter verschiedenen Verhältnissen. Der Aërosack blähte sich im Winde sofort voll auf, zeigte jedoch, wenn man ihn an einer an der vorderen Öffnung befestigten Schnur festhielt, einen überraschend geringen Widerstand im Winde. Mr. Alexander hielt sodann mehrmals ein Taschentuch vor die vordere Öffnung.

The Russians considered that all balloons should be easily identifiable as being military or civil, and should carry flags and pennants accordingly. Any balloon without a flag was regarded as being a recording balloon, with instruments for the return of which a reward was generally offered, and so the Russian soldiers would shoot it down. Colonel von Kowanko admitted that "certain unfortunate occurances have taken place due to the want of an easily recognisable signal. German and Austrian balloons carrying aeronauts had been fired upon by some Cossacks stationed along their frontier . . ." It appears that military balloons would be fired upon, but any balloon floating above a fortress was very liable to be treated as a spy. Since balloonists could not control the direction of their flight, and if they descended they would be treated as spies, they tended to try to escape by gaining height and hoping to find a favourable wind away from the unfriendly frontier.

Patrick Alexander made several visits to Russia, the first probably in February 1897, the evidence being his letter to Captain Baden-Powell dated May 1897; "I saw one of your kites being used in Trans Caspia last February." (Russia Central Asia = Trans Caspian Territory). He is reputed to have assisted the Tsarish government with railway construction. Mr. J.I.M. Forsyth states that "Wherever he went in Russia particularly he found scientists eager to discuss the problems of flight."

An enquiry addressed to the U.S.S.R. has brought no reply to date.

Dr. K. Danilewsky's Flying Machine had been one of the papers read at the Aeronautical Society meeting on July 17th, 1900. The notice of meeting dated April 1900 being the one at which Patrick Alexander's election to membership was recorded. Dr. Danilewsky had supplied photographs to illustrate the talk. His machine was described as a cross between a balloon and a flying machine, with the balloon supporting the weight. Another machine which was described, "The Weczera Flying Machine" from Hungary was shown in model form, and Major Baden-Powell's latest kite experiments were the subject of slides shown during the evening.

By 1901 articles from Russia in Cyrillic script were appearing among the cuttings kept by Patrick Alexander, some illustrated. He annotated one that it was "about the exploration of the atmosphere."

Prince Kroptkin in his paper, "Recent Science" described what had been done by September 1901 by Continental observers to collect data about the upper layers of the atmosphere using kites, manned and unmanned balloons and automatic registering apparatus. It was being ascertained where cold waves and heat waves came from, and how much colder it was at 30,000 feet that anyone had ever supposed. The Prince complained that Great Britain had not joined in the great international work. He thought that the time had come for co-operation, and the Sussex News dated 18th September, 1901 concurred.

At that time the Boer War was nearing its end, having revealed the weaknesses of the British Army. Balloons had been of limited value, and any funds available at the Treasury were being seized by the Admiralty which had evidence that Germany was building a fleet to challenge the Royal Navy. The Navy was not interested in balloons - yet. Only the Aero Club and Patrick Alexander took part in international research.

In May 1902 the International Conference in the Reichstag, Berlin, was attended by the War Offices of all the European powers except France - who sent civilian aeronauts - including Russia, who sent a General. Japan was also represented by members of its War Office. A sub committee was elected to consider the steps to be taken for petitioning all the Governments to agree upon suitable measures connected with the landing of balloons in a foreign country, so as to avoid the arrest of the travellers and the destruction of their instruments, "such as takes place in Russia." Major Trollope, who represented the Aeronautical Society of Great Britain was elected on this sub committee.

Patrick Alexander refers in his letter to Major Baden-Powell to the giant balloon "Le Geant" which was being prepared for a duration flight into Asia, and which he was to be asked to assist, probably with equipment and as an aeronaut, and possibly financially. He mentions the Aeronautical Congress of 1900, and his big propellers designed to make balloons navigable.

Major Baden-Powell's famous brother, Colonel Baden-Powell, later to become the Chief Scout, was stoutly defending Mafeking with a little garrison on short rations against a besieging force of Boers. The siege began on 11th October 1899 and did not end until it was broken by a mounted column under Colonel Mahon who made a 13 day dash to reach Mafeking. There were "Mafeking" celebrations in London, but the war dragged on for two more years.

Patrick Alexander referrred to the lack of support for aeronautical research by the British Government, while the Germans and French in particular were receiving financial assistance from their Governments. He was spending large sums on aeronautical and scientific research. In 1900 he was 33 years old, and thinking he would not live beyond 50, he spent accordingly.

Chapter 10

The First Zeppelin flies at 8 p.m.
on July 2nd, 1900

Descriptions of the first Zeppelin that was nearing completion at Lake Constance must have intrigued every aeronaut, and not least Patrick Alexander who was reputed to be the official British observer. Described in the New York Times as "an Aerial Train", and "a series of Airships joined to each other", the "launch" had been expected within a few days of August 16th, 1899. It would be witnessed by Emperor William, better known as the Kaiser, with the Empress, the King and Queen of Wurtenburg, the Grand Duke of Baden, and many members of their Courts. The name General Count Ferdinand von Zeppelin, a Wurtenburger, became known everywhere. The story of a famous cavalry charge he made in the Franco-Prussian war recalled his brilliant service as an officer. The now venerable gentleman with his long white hair but still preserving the litheness of movement, fiery courage and unbending tenacity of his youthful days was linked with his reputation for grappling with the problems of aeronautics and the mathematical riddles posed by the great airship. Despite the many ill-conceived ideas of other designers, who failed to achieve success with their schemes and lost the money of their supporters, the necessary huge capital had been raised by German bankers, financiers, famous scientists, and members of the royal families. A huge floating bridge, 200 yards long, and a depot had been built at Friedrichshafen, where the "train" was to be assembled after being fabricated in various foundries and factories. The airship was described as an aerial tube, composed of tubing and cordage, with a car for passengers, another for the Daimler motor, with "boats" for the Captain, engineers and crew hung under the great balloon. The article admits that the description is neither clear nor explicit, but blames the patent, "which in true German style is even more abstruse and unintelligible." The airship was, assured the worthy General, able to carry a freight of 1,900 kilogramms (1.87 tons), rise to 1,500 metres (4,100 feet), remain airborne with ease for a week, and have a speed of 10 metres a second (over 18 miles an hour).

Count von Zeppelin's experiments had begun in 1892, and after several postponments, it was finally announced that the first flight would be at the beginning of July 1900, weather permitting. The press referred to it variously as an aerial ship, an aerial train, a steerable balloon, and a flying machine and credited the Count with an age of 83, (he was 62).

On Sunday July 1st, the Zeppelin LZ1 was waiting for the wind to drop, to permit it to be brought out of its floating hangar for the first time. Forty thousand people - including three thousand cyclists - waited for hours in the hope of seeing the historic first flight. Two small balloons were released to test the wind direction and strength, and then there was alarm as two explosions were heard. It was said that one of the seventeen balloons inside the airship had exploded. Then the motor of a benzine boat exploded, setting the boat on fire. The local Fire Brigade extinguished the flames, and rescued those on board.

The crowd was becoming irritated, hissing and cries of "treachery" followed, but eventually the airship was brought out as the engines started. The airship was allowed to ascend a few yards to test its carrying power and the action of the

A Souvenir of Friedrichshafen, July 2nd, 1900

propellers. As darkness was falling, and everything was apparently satisfactory, it was towed back into the floating hangar. It was announced that the first ascent would definitely be the next day, weather permitting.

On Monday, July 2nd, 1900, Count Zeppelin's LZ1 was brought out of its floating hangar, and at 8p.m. it started to move, powered by its two Daimler engines, each of only 16 horse power, driving four screws 44 inches in diameter, one pair being at the bow and another at the stern. The speed travelling against a light wind was stated to be 18 miles an hour. On board were Count von Zeppelin, Baron Conrad Bassus, Herr Eugene Wolf, Engineer Burr, and Mechanical Engineer Gross.

As British Observer, Patrick Alexander was in a lauch that went as near as it could to the scene, and he brought back picture postcards of the airship flying above the launch. No doubt he could have marked himself with the traditional "X".

Patrick Alexander observes the first Zeppelin flight
from the launch, 'Schwaben'

The first flight of the first Zeppelin was reported as being for 35 miles to Immenstadt, according to Reuter, but actually it was only 3.5 miles to Immenstadt, 1/10th the distance reported. The decimal point had disappeared in the process of telegraphing to England. The correction "very much diminishes the wonder of the flight, though even so it is no doubt an achievement", reported the Evening News, 18th July, 1900. The flight had been hailed in England as a great success.

The flight was not really a success. The engines were hopelessly underpowered for such a huge craft, but at last a metal ship had floated in the air, which many had said could not be done. Earlier doubters had refused to believe that a metal ship could sail the seas, and such proposals had been ridiculed. Balloons could rise and fall but only travel with the wind. The French had built small airships that had flown, and even returned to the starting point but Count von Zeppelin planned greater things - a navigable craft that could cross the Atlantic in 4 days was among his projects. Patrick Alexander had studied the problems involved, and made trials, but this was on a scale as great as anything dreamed of. There would be bigger and more powerful airships to follow.

Zeppelin IV was to make a flight of 378 miles on her acceptance flight for the German Government, only to be wrecked in a sudden storm while engine repairs were being made to the twin 110 h.p. motors. Public reaction in Germany was immediate - £250,000 was raised and eight more Zeppelins were to be completed within a year. Count von Zeppelin was decorated with the Order of the Black Eagle. In England, the War Office deliberated and did nothing. By 1909 the Zeppelins were sufficiently reliable and controllable for a commercial airline to operate daily flights for fare paying passengers. DELAG were the initials of Zeppelin's joint venture with the Hamburg-America Steamship line. LZ5 flew 750 miles in 39 hours in 1909, and the war was in sight that would replace a passenger load by bombs.

Patrick Alexander, the Hon. C.S Rolls, Colonel Templer and other like-minded aeronauts pressed for progress and a British reply, but this when it came was on a shoe string. Only one engine was available and that was the French made "Antoinette", which at one time had to be transferred from one machine to another.

"The short flight was due to a mishap in the rudder", said Patrick Alexander at a meeting of the Aeronautical Society on 17th July, 1900. He was replying to a criticism of the Zeppelin by Hiram Maxim who had been invited by the Chairman Major H.C. Roberts to criticise Count Zeppelin's experimental flight earlier that month at Lake Constance.

The dynamic inventor Hiram Maxim had designed and built a great biplane. "The Maxim Flying Machine" had attracted the attention of the airminded Prince of Wales, (George V of later years) and the machine had actually lifted itself and its crew into the air on 31st July, 1894, only to immediately suffer serious damage. Financial difficulties prevented him from completing a replacement aircraft.

Hiram Maxim opened his criticism by repeating the view he had expressed in an interview with a Daily Chronicle representative, saying that the machine did not, in his opinion, develop anything new. This put a damper on discussion. He continued "Flying machines are certain to come in the immediate future, unfortunately I have not seen a reliable account of what took place, but it would seem, so far as I can gather, that the Count's balloon slid along in the wind very much like any other balloon". He repeated his prophesy about flying machines, adding "we certainly have enough skill in England to build flying machines", and sat down.

Patrick Alexander immediately got up to announce that he had been present as one of Count Zeppelin's assistants and had been an observer at the trial of Count Zeppelin's machine, whereupon Mr Maxim looked apprehensive and apologetic.

"The stability of the machine" said Alexander severely," was perfect, for three and a half miles we went against the wind at a speed of eighteen miles per hour; the experiment, as far as it went, was completely successful but our steering gear went wrong and we had to come down."

At that time the steering was carried out by wooden frames 13 feet square placed horizontally and vertically, and moved by a screw worked from the control platform.

One result of the flight was noted by a London patent agent, who said to the Daily Mail reporter "Genius asserts itself in a peculiar way. One month it is bicycle tyres, another month electrical contrivances which will benefit humanity; and the next month something of equal importance. Now it is flying machines . . ."

Chapter 11

Berlin's Biggest Balloon

In their journal dated July 1900 the Aeronautical Society drew attention to the preparations in progress in Berlin for the construction and equipment of a very large balloon for a scientific expedition, the principal object of which was to determine the duration of the lifting power of balloons.

The passengers in the balloon would be Dr. Berson and Dr. Suring of the German Meteorological Institute, Herr Zekely, an engineer of Postdam, and Patrick Alexander of Bath, the aeronaut and meteorologist.

The world's headlines read "AN ASCENT OF CONSIDERABLE SCIENTIFIC IMPORTANCE AT BERLIN". The October number included a telegram from Patrick Alexander announcing the departure of the balloon from Friedman, Berlin, on Sunday September 23rd, 1900 at 5.53p.m.

In his letter to Baden-Powell dated 30th June, 1900 Patrick Alexander had mentioned his invitation to join the expedition which was to use the world's biggest balloon, and establish endurance records, besides taking scientific and meteorological readings. The planning was being done by the Berlin Meteorological Institute for an ascent in September 1900 as soon as the wind was favourable. They were to have the use of Herr Zekely's gigantic balloon which had a capacity of 9,000 cubic metres of gas which was variously calculated as 11,772 cubic yards or 317,844 cubic feet. At that time the standard British "War Balloon" contained 10,000 cubic feet and the maximum size of a Gordon Bennett Race balloon was 77,000 cubic feet. Only the captive balloon of the 1879 Paris exhibition was larger, with 880,000 cubic feet.

The total weight was stated to be 7.25 tons, plus 3.50 tons of ballast and a trail rope 300 metres long which weighed 0.25 ton. This was to control the height of flight.

The basket or "car" as it was called weighed 0.25 ton, and was provided with every possible up-to-date requisite of the day, including provisions for several weeks, and maps of the foreign lands it might drift over, including Russia and Scandinavia. The French, who treated the matter with scant respect, added "and China" - after all, were they not THE balloon experts of all time? The expedition carried what was described as "rapid fire armament, rifles and revolvers," (to fire

73

back if attacked over Russia?). The car was over 2 yards square, and would float if they came down in the sea. It contained two iron bunk bedsteads, a collapsible dining table, three of the new electric lamps to be powered by lead/acid accumulators which would give 300 hours of lighting. These were carried outside the car, with three zinc tanks each containing 55 litres of water. The provisions included eggs, tinned milk, fruit and wine, biscuits and jam. The provisions were calculated to last 20 days. The total load was put at 4 tons, and it took ninety men

Inflating "Berlins Biggest Balloon" — 23rd September 1900

Die erste wissenschaftliche Ballon-Dauerfahrt: Der Ballon beim Beginn der Gasfüllung.

Berlin's biggest balloon - one hour after inflation commenced

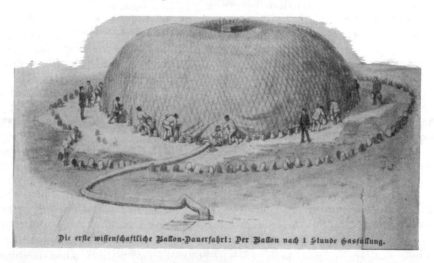

Die erste wissenschaftliche Ballon-Dauerfahrt: Der Ballon nach 1 Stunde Gasfüllung.

After four hours

After nine hours

of the Military Ballooning Detachment, and forty men of the Railway Regiment 3 hours to carry out the loading and to hold down the balloon.

The ground crew was under the command of another famous German aeronaut, Captain von Tschudi.

From left to right: Prof. Suring of the Prussian Meteorological Institute, Patrick Alexander, (seated), Prof. Berson and Herr Zekely. The basket contains trained pigeons for communication with Berlin.

A large basket was also carried outside the car, containing a number of trained pigeons for purposes of communication with Berlin. This basket can be seen in the photograph taken on Sunday 27th September, 1900, just before the take off. Patrick Alexander is sitting cheerfully on a box, with the three Germans standing behind. Behind them is the great balloon, with some of the ground crew.

Why had Patrick Alexander been invited to be one of the party on such a prestigious occasion? The Kaiser planned to attend the ascent, (in the event he was unable to do so) and thousands of Berliners crowded into the area, and on to roofs. There were several very competent German aeronauts, who could have joined the party. All the senior officers of the Balloon Detachment and Meteorological Institute were present, possibly anticipating the presence of the Kaiser, who was keenly interested in aeronautics and meteorological work, and helped whenever funds ran out. One officer that Patrick Alexander may have displaced was Captain A. Hildebrandt, Instructor of the Prussian Balloon Corps, sometimes referred to as Captain of the Kaiser's Balloon corps.

It is possible that Patrick Alexander's financial and other assistance, including equipment, plus the loan of his Majestic balloon could be the answer. Herr Zekely had designed the balloon, which was made at the Hanover works of the Continental Caoutchouc and Gutta Percha Company.

First a military balloon took off, to show the wind direction, and at 5.45p.m. on Sunday, 24th September, the aeronauts entered the car, final orders were given during a nine minute period, then the tethering ropes were cast off and the balloon rose majestically, swept gently along by a breeze towards the north east. There had been a calm while the balloon was inflated, and this had facilitated filling and balancing the balloon and its load. They drifted towards the Baltic and Sweden, and were soon out of sight of the thousands of spectators around the military enclosure, and those who swarmed on the roofs.

The balloon was not intended to rise very high, and the aeronauts relied upon the great 300 metres of trail rope to keep them from rising higher. The rope had been a great inconvenience, as it was coiled into the car, almost filling it, and they paid it out as soon as possible. At first the weight of the part dragging along the ground resulted in the balloon rising, but as the extra length became suspended, its weight pulled the balloon down again. All seemed to be going well, as they floated along in the late summer dusk over the northern suburbs of Berlin, into Brandenberg, when trouble arose. Their cable swept through the telegraphic line from Bernau to Wandlitz - not that they knew much about this - but the end of the great cable was becoming unravelled, and soon it became entangled with the trees, bringing them to a standstill. All struggles to release it were in vain although the wind was still light. They decided to have a meal and wait for daylight which might bring someone who could cut them free. It was decided inopportune to release a pigeon carrying the news. After all, the pigeon would have to fly back against the wind to Berlin which would affect its performance, and it was thought that as it was dark, the bird would either wait for sunrise to get its bearings, or would lose its way.

They settled down for the night as comfortably as they could in the cramped car, waiting for dawn and someone with an axe. But the wind was increasing, the balloon became restive, and the car swayed more and more. At about 10.30 p.m. a squall hit them, and the balloon was beaten down until it touched the trees. Afterwards it was estimated that the wind velocity had quadrupled, to something over 20 miles an hour. In the dark, and with the great balloon plunging madly out of control, they decided to open the valve that would release all the gas. They dropped into the trees, and so to the ground, luckily without injury, but the balloon was badly damaged. In the confusion, one pigeon was released, but either no message was attached or it fell off, and when it was received in Berlin at 8a.m. it was found to carry no despatch. By 11p.m. they were safe but bitterly disappointed.

They were near the town of Bernau, to which they eventually made their way to send telegrams.

"GIANT BALLOON A FAILURE" was a typical headline around the world. The French had been having a lot of fun referring to "M. Pickwick Alexander," and to the proposed flight to Siberia - or China - and there they were with their great balloon, stuck in a tree 20 kilometres from the start. . . . .

The Americans had asked that the great balloon be brought to their Exposition at St. Louis in 1904, and that had now become unlikely. The balloon was salvaged and used for another flight, which almost had a tragic ending. Once again it floated near Bernau, this time caught in a very strong wind - "une vitesse fantastique" said the French, and on towards the Baltic. Fearing to descend into the sea, the two aeronauts crash landed the balloon on a sand spit between the sea and a lake, throwing one aeronaut out. The loss of his weight made the balloon rise rapidly, the other aeronaut hurriedly dropped into the lake, and was lucky to be rescued by a fisherman. The balloon was never seen again.

At a discussion about the accident, it was realised that if Patrick Alexander and his companions had cut the trail rope near the car, where they could reach it, the loss of weight would have resulted in the balloon rising out of control besides nullifying their height control arrangements. It appears they had no gas control valve, as these tended to leak gas, and a duration record was being aimed at.

Trail ropes became increasingly unpopular, they could snag if fitted with steel tips, and fray if not so fitted, when the frayed ends could also snag. The loss in 1897 of Andree's North Polar Expedition balloon was attributed to to the end weights coming unscrewed and lost from the trail rope, upsetting the balance of the balloon.

Griffith Brewer used a bundle of hemp at the end of a trail rope 60 feet or so in length, and when hung from the basket at night, in light winds, this gave warning if trees were approached too closely - he described it like going fishing, and a 'bite' would attract attention, even when the trees were invisible in the dark.

What happended to Patrick Alexander? He went on to Friedrichshafen, and the first Zeppelin but first he sent this report to Monsieur Aime, Secretary of the Aeronautical Club of Paris, which was printed in The New York Herald, 30th September, 1900:

MR. ALEXANDER WRITES
Describes His Experiences on the
Giant German Balloon

M. Emmanuel Aime, secretary of the Aero-Club, has received the following letter from Mr. Patrick Alexander, of London, describing the unlucky voyage of the giant German balloon:-

"We left the Friedenau Sports Park on Sunday evening, The first thing we did was to pay out the guide-rope, which completely filled the car, and therefore greatly inconvenienced us. It took us exactly an hour to get rid of it, which is not surprising, seeing that it is 300 metres long and weighed five quintals. For some time all went well; the balloon was perfectly balanced. A little after seven o'clock we arrived above Bernau, and passed over a wood. The guide-rope had not been strengthened with steel wire at its lower end for fear that it should get entangled, so that it quickly became unravelled. The end caught in a tree, and we were hitched.

"As the wind was not blowing more than two to three metres a second, we decided to remain in the air, and wait for daylight to get the peasants to cut our cable and continue on our voyage if the wind proved favourable. Unfortunately, at half-past ten, the wind rose to great violence, and began beating the balloon down upon the trees at a speed of eight or nine metres per second.

"As the balloon was enormous (displacement 9,000 cubic metres and of 25 metres diameter) it would have been madness to remain as we were. We decided to land, and opened the valve. We fell on the trees, which broke the shock. At eleven o'clock in the evening we were on land, thoroughly disappointed, but I think we did what was best. Write to me in Switzerland where I am going to witness Count Zeppelin's experiments on the Lake of Constance.''

He arrived at Friedrichshafen about the time of a serious mishap to the Zeppelin on the night of 25/26th September. Arrangements had been made to refill the balloons with hydrogen, when during the night, the fastenings from which the airship hung broke from their chains, and some 10 tons of airship fell with a tremendous crash, twisting the ribs. Repairs would take at least two weeks, and Patrick Alexander returned to England. It had been a bad week.

Chapter 12

The L'Aerophile

The French may have made fun of Patrick Alexander and other British aeronauts upon occasion. They once called him Monsieur Pickwick Alexander, but his work was well known and appreciated, and he was an active member of the French Aeronautical Club.

L'Aerophile featured him in their series "Portraits D'aeronautes Contemporains." The article is dated August 1900, but includes a mention of the Giant Berlin Balloon accident which took place on Sunday 23rd September, 1900.

Translated by Mr. J. Marson.

PORTRAITS OF CONTEMPORARY AERONAUTS

PATRICK Y. ALEXANDER

"Independent, a bachelor, the only one in the world according to his own energetic expression, a globe trotter gifted with a supreme level of mobility, I was going to write about British ubiquity, (being everywhere, or in an infinite number of places at the same time.)

He is known for having seen all that exists, men and things about the air, in England, France, Germany, Switzerland, Austria, Russia, America, China, Australia, in the whole world—and in the Transval.

He is in touch with Santos Dumont, Count Zeppelin, Rotch, Berson, Heigsel, Besancon, Hermite, Roze, Busson, Langley, Kowanko, Mallet, Lachambre, Renard and the Emperor of Turkey*.

He has been up in a balloon, in a hot-air balloon, and parachute—or more exactly came down by the latter. He will be going up into the thermosphere—and probably by kite.

* Anglicised: (Author's note Uncle Tom Cobley and All).

He went up from Crystal Palace, from Bath, from Paris, from Berlin, from Vienna, from St. Petersbourg, from Moscow, from Nijnii- Novgorod (Gorki) and came down all over the place, on the ground and at times, in the sea.

L'AÉROPHILE

Directeurs : Georges BESANÇON et Wilfrid de FONVIELLE

8e Année — N° 8   Août 1900

PORTRAITS D'AERONAUTES CONTEMPORAINS

Patrick Y. Alexander

Indépendant, célibataire, « seul au monde », selon son énergique expression, globe-trotter doué au suprême degré de la mobilité, j'allais écrire de l'ubiquité britannique.

Connaît pour l'avoir vu tout ce qui existe, hommes et choses de l'air, en Angleterre, en France, en Allemagne, en Suisse, en Autriche, en Russie, en Amérique, en Chine, en Australie, dans le monde entier et dans le Transvaal.

He went through the atmosphere with Spencer, Berson, Suring, Zekeli etc., and also alone with his shadow, in his second ascent in July 1891.

He crossed the Channel by balloon from Dover to Gravelines in the 15th Sept. 1899, and also the Baltic Sea to make the double.

And of course he took part in the ascension of the huge balloon from Berlin on 23rd Sept. 1900 and remained stuck in that unfortunate tree which stopped the '8,000 Cubic Metres' 30 kilometres from the start, supposedly for the exploration of Siberia.

At the moment he is following up the manoeuvres of Zeppelin's balloon over Lake Constance.

He has a passion for aeronautics as with all the sciences and the means to satisfy it with that rare originality of being at the same time clever and wealthy.

He has pursued massive research in his Experimental Works of Bath, on the output of aero engines and particularly on propellers of which the span reaches up to 10 metres.

He has published one of the most interesting and useful books in aeronautical literature. An abridgement of aeronautical specifications where he has brought together all the patents taken out in England concerning aerial navigation and all projects carried out previously by inventors from the most serious to the most Bizarre.

He is himself the author of the most audacious idea ever to have come out of aeronautics; being given a little elongated balloon carrying the Indian Mail without a pilot to direct it from the coast over the Straits of Dover sending it radio waves to operate an impellor controlling the take off, descent and movement to left and right.

He believes the problem not only possible but simple—and he will resolve it.''

The last year of the 19th century had brought halycon days for Patrick Alexander during which he was able to travel widely and participate in the excitement of aeronautical progress. The 20th century was to bring greater progress than most people dreamed of, but Patrick Alexander's health—possibly due to his bad leg—tended to put a brake on his activities.

Chapter 13

Meteorological Work

The Meteorological Office was originally a department of the Board of Trade. Established in 1854, it is now part of the Ministry of Defence.

Man has studied the weather for many centuries. Once folklore was the extent of knowledge, but the science of meteorology depends on facts, and aeronauts were quick to appreciate that they could obtain facts in the course of their ascents. For as long as men had sailed the seas, lives had been lost, and ships sunk by lack of accurate weather forecasting. One of the first examples of international co-operation was the Conference which met in Paris in 1896, when the International Commission for Scientific Ballooning was inaugurated, to be followed by conferences every two years. These were held at Strasbourg (1898), Paris (1900), Berlin (1902), St Petersburg (1904), and Milan. Previously, research had been sporadic and depending upon individual effort, one of the foremost meteorologists was James Glaisher who founded the Royal Meteorological Society in 1850, and adopted really scientific methods for his twenty-eight ascents. Several meteorologists lost their lives when they ascended too high, and unmanned balloons (sondes) came into use.

Unmanned balloons carrying automatically registering instruments were first tried by the French aeronauts Hermite and Besancon in 1893. These balloons were so successful that subsequently, at the Meteorological Conference held in Paris in 1896, simultaneous ascents on prearranged dates were agreed upon, and balloons, both manned and un-manned, were launched from places all over Europe. Valuable data regarding meteorological conditions was obtained. Similar experiments were made in U.S.A., including those by Lawrence Rotch of the Blue Hills Observatory, near Boston, Massachusetts, who also used kites, as did the Germans. The sondes carried instruments above the height limit that human beings could survive in. They were set to burst at prearranged altitudes, then to parachute to earth for return to the laboratory concerned.

In almost every European country such ascents were made on a fixed day in each month. In England only Patrick Alexander's private enterprise ascents and balloon sondes did something to remedy the deficiency. The Daily Telegraph observed that "even in science our 'splendid isolation is visible", (January 1902).

Charlie Poole preparing paper 'ballons-sondes'
at Patrick Alexander's Experimental works, Batheaston

Europe noted that no-one from England attended the 1898 conference, but Patrick Alexander provided his balloon "Majestic", this time for use by the Prussian Balloon Corps at Tegel, Berlin. With a capacity of 3,000 cubic metres of gas, it was the largest captive balloon used.

Interest in the subject was increasing, and one of the first weather maps to be printed in a British newspaper appeared in The Times dated 15th September, 1899.

Interest in Scientific Ballooning was slight in England, but by January 1902, the scientific ascents in Europe were being reported. Great variations of temperature had been found at different localities in the uppermost layers of the atmosphere. The coldest were at the northeast, the warmest at the southwest. At 5,000 metres the temperature was 20 degrees Centigrade above Paris while above Vienna, it was only 11 degrees Centigrade. Isothermal lines were found to run from south towards the northeast, those of minus 10 degrees Centigrade extending from the north of the Adriatic westwards to Moscow, and those of minus 15 degrees Centigrade from south west France to St. Petersburg. The lowest pressures were above England, the highest above south west Europe. Wind speeds at various altitudes were recorded. ("Christian Work" 29th January, 1902).

The comments of the press were to the effect that improved weather forecasts were to be hoped for as a result.

International ballon sonde. The Swiss ascent of 3rd September, 1903.

Patrick Alexander became a Fellow of the Royal Meteorological Society on February 20th, 1901 and Secretary of the International Aeronautical Commission in 1902. He combined ascents in his own balloon from the Crystal Palace with simultaneous ascents by sonde balloons from Bath. The Reverend John M. Bacon, who became a keen balloonist, wrote in his book "The Dominion of the Air", "Mr. P.Y. Alexander of Bath, who has long been an enthusiastic balloonist, and who had devoted a vast amount of pains, originality, and engineering skill to the pursuit of aeronautics, was at this time giving much attention to the flying machine, and was indeed, one of the assistants in the first successful launching of the Zeppelin airship" . . . . "The first occasion when the writer was privileged to occupy a seat in the balloon furnished by Mr. Alexander was on November 8th, 1900. It was equipped with the most modern type of instruments. It was a stormy and fast voyage from the Crystal Palace to Halstead in Essex, 48 miles in 40 minutes. Simultaneously with this, Mr. Alexander dismissed an un-manned balloon from Bath, which ascended 8,000 feet, and landed at Cricklade . ."

The Daily Mail dated 8th December, 1900, included an account of Patrick Alexander's release from Bath of sondes balloons carrying self recording instruments, in co-operation with continental meteorologists, using varnished paper balloons costing £2.10s (£2.50) instead of £25, the cost of a small silk balloon. The first paper balloon was released on Thursday 6th December, 1900.

Baro-thermo-hygrograph, designed for recording balloons by Dr. Hergeschell and made by Bosch of Strassburg.

Whenever Patrick Alexander sent up a sonde balloon fom the Mount, Batheaston and it was found and returned, he would notify the meteorologist, Professor William Napier Shaw, F.R.S., with details of time and place of ascent and descent, and forward the record charts. A typical letter is dated 11th January 1901:

"We had an ascent yesterday at 12.40, the balloon descended 1.5 at Chipping Sodbury. I hope to show you the records next Wednesday. Dr. Symons has a usual very kindly assisted me.

Believe me,
Very sincerely yours,
Patrick Y. Alexander"

A previous ascent "at noon from Bath" descended near Cricklade three quarters of an hour later. The record was detached and torn and the instruments damaged. The temperature at ground level had been just below freezing. The descent had commenced at about 12.20 p.m. at an altitude of 2,300 metres, with a temperature 15 degrees below zero. Another balloon was launched early in February 1901 at 9.50 a.m. and was picked up at sea at 2 p.m. about 15 miles south west of the Casquet rocks, by Captain Rualt's steamer 'Vulcan'. The captain sent a telegram on his arrival at West Hartlepool to Patrick Alexander.

Patrick's next letter to Professor Shaw is dated 25th March 1901:

"I have been ill for a month and not able to attend to the enclosure before.
I was in Berlin 6 weeks ago to witness private trials of Hofmann's flying machine the model of which I thought would be very suitable for carrying self registering instruments and controlling its direction with Hertzian wave power.
The machine travelled very well without control but unfortunately about three weeks ago at a public evening demonstration a jigger arrangement jammed with the result that it came to the ground like a brick and smashed, 'twas ever so, however we are building another and trying once more.
I enclose cheque for D.W. reports (*) for which kindly let me have a receipt.

Believe me,
Very truly yours,
Patrick Y. Alexander

P.S. How is the S. Polar expedition getting on. I met some of the German expedition in Berlin they were talking over several arrangements of kites to take with them. I am sorry the wireless kites will not be ready in time."

*D.W. = Daily weather reports.

The wireless kites may have been Cody's kites, which were being used for this purpose by the Navy in a number of trials to carry wireless aerials higher than the smaller ship's masts were capable of doing.
Cody's kites were attracting attention, but he and his theatrical bookings were in the north. Patrick Alexander and E.S. Bruce, Hon. Secretary to the Aeronautical Society, wanted a demonstration near London. A letter dated 14th July from S.F. Cody to E.S. Bruce about kites and the prospect of a demonstration ends with the following information:

"I may mention that I have supplied Mr. Bruce who is at the head of the Scottish Antarctic Expedition - which starts in August - with one of my No. 1 size aeroplanes." (The latter is one of Cody's terms for his kites).

H.M.S. Hector towing a kite in 1903

87

The demonstration of Cody's kites took place as part of Patrick Alexander's centenary celebration of the 1802 balloon ascent at Bath, on 9th September, 1902, and was a great success.

1902 was also the year of the Fog Enquiry, and he lent his small signal balloon to the Meteorological Office. The balloon had a capacity of 3,500 cubic feet of gas, and was to be flown captive at 1,000 feet. Unfortunately, it broke loose, and most of the references to Alexander in the Report of the Fog Enquiry arise because of this, and nothing very significant appears to have resulted from the Enquiry.

About this time he "went to the Amazon to Hunt the Cyclone" according to Major C.C. Turner. Between 1887 and 1900 there had been several books published on the relation between tropical and extra-tropical cyclones, and it was known that the unstable climate of the British Isles was in the main due to cyclonic areas. No other references to this "hunt" have been found, and it may have been a good excuse for a holiday, after his illness of March 1901.

The Southport Exhibition of September 1903 included a section devoted to meteorological research of the upper atmosphere by kites and balloons. Mr. W.H. Dines, (Secretary of The Meteorological Society), exhibited charts obtained from self recording instruments sent up by kite at Crian, North Britain, in July and August 1902, and Dr. W. Mansergh Varley exhibited apparatus used by Patrick Alexander for balloons - sondes experiments.

Extract from The Aeronautical Journal
October 1903
Dr. W. Mansergh Varley exhibited for Mr. P.Y. Alexander apparatus used for balloons-sondes experiments:-
1. The smaller of a pair of india-rubber balloons used for the ascent from Bath in July 2, 1903. This balloon landed at Alfreton, in Derbyshire, five hours later, having been to a height of over 20,000 metres.
2. Two new rubber balloons similar to those used in the ascents from Bath, made by the Continental Gutta-Percha Company of Hanover.
3. Barothermagraph for sounding balloon work, of Professor Hergesell's pattern, made by Bosch, of Strassburg.
    This instrument has already made two ascents from Bath, the first in July 2, when it fell at Alfreton, Derbyshire, having travelled 126 miles in five hours, and attained a height of over 20,000 metres, and the second on August 6, when it fell at Eccke, on the Franco-Belgian frontier, having travelled 229 miles in three hours and attained a height of 13,700 metres.
4. Record obtained for the ascent from Bath on June 4, 1903. The balloon fell in the sea and the records are somewhat damaged by water.
5. Record obtained for the ascent from Bath on July 2, 1903.
6. Record obtained for the ascent from Bath on August 6, 1903.

Alexander tested the new rubber balloons mentioned in (2) and (3) above, successfully making the balloon-sonde ascent from Bath that reached over 20,000 metres. He presented some to the Aeronautical Society in September 1903.

In 1905 he supplied a couple of his record-breaking balloons to William Marriott, Secretary of the Royal Meteorological Society for their exhibition in March 1905. They were inflated and suspended complete with the apparatus used. As the latter

The Falmouth Observatory

cost £60, repeated losses were a serious expense. The Society wished to give publicity to their work and to urge that any apparatus found was dealt with in accordance with the attached instructions.

Alexander resigned his Fellowship of the Society at the end of 1908, but rejoined early in 1917, when he was being appointed Meteorological Officer to the recently formed Air Ministry at the Falmouth Observatory, a position he held until the end of the 1914-1918 war on November 11th, 1918.

In February, 1901, Patrick Alexander was in Berlin to witness private trials of Professor Joseph Hofmann's flying machine, the design of which he had been consulted about, and therefore regarded with favour.

The trials were widely reported, Patrick Alexander was photographed with Regierungsrath (Professor) Hofmann in the latter's workshop.

The 'Morning Leader' carried one such account, with three illustrations showing the "air-ship" on the rails preparatory to flight, also when about to commence its flight, and when "suspended in the atmosphere".

Professor Hofmann was an elected member of the Aeronautical Society in January 1903, and once mentioned to Patrick Alexander that he had not received a receipt for his subscription. Apparently the Secretary was somewhat lax in such

The view from Patrick Alexander's Falmouth Observatory rooms

matters, and the next year Patrick paid the subscription himself (£1.05, one guinea per annum), and demanded that the receipt be sent to him.

The Professor had been working for 27 years upon his invention, which was a 9ft. dragon-fly shaped "air-skimmer", weighing 7lbs, consisting of a tripod collapsible frame like a camp stool, with wheels or rollers to run on a short track, a vertical donkey engine boiler with 72 copper steam tubes and superheater on the Belleville principle, heated by alcohol. This generated a steam pressure "of 11 atmospheres" (165 pounds per square inch) which was piped to the cylinder of a small steel steam engine jacketed by hot gases and exhaust steam. This drove two double propellers revolving at 30 to 50 revolutions per second, a terrific rate of speed. As soon as the engine got up speed, the machine commenced to move forward, and before it reached the end of the short track, springs tucked up its tripod supports "just as a stork does its legs when in flight". Robbed of its supports, the machine fell, driven forwards by its propeller, but only for a split second, then the air beneath the wings supported the machine, which then gained height. The legs remained raised front and back while in flight, and acted as an undercarriage on landing. During flight, steering was effected by raising or lowering a "sail", (or aerofoil) behind the propellers. A full size machine would have a crew of two men, and burn coal or petroleum. The railroad start was not new, Hiram Maxim used a track for his great machine ten years earlier, and the Wright brothers were to use a track at first in 1903. After several successful trials, the model Hofmann Flying Machine smashed itself to pieces while Patrick Alexander was present. He later wrote to the Secretary of the Aeronautical Society:

"The Mount Batheaston Sat 30/3/1901

Can I exhibit some of the instruments that are being used in the International ascent at the next Annual Meeting which I think you said would be April 15.

I should also like to show some photographs of the Hofmann Flying Machine, the successful flights of which I witnessed in Berlin before it finally smashed itself to pieces. I can explain the accident.

I see you are giving a lecture at the Birkbeck. The vertical propellers or lifters are only a type of machine but I think they will be suitable for carrying meteorological instruments and control their movements in the air by my system of "Hertzian Waves force".

What a good discovery this is of the Diesel method of gas engines it will be a good lift for flying machines. It has long been an open secret.

When I last saw you at Bryans' lecture I said I would financially assist the Society if I may - This I am quite prepared to do with the extent of £100 annually for 5 years - Aeronautics only wants pushing in this country and it is quite time the Authorities commenced to seriously undertake the building of flying machines. If the Council will accept my offer I shall be very pleased to assist -

Trusting you are well and with kind regards-

Believe me,
Very sincerely yours,
Patrick Y. Alexander"

Professor Hofmann (left) and Patrick Alexander, Berlin, 1901

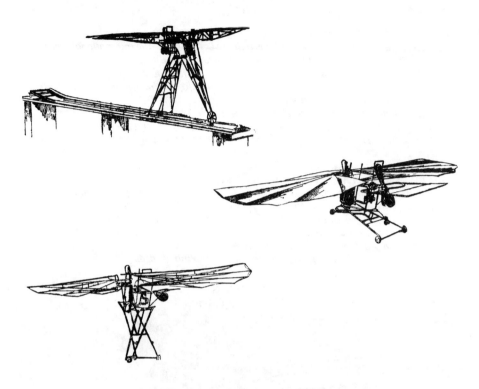

"The Hofmann 'Flying Machine'

The Mount   *Weds 1/5/1901*
   Thanks for yours of yesterday acknowledging the £100. I hope you have not "blued" the lot in drinking my health at the Buckingham Palace Hotel.
   I wrote you at Palmeira Avenue asking if you have anyone going to see the trial of Veryara's machine in Glasgow. May I ask if you have any news of Baden-Powell?

Very sincerely yours,
Patrick Y. Alexander"

At the General Meeting of the Aeronautical Society on 4th December, 1902, with Major Baden-Powell, the President, in his chair, the Secretary gave details of the finances of the Society, showing that they had 100 members, an income of £355, and expenditure of £151, leaving a balance of £204. Thus Patrick Alexander's donation had virtually doubled the balance of income over expenditure as the ordinary subscription was one guinea (£1.05) per annum.

One consequential benefit that Patrick Alexander appreciated was a supply of free tickets for Society events and additional copies of the Journal to pass on to his friends. When later these perquisites failed to reach him, he was far from pleased.

Chapter 14

Halcyon Days for
Patrick Alexander and the
Aeronautical Societies

In April 1900 Patrick Y. Alexander was elected a member of the Aeronautical Society. (Aeronautical Journal April 1, 1900).

The next journal dated July 1900, ended with a list of applications for patents, the last being:- "5,092. P.A. Alexander, of the Experimental Works, Bath. Improvements in or connected with Air Propellers".

The programme of papers read during the 1900 season of meetings of the Society included:

1. "Cloud Photography from Balloon", by the Rev. J.M. Bacon, illustrated by photographic lantern slides.
2. "Portable Electric Balloon signalling in War", by Mr. Eric Stuart Bruce, M.A., Oxon, illustrated by lantern views, working models, and experiments. (He was temporary secretary).
3. "The Weczera Flying Machine", by Mr. L.W. Broadwell. A model of the machine, which had lately arrived from Hungary, was exhibited.
4. "Dr. K. Danilewsky's Flying Machine", illustrated by photographs supplied by the inventor.

During the evening some lantern views depicting Major Baden-Powell's latest kite experiments at the front (the Boer War) were projected. The meeting had been arranged as late as possible in the season in the hope that Major Baden-Powell might return in time to take part in the proceedings.

Lord Rayleigh had given the Friday evening discourse on "Flight", when it was hoped that the expected model would really fly round the theatre, unlike most models shown to the Society. The members were disappointed again.

The Society's meetings were among the best sources of information about aeronautical progress - and failures - and there was an exchange of speakers with the members of La Societe Francaise de Navigation Aerienne, whose President, Monsieur de Fonvielle came to England to address the Society upon his scientific balloon work. The temporary secretary, Mr. Bruce, was fulsome in praise of the progress of France in the science of aeronautics, and recounted the experiments of the previous secretary, Mr. F. Brearey, whose models included some that had flown round the hall - and were, it seemed, akin to those of Monsieur Penaud. There was the work of Major Baden-Powell, whose kites were in use in South Africa in connection with M. Marconi's wireless telegraphy, as no poles were long enough to carry the apparatus to the necessary height. Captive observation balloons were of the utmost value in South Africa, while officer training was the responsibility of Colonel Templer, Instructor of Ballooning at Aldershot, and an intrepid aeronaut, who had been shipwrecked on the way out with all his horses and traction engines. Mr. Bruce referred to the British war balloons of goldbeaters skin, inflated by hydrogen compressed in steel cylinders; the observations from balloons made at the siege of Ladysmith, at Maggersfontein and Spion Kop, which saved the troops from a 'death-trap'. His general review of British science included Sir William Crookes and Rontgen radiation, Mr. Glaisher the scientific balloon expert, and Hiram Maxim the inventor of the Maxim gun used in the Boer War, and the great experimental flying machine that bore his name.

Other papers at the English meeting were concerned with the flight of birds, Major Baden-Powell had studied the Secretary Bird, a type of 'Road Runner' that could take off after violent running. Mr. F.H. Wenham recalled his paper of June 1866 on Aerial Locomotion, and his conviction that flight was not impossible for man, considering the apparent ease with which large birds traversed the air, and the progress made with 'screw vanes'.

Patrick Alexander collected all such papers and reports, and was spending his fortune and his energy in getting first hand knowledge of what was happening all over Europe.

The attitude of the Aeronautical Society and the Aeronautical Club to Patrick Alexander seems to have been ambivalent. He was usually generous almost to excess with subscription lists. From 1901 to 1906 his name headed (alphabetically) many committees nominated by the Aero Club. But despite his years of ballooning, he was never awarded the Club's certificate as an aeronaut. These certificates were issued from June 14th, 1905, the first going to C.F. Pollock, with Alexander's friends F.H. Butler, the Hon.C.S. Rolls, Griffith Brewer, and J.E. Capper in the first half dozen. He was a member of the Aerotechnical Committee, and was accepted as an aeronautical scientist. The Aero Club was founded primarily by motorists, but there is no evidence that Patrick Alexander ever owned or drove a motor car.

The Aero Club had been first proposed in a balloon in which were Frank Hedges Butler, his daughter Vera, the Hon. C.S. Rolls and Stanley Spencer, the balloon manufacturer. They were chafing at the restraints of the Royal Automobile Club - of which they were active members - and after a whirlwind negotiating period, an Organising Committee was set up that included Mr. Patrick Alexander and 22 other aeronauts, among them being the Hon. C.S. Rolls, Colonel Templer and Major Trollope.

When the list of members was printed, those with their own balloon were indicated by an asterisk, and Patrick Alexander's name was one of the very small number so indicated.

The first ascent of a balloon under the auspices of the new Aeronautical Club was on November 15th, 1901 by the balloon "City of York" which flew a pennant

"AERO CLUB". The second outing from the Crystal Palace had the use of Patrick Alexander's smaller balloon of 35,000 cubic feet, "Queen of the West". The Club ordered their own balloon which was paid for by every member subscribing £10.

The agreed purposes of the Club were to include the organising of congresses, exhibitions, races and contests, and the granting of certificates of competency to members who made sufficient ascents under certain conditions to be recognised as competent to take control of a balloon. Candidature was to be open to all in a wide field of scientists and aerial experimenters.

Santos Dumont had performed the then remarkable feat of flying his one-man airship from St. Cloud, Paris around the Eiffel Tower and back to the starting point on October 19th, 1901. This had aroused great acclamation, and to crown the emergence of the Club as a force in aeronautics, Santos Dumont was proposed for Honorary membership, and invited to be guest of honour at a banquet under the chairmanship of Colonel Templer. The ad hoc committee to deal with arrangements included Patrick Alexander, the Hon. C.S. Rolls, Colonel Templer and Major Trollope, with F.H. Butler in the chair, and six other members. The banquet on November 25th was a brilliant success, attended by peers, scientists, members of the diplomatic corps, leading engineers, and many other important personages, plus the Editors of the world's press. They were halcyon days for the Club - and Patrick Alexander.

Everyone who was anyone in aeronautics was present, much to the satisfaction of the ad hoc committee. Reporters from all over the world attended, and been impressed not only by the flight of Dumont but also his prize money of £4,000 - an immense sum in those days.

After the banquet, Santos Dumont agreed to his airship, (with which he had won the Deutsch prize of £4,000) being moored in a special 'aerodrome' built for him by the Crystal Palace Co. in the balloon ascent enclosure. It had been on view in the concert room at the Palace since Easter, and members of the Aero Club could view it for free, while others had to pay at least one guinea (£1.05). Club membership cost two guineas per annum.

For some few years every committee set up by the Aero Club included Alexander. The second meeting of the new Aero Club was arranged to take place on 31st March, 1902 at Ranelagh, where a big gas main had been laid for the purpose of inflating the Club's balloons. Patrick Alexander was programmed to ascend in his private balloon with members of the Club if he was back in time from the International Aeronautical meeting in Berlin, where a fellow committee member with Alexander was Professor F.W.H. Hutchinson of Cambridge, who pinned his ideas on ornithopters. His apparatus ("No other word suffices", wrote B.J. Hurren in "Fellowship of the Air") had feathered, flapping wings which flapped at between 360 and 400 beats per minute, but did not fly.

Patrick Alexander was noted for the equipment he always carried when ballooning, and the Aero Club published a list of "Aeronaut's Equipment":

AERONAUTS EQUIPMENT
FOR LONG TRIPS AND CROSS CHANNEL VOYAGES

1. Light 'rucksac' to carry pyjamas, pair of slippers, tooth brush, etc.

2. Sleeping bag.
3. Washing basin Willesden canvas.
4. Folding table for maps & charts etc
5. Calorit tins to heat coffee & soups
6. Clothes, thick alpine guide suits to prevent cold, light waterproof coat.
7. Leather gaiters.
8. Snowshoes over ordinary boots for warmth.
9. Luncheon and tea basket.
10. Light mattress, pillow & blankets.
11. Light lifebuoy belts.
12. Crimean cap with flaps for ears.
13. Statoscope, registering thermograph barograph & hydrometer, aneroid and compass, and small rule, charts & maps.
14. Basket for wine, mineral water, aluminium gallon flasks for water, cups of aluminium, field glasses.
15. Knife for ropes, knives & forks, paper plates.
16. Electric lamps for night work.
17. Folding lamps for night work.
18. "Bradshaw" and "A.B.C." and camera.
19. Small notebook for diary & log of run.

The trophy presented to Patrick Y. Alexander in September, 1898 in Berlin

The Aero Club was more concerned with social functions and competitions than the Aeronautical Society, which was more a scientifically inclined body, without much public appeal and people failed to realise that there was such a Society, nor that it had been in existence for over 50 years.

The Daily Mail gave a series of very large prizes in the early days of aviation. The prize of £10,000 for a flight from London to Manchester was subject to a condition that the authority should be the Aero Club of the United Kingdom.

The problem was largely one of power in a light, reliable form. The Daily Mail remarked that the engines of the old days would seem as barbarous to posterity as the Puffing Billy, but that with the evidence of science, "it may soon be possible to unlock the infinite source of the electron."

Patrick Alexander began to plan how the engine problem could best be dealt with.

To obtain information about aeronautical progress, and to meet the aeronauts and designers in Europe, Patrick Alexander joined the Aero Clubs of Berlin and Paris and the Aero Club of America. At one time he was also a member of the Austrian Aero Club - Wiener-Flugtechischer Vereises Austria.

In Berlin he was given a trophy inscribed in German "DEDICATED TO PATRICK Y. ALEXANDER IN MEMORY OF THE ASCENT OF THE 15TH SEPTEMBER, 1898, BY THE GERMAN SOCIETY FOR THE FURTHERING OF AERONAUTICS IN BERLIN". The records of the Society have not been found. The trophy is in the Windsor Collection of the Royal Borough of Windsor and Maidenhead. A similar trophy is in Augsburg, in the collection of Herr Horst Hassold, of Ballonfabrik, and yet another was the subject of an illustration in the New York Herald dated 11th October, 1906 "SILVER TROPHY PRESENTED BY BERLINER VEREIN FUR LUFTSCHIFFAHRT FOR COMPETITION".

Patrick Alexander was well known and appreciated at the Berlin Aero Club. The Secretary Captain A. Hildebrandt referred to Alexander's valuable work in connection with Scientific Ballooning and meteorological research in the early years of the International Commission, and mentions his work with Herr Hofmann of Berlin, and their working model of a flying machine which was often demonstrated successfully.

Captain Hildebrandt wished to make a channel crossing from England, and in April, 1906, Patrick Alexander put his own balloon at Hildebrandt's disposal, having it prepared at the Crystal Palace. Captain Hildebrandt arrived with two friends, Geheimrat Busley and Baron von Hewald, another well known German army aeronaut. The wind was in the wrong direction, being easterly instead of the north wind needed, and Patrick Alexander arranged for the visitors to make an ascent from Wandsworth Gas Works with Mr. Frank Butler of the Aero Club of the United Kingdom. The Hon. C.S. Rolls was to be one of the party, but the wind was so troublesome - and the other trio so weighty - that he and Busley had to be left behind. "The Car" dated 18th April, 1906 reported that "The ascent was quite a success, and the balloon went away at a very good pace assisted by a favourable wind. Captain Hildebrandt has made about 200 ascents and is noted on the Continent for his daring exploits in ballooning."

The wind at first was easterly, and the balloon passed over Richmond Park and then Windsor Castle, to the delight of the German officers. Then, as the wind became more north easterly, they floated over Hampshire,and came down on Sir Anthony Cope's estate, Bramhill Park, near Winchfield. This was convenient for Hook station on the London - Basingstoke railway, and with the balloon deflated and packed into the car, the party was soon speeding towards Waterloo.

Baron Hewald had planned that the Channel crossing should aim at landing as near Paris as possible, so that the party could proceed to Milan where the German aeronauts were to give displays at the International Exposition. The displays were to include the use of a "Balloon Brake" invented by the Baron. This consisted of an iron bar with teeth, similar to a garden rake in appearance, to be fitted to the side of the balloon car and in the event of landing in a strong wind, the operation of a lever inside the car would cause the rake to clutch the ground, and bring the car to a standstill.

Mr. Frank Butler gave a press interview about the flights made that week. He gave as an example a flight made near Derby with two companions, claiming that ballooning was cheaper and quite as exhilarating as motoring.

In 1902, the name of Patrick Alexander led the list of "Pilotes de la Societe" in L'Aero Club de Paris. Other names included E. Archdeacon and Maurice Farman - both he and his elder brother Henry were English born but French speaking sons of an English journalist who had made his home in France.

Patrick Alexander wrote to E.S. Bruce, Secretary of the Aeronautical Society, in a letter dated September 7th, 1900 from the Elysee Palace Hotel in Paris -

"We are going to make you Membre d'Honneur of the Aero Club here as Monsieur Faure appreciates your assistance on the occasion of his cross channel trip. You are reported in the French Newspapers as Sir Eric Stuart Bruce, if this is correct, please let me know at once as I thought you were a Reverend gentleman . . . Santos Dumont's balloon goes very nicely and I think will be a success when the full power trials take place.

Are you coming to Paris for the Congress?

May I ask if you have any news of Baden-Powell and when he is likely to be back in England?

> *With kind regards,*
> *Believe me,*
> *Very sincerely yours,*
>
> *Patrick Y. Alexander"*

The Congress referred to was the International Permanent Aeronautical Commission of which Patrick Alexander was the Foreign Secretary for Great Britain.

Patrick Alexander was to resign from membership of this and the Aero Clubs of England, France, America and Germany in letters dated December 7th, 1907. He wrote a letter of explanation to Baden-Powell: "They're getting too prominent for me, so I am clearing out and going to take up gardening"."

About this time his letter headings became 'United Services College, St. Marks, Windsor'.

Chapter 15

The Balloon Centenary at Bath in September 1902

Patrick Alexander had long planned to celebrate the ascent by Jacques Garnerin at Bath on Monday, 8th September, 1802 from Sydney Gardens. The ascent was to be made at the same place and at the very hour (6.10p.m.) on which Garnerin ascended a hundred years before. The enterprise and hospitality of Patrick Alexander were to be extended to their greatest possible extent.

As Secretary for Great Britain of the International Aeronautical Commission he invited a truly representative gathering to witness how much progress had been made regarding aeronautics and science. The Garnerin ascent of 1802 had been a public affair, with 5 shillings (25p) charged for admission. The Bath Journal remarked in 1902 that the centenary proceedings were not quite so sensational in character. They were virtually conducted in private, with a number of gentlemen present who were interested in ballooning and science.

It was to be more than a commemorative balloon ascent, with also a display of the latest aeronautical and meteorological material and scientific apparatus that Patrick Alexander had assembled in his famous Experimental Works with the aid of Carter, his burly engineer.

Patrick Alexander had much organising to complete before the two days' celebrations. There were guests to invite, accomodation to arrange, mostly at The Mount, Batheaston - and transport from the station, also hospitality including a centenary dinner at Fortts' restaurant to complete the first day's programme.

Guests arriving at Bath Station were conveyed to Sydney Gardens, which is between the Kennet and Avon Canal and the River Avon, nearly 3/4 mile from the station. The Sydney Gardens had been in existence from the end of the eighteenth century. The Mount, Batheaston is over 4 miles north-west of the gardens, and up a long, steep hill. This presented a tiring journey for the carriages, and the rare motor cars of the day.

There is no record of Patrick Alexander getting the city's approval to his centenary ascent, nor of any civic dignitaries being in attendance, and it is possible that the Gardens were still private. The South West Gas records indicate no sign of a gas main being laid into Sydney Gardens for the purpose of balloon ascents.

Inflating the Alexander Balloon at Sydney Gardens, Bath,
September 8th 1902

The proceedings opened at 4.20p.m. on Monday 8th September 1902 by the dispatch of a small sondes balloon equipped with self recording instruments, and at 5 o'clock a pilot balloon was released to test the wind direction and strength. The great balloon "Alexander" had been inflated with coal gas, and its bulk loomed above the trees. Around the basket were Patrick Alexander's guests, about a dozen in number. By ten minutes to six o'clock, the aeronaut, Professor Gaudron, entered the basket accompanied by his assistant, the cheerful little Charlie Poole, also of London.

Illustration (Page 101)

Patrick Alexander and his guests awaiting the exact Centenary Hour for 'lift-off' of Garnerin's 1802 Ascent. The guests include (from left to right):
Mr. Baker, Major Trollope, The Hon. C.S. Rolls, Major Brain, Major Baden-Powell, Mr. Carter, Patrick Alexander, Mr. Bruce, Samuel Franklin Cody, Mr. Pearson, Augustus Gaudron, Dr. F. Alexander Barton, Mr. P. Spencer, Mr. Taylor, Charlie Poole, Captain Templar, Mr. R.A. Dykes and Mr. Groombridge.

100

Hon. Chas Rolls. - KILLER AT BOURNEMOUTH. -

MAJOR BADEN - POWELL. -

SAMUEL FRANKLIN - CODY - KILLER AT ALDERSHOT -

AUG°. E. GAUDRON, LONDON to RUSSIA IN BY A BALLOON -

Capt. TEMPLER IN A BALLOON WITH

101

Ready for the ascent from Sydney Gardens

The balloon had a lifting capacity of 5cwt. It made what was described as a "majestic ascent in the still atmosphere" and disappeared in a westerly direction while the guests cheered and waved their hats. Patrick Alexander's guests included the President of the Aeronautical Society of Great Britain, Major Baden-Powell, brother of the famous defender of Mafeking; the Hon. C.S. Rolls, of the Aeronautical Club, a keen balloonist; Major Frank Trollope, Vice President of the International Aeronautical Commission and Superintendent of the Army

102

Balloon Factory at Aldershot; Dr. F. Alexander Barton and Mrs Barton - he was a balloonist, a physician, surgeon and designer of an airship for the War Office, he had crossed the Channel by balloon with Gaudron; Mr. Groombridge, inventor of the propeller that bore his name; Mr. Richard Young - who appears to be a relation of Patrick Alexander's mother; Mr. Eric Stuart Bruce, Honorary Secretary of the Aeronautical Society; Mr. O. Field, Secretary of the Aeronautical Institute and Club; L.C.S Cody of Texas, who had been appearing on the halls at Newcastle, Glasgow, Gateshead and other theatres in the North and Midlands, where he spent his spare time flying his great kites sometimes above a theatre to the astonishment of the populace. He was appearing in his autobiographical melodrama "The Klondyke Nugget" based upon his experiences in the Klondyke goldfields in 1883 and 1884. He was extremely skilled in the use of the lasso and rifle, and an excellent shot with any gun. His show was very popular, and he was making money. This he was to spend on British aviation. One aftermath of his visit to Bath and the display of kite flying that he gave the next day at Patrick Alexander's request was that he would leave the stage and become not only Chief Kite Instructor to the British Army, but the first man to build and fly an aeroplane in England.

After the balloon ascent, Patrick Alexander entertained his guests at the prestigious Fortts' Restaurant, where Charlie Poole and Professor Gaudron joined them after their flight to Chew Magna, 5 miles from Bristol. The dinner table was beautifully decorated, everything having an aeronautical motif. Above the table

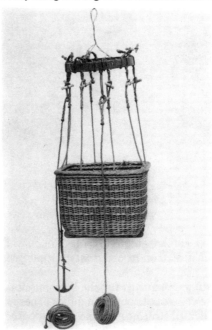

The car of the model balloon centrepiece

103

hung a model of a fully equipped balloon complete with its car. (The car survived to become one of the exhibits in the 'Alexander' section of the Windsor Guildhall Exhibition, now alas closed by the Borough Council).

The dessert and petit fours were in the shape of balloons, the wines of France and Germany reflected their aeronautical background, and everyone had a great time.

The next morning the guests met at The Mount, where several experiments had been arranged together with items of aeronautical interest in the Experimental Works. Mr. Groombridge had one of his propellers on show - he claimed that his patent propeller would effect a revolution in aeronautics.

FRONT VIEW.

The Mount, Batheaston

There was one of Alexander's man carrying gliders, which had made some short flights, and he demonstrated another patent multiple propeller driven by an electric motor.

He also showed some apparatus for the transmission of wireless telegraphy, which he used for the control of flying machines. There was one experiment that drew great interest; demonstrating extreme cold by carbonic acid gas. They then adjourned to watch a display of kites by Cody, who explained that his largest man carrying kites were too big to bring, as they required a crew of 8 men. Nevertheless, the display he gave afterwards was voted the "piece de resistance" of the day. The party went to the top of Bannerdown, the hill above The Mount. An easterly wind was blowing, and Cody sent up one of his "War Kites", which many military experts were to consider to be the best in the world, although Baden-Powell, who also designed and flew man carrying kites, for a long time preferred his own type.

Cody's kite soared up to a great height, almost a mile of wire being taken up, until it was flying steadily some 1,800 feet above the ground. He then sent up another smaller kite on the same wire, and then another, each arranged so that it stopped a short distance below the previous kite, until there was a long string of kites.

The last kite carried an explosive charge, which Cody fired high above the spectators, who by then included a number of residents of the area, and some small boys. They were highly delighted. Finally he sent up a Stars and Stripes American flag, then more kites, the uses and advantages of which he explained in his very entertaining manner, after which the guests returned to The Mount for lunch. It had been a most interesting morning.

At The Mount two of Patrick Alexander's balloons were to be seen. One inflated balloon was tethered between the house and the large glasshouse, and another bearing a Union Jack flag was inside the balloon shed. Both balloons were used as backgrounds to photographs taken as a record of the celebrations.

After lunch, a small sonde balloon which Carter and Charlie Poole had prepared, was sent up with its load of automatic self recording instruments to take meteorological recordings of atmospheric pressure, humidity, and temperature on clockwork driven drums carrying paper charts. These were in common use in Germany and in France, where they were sent up from Trappes, near Paris. Patrick Alexander was the only meteorologist operating with sondes in Great Britain at that time. The balloon disappeared rapidly in a north easterly direction, and the return of the instruments and charts were awaited. Patrick Alexander explained that about 60% of such experiments resulted in their return, which was fortunate as each set cost about £60.

He then showed a smoke-ring machine, which demonstrated how vibrations of the air carry for a considerable distance, after which a charge of gun-cotton was fired from what looked like a large megaphone. It was claimed that this instrument, a ring gun, was capable of bringing down a balloon or a kite. Finally, what was one of the most striking exhibits was the use of a new chemical compound which when ignited, reached a temperature of 5,000 degrees Fahrenheit, and burnt through a ¾″ iron plate in a few seconds, the metal shrivelling up like a piece of paper, with an intense white light. The thought struck those watching that this material, a mixture of oxide of iron and chemicals known as Thermite, would be of considerable interest to burglars and safe cracksmen. There were several other items of scientific interest, including instruments and tools useful to balloonists - Patrick Alexander was famous for the kit of tools and instruments he had perfected for aeronautical use. The guests finally left The Mount late in the afternoon, after what they all regarded as a most interesting couple of days in the beautiful country, with fascinating displays of the science to which they were devotees.

Samuel Cody later gave a series of successful demonstrations of his manlifting kites to the Navy, who purchased four complete sets of his kites for use on ships at sea. Their problem was lifting aerials high enough for long range wireless communication. They also hoped to be able to detect submarines by man carrying kites towed by warships. The latter tests went well, until the captain apparently forgot that he was towing a man carrying kite into the wind, and changed direction, with the result that the kite with the unfortunate Cody was dropped in the sea, nearly drowning him.

Kites had been tried with some success during the preceding South African war. Balloons were found best in light winds, and kites in the strong ones, but the war had shown the need for complete re-organisation, and kites were a minor matter to the War Office. An enterprising Army Commander - Sir William Butler of the Western District - had been impressed by the Cody kites he saw demonstrated at Devonport, after Cody delivered his Naval order, and Cody was invited to bring his kites and team of men (up to 8 were required for the more advanced man lifting kites) to Farnborough for tests under the supervision of Colonel Capper. The tests

Patrick Alexander and his guests at the Mount, Batheaston, including (from left to right), the Hon. C.S. Rolls, Miss Gladys Young, Charlie Poole, Major Trollope, Col. Capper, Patrick Alexander, Augustus Gaudron, Samuel F. Cody, Major Baden-Powell, Mr. Field, Doctor F. Alexander Barton, unknown, Mrs. Young, R.A. Dykes. (Front), Mr. Young, Mr. Carter. Inside the shed is Patrick Alexander's small balloon.

Another of Patrick Alexander's balloons at The Mount

took place in June 1904 and were entirely satisfactory. Colonel Capper went up with Cody on one occasion, and on another went up solo to 1,000 feet, the second highest ascent made. The highest ascent was to 1,300 feet in a wind of 17 m.p.h. One great virtue of Cody's kites was the absence of accidents. Pioneers trying out gliders and powered aircraft were being killed or seriously injured, but not one fatal accident occurred with the Cody kites, even when a main cable broke - an accident that had been feared. The kite and its basket came gently down to earth without damage. The Baden-Powell manlifting kites were less satisfactory, a fact that did not help Cody at first, as military men tended to say 'How can this cowboy showman succeed where the great Baden-Powell has failed?' Cody was not always accepted at first in other quarters. The Aeronautical Society granted him membership in 1903, but the Aeronautical Club refused his application at first. The rebuff was to be made good in 1909 when he was granted membership and later its highest award, the Club's gold medal in 1912. This was shortly before Cody was killed on 7th August, 1913 flying the big new aeroplane he had just finished for the Round Britain race. Without the recognition that Patrick Alexander had given Cody as a pioneer in man carrying kite flying with the opportunity to show his kites before an important group of aeronauts at the Bath Centenary celebrations, progress in aeronautics in England would have been slower.

The original scheme to enable Cody to display his kites at Bath before officers from the Balloon Section of the British Army may have come from Eric Bruce, Acting Hon. Secretary of the Aeronautical Society while Major Baden-Powell had been serving in South Africa. Bruce is reputed to have done much to smooth the way of the somewhat rough and ready Cody into the scientific world of the Aeronautical Society. When Cody was appearing at the Metropole Theatre, Gateshead, Bruce had written asking if his kites could be demonstrated near London. Cody replied at length, explaining that his theatrical enterprise kept him in the North and West Midlands, and describing his range of kites, from 7 to 38 feet across. The small 7 foot kite carried a spread of 1010 square feet, three were silk, the others canvas. The equipment included 8 to 10 miles of piano wire and

Samuel Franklyn Cody's kite which he demonstrated at Bannerdown, Batheaston
1. Augustus Gaudron. 2. Doctor F. Alexander Barton. 3. Mrs. Barton. 4. Mr. Carter. 5.
Rev. Winwood. 6. Col. Capper. 7. Patrick Alexander. 8. The Hon. C.S. Rolls. 9. Mr.
Young. 10. Miss Gladys Young. 11. Miss Young. 12. Mr. R.A. Dykes. 13. Major Baden-
Powell. 14. Samuel F. Cody. 15. Miss Young. 16. Mrs. Young. 17. unknown.

much cable. The larger kites required several men to handle them, the largest needed eight men.

Patrick Alexander was inviting some of the most eminent men in British aeronautics to come to his celebrations at Bath. The opportunity was too good to miss, and he sent Cody an invitation that explained the opportunity for him to show his kites to important military representatives, who previously had not shown much interest. Cody had a succession of aeronautical successes and built and flew British Army Aeroplane No. 1 on October 16th, 1908, the first aeroplane flight in Britain. Despite intermittent Press derision, he became Britain's most distinguished and popular aviator. His fatal crash was a painful shock to the entire nation, and he was the first civilian to be buried in the Military cemetary at Aldershot, with unprecedented Military honours.

The display Cody gave at Patrick Alexander's centenary celebration at Batheaston in September 1902 seems to have been more significant than it appeared to be at the time.

The Experimental Works at The Mount, Batheaston, and Bath

111

Chapter 16

Patrick Alexander and Radio Controlled Model Airships

"Atmospheric Electrification" had been known for many years when Oliver Lodge gave a talk on the work of Hertz and electric waves about 1888 to the Royal Society. Because his audience was largely in the predicament of not knowing anything about the subject, Oliver Lodge had to hastily summarise the subject so that his audience could appreciate the importance of syntonic or tuned electric oscillations. He then showed several examples of tuned circuits exciting similar tuned circuits. It is known that Patrick Alexander was with Oliver Lodge at Liverpool University, who had several assistants, but he is not one of those referred to in Oliver Lodge's book "Signalling Without Wires. The Work of Hertz and his Successors." This was before wireless had been demonstrated by Marconi in 1895, and developed to the point of transmitting across the Atlantic.

Before the end of 1900 Patrick Alexander was noted by L'Aerophile of Paris as "the author of the most audacious idea ever to have come out of aeronautics, being a little elongated balloon carrying the "Indian Mail"- without a pilot to direct it - from the coast over the Straits of Dover, sending it radio waves to operate an impellor controlling the take-off, descent, and movement to left and right."

In 1899, Patrick Alexander was interested in the wireless experiments of H.M.S. Jasseur, a tender to H.M.S. Vernon at Portsmouth. The smaller ships of the Royal Navy did not have masts tall enough to allow long distance reception with the apparatus of those days, and balloons and kites were tried experimentally (and, at first, unofficially - "The Admiralty does not encourage originality," noted Patrick Alexander). In July, 1900, Major Baden-Powell's kites were tried, and in 1904 Samuel Cody's kites were found to be satisfactory.

The experiments at Portsmouth were always of interest to Patrick Alexander, and towards the end of 1905 he was living at 'Rothesay', Spencer Road, Southsea. Shortly afterwards - probably January - he had opened an office at 73, Pearl Buildings, Portsmouth. The naval experiments with great kites could sometimes be viewed, and man carrying kites were repeatedly used for trying to spot submarines. With his international reputation as an entrepreneur, anyone interested in such work could, no doubt contact him if, say, kites, baskets and special gear was required, to ascertain "where to buy".

Patrick Alexander exhibited his device for steering a balloon by electric waves - Hertzian waves he called them - at a meeting of the Aeronautical Society held at the Society of Arts on 14th July, 1901. He also showed his "furrowed airscrew for getting a better grip on the air", resulting in more driving power for the same number of revolutions. He displayed his horizontal wheel of revolving cones, designed to increase the lifting power of kites, and "a new arrangement of the wings in skimming machines by which the flapping took place, not from the centre of the two wings outwards, but the tips being fixed in a perpendicular motion through the centre axis."

Percival Spencer, the balloonist, in another talk stated that Patrick Alexander's grooved propellers gained a much greater thrust. He described the grooves as similar to small corrugations.

In May, 1902, the International Commission for Scientific Ballooning met in the large chamber of the Berlin Reichstag. Patrick Alexander and Professor F.W.H. Hutchinson of Cambridge were the representatives of the Aeronautical Club of the United Kingdom.

Patrick Alexander, announced as a leading English Aeronaut, read a paper before the delegates on "The Steering of Flying Machines that have Meteorological Instruments on them for Taking the Temperature, Pressure, and Moisture of the Atmosphere" and explained a method of his own invention. He said "these machines can be sent away, within a radius of 50 miles, by day or night, and can be steered back to the same place. They are not only applicable to Meteorological research," he added, "but can also be used for military and naval purposes".

This was at a time when Wilbur and Orville Wright were over eighteen months from making the world's first powered sustained and controlled flight on December 17th, 1903. The round trip of 100 miles implied by Alexander's 50 mile radius was not remotely achieved even by the Wright brothers, until Wilbur Wright made the first flight of over 2 hours 20 minutes on December 31st, 1908, when he covered 78 miles. Only balloons flew longer and further - but neither were steered or controlled, so he may have had Count von Zeppelin's great airships in mind.

The Berlin meeting was expected to produce some important results, not only for meteorology, but also for military and naval purposes, and the Aeronautical Section of the German Army acted as host to the foreign deputies. The War Offices of every European power except France had sent official delegates - and France was represented by some well known civilian aeronauts. Russia sent a General and a Staff Colonel, and the Japanese War Office was represented. Major F.C. Trollope, Grenadier Guards, represented the British War Office and Lawrence Rotch, the eminent American meteorologist was present, and read a paper about the Blue Hills, Boston experiments with kites and balloons for carrying instruments.

A sub-committee was elected to consider the steps to be taken for petitioning all the Governments to agree upon suitable measures connected with the landing of balloons in a foreign country, so as to avoid their confiscation and arrest of the travellers and the destruction of their instruments, such as had taken place in Russia.

Alexander's ideas on the subject of guidance by "Radio Waves" were recalled in 1903, when the brilliant Hungarian engineer Mr. Telsa put forward the possibility of using electrical waves for the purpose. According to a report in a French journal Le Figaro, 11th February, 1908, arising from a Monsieur Branly's invention for the guiding of torpedoes by radio waves; Telsa said:

"It seems that Mr. Branly may have discovered the guiding of torpedoes by means of radio waves."

The report continued . . .

"This news, true or not, reminds us of certain schemes from a Hungarian engineer Mr. Telsa, who in 1903 put forward the possibility of supplying electrical waves to guiding in the air. He said, from the moment that a current, quite weak in effect, is capable of operating telegraphic apparatus from one continent to another, it seems certain that with sufficiently powerful equipment, it will become possible to create currents of enormous power over continents and seas, which will constitute aerial electrical tracks by analogy with railway lines on the ground, and on which aircraft will travel in the manner of our locomotives for the general transport of travellers.

The idea was not new. In 1900 an English aeronaut Mr. Patrick Alexander put it forward and was himself proposing to try some tests over the Pas de Calais.

The problem is not only possible but simple, he concluded.

It goes without saying that we will leave all the responsibility for their assertions to Mr. Patrick Alexander and Mr. Telsa the engineer."

"Your passports please," shouts the douanier.
"Come up and get them,' was the usual retort

114

Chapter 17

Patrick Y. Alexander goes to America

The Bath Centenary Celebrations of September 1902 were over, and it was late in 1902 when Patrick Alexander reached America, travelling first class on the luxurious Campania. He knew that the most serious student of aeronautics in the U.S.A. was Octave Chanute, who had brought over from Europe Lilienthal's work, together with Penaud's tail for longitudinal gliding stability. Chanute was 70 in 1902, and did no flying himself, but had several proteges who tested his gliders and their own designs. He advised the Wrights concerning glider construction. Aided by Chanute's letters of introduction, Patrick Alexander learned about the various aeronautical experts in the U.S.A., and was able to make their acquaintance. The aeronauts and aviators and their machines and balloons were the subject of a good deal of scorn in the U.S.A. especially the optimist who exaggerated the capabilities of his design, only to become something of a laughing stock when it failed to fly, but Chanute was different.

Patrick had learned enough for evaluation of some designs and projects not to be difficult. In 1900 there were a few glider designers who were no better than Lilienthal or Pilcher, but he was very favourably impressed by Octave Chanute who made no rash claims or promises. He wanted to visit the Wright brothers, who at first, only left their bicycle business in Dayton, Ohio, between September and January. Their first kite had been flown by Wilbur in August 1899, when Orville was away on a camping trip. Orville found that he could control his kite both laterally and longitudinally. With a wing span of 17 feet and an unladen weight of 50 pounds, it could carry a pilot weighing 10 stones in a prone position, the wing loading being just over 1 pound per square foot. (For comparison, a high performance sail plane might today have a wing loading of 5 pounds per square foot). Their original idea had been to fly the kite from a tower, tethered by ropes, the object being to gain experience of being a pilot without the risk of free flight. They asked Chanute's advice as to places where steady winds could be expected during the period September - January, and he suggested Kitty Hawk, 8 miles east of Dayton, Ohio, should be investigated.

When the U.S. weather bureau confirmed his advice, they set up camp for the first time at Kitty Hawk on the coast of North Carolina.

As Patrick Alexander was to find, it was a difficult journey to the small isolated settlement. The Wrights had to transport not only their aircraft, but also their tools and other equipment, camping impedimenta, and have the materials delivered for the tower.

I am indebted to the Researcher, Mr. Jerry L. Cross, Division of Archives and History, North Carolina, Department of Cultural Resources, North Carolina, U.S.A. 27611, for the following:

"By 1900 the normal route from New York to Kitty Hawk was a four step procedure. One took the train from New York to Baltimore, Maryland, then boarded a steamer to cross the Chesapeake Bay to Norfolk, Virginia. At Norfolk another train (the line now known as Norfolk and Southern) was taken to Elizabeth City, North Carolina, where a boat carried passengers across Albemarle Sound to Kitty Hawk on the outer banks. The last step of the journey was described in a letter from J.J. Dosker of the Weather Bureau to Wilbur Wright dated August 18, 1900; "You can reach here from Eliz. City, N.C. (35 miles from here) by boat direct from Manteo (Dare County) 12 miles from here by mail boat every Mon., Wed. & Friday." The route from Manteo principally served travellers heading to Kitty Hawk from the south and west. If Patrick Young Alexander had made the trip to Kitty Hawk in 1903, he most likely would have travelled from New York by the route described above."

The summer camp of the Wright brothers was near Kitty Hawk, a small settlement in a sandy area of a strip of land separating the Albemarle Sound from the Atlantic Ocean. There were a number of sand hills of varying heights and machines could be tested in different wind conditions. Four miles to the south of the Wright's camp was the Kill Devil sandhill rising to 100 feet from the flat, where the brothers tested their gliders in the three years before the first powered flight. Their glider No. 1, based on recognised data, was flown in 1900, mostly as a kite. In 1901 they flew glider No. 2, again using published data - which was found to be unsatisfactory. In 1902 they mastered flight from their own wind tunnel measurements with their No. 3 glider, using rudder and 'warping' co-ordination.

'Warping' - actually 'wing warping' - was the method of applying twisting to the wings to increase or reduce the curvature simultaneously with the rudder movement. This gave the pilot flight-control, and with their wind tunnel results, was the key discovery of the Wright brothers.

They were largely ignored and dismissed by the European aeronauts, who did not take the trouble to understand the problem, and thought of an aeroplane as a winged motor car to be driven into and steered around the sky. The problems of proper flight control were learned by gliding, which few Europeans were studying and the Wright brothers' successes were not entirely believed. Some French aeronauts implied they were false.

Their experimental flights were checked by spring scales inserted in the mooring ropes, but they found that learning the arts of piloting was hard and difficult. There were several crash landings, but their design was easy to repair. Having found that the data by Lilienthal and others was unreliable, they stopped relying on such works, and produced their own data from their own discoveries. In 1901 they made flying experiments from July 10th to August 29th, the revised period being the result of changed business pressures with the cycle business. There were, they

116

found, defects in their designs, and these they sought to eliminate by experiments during the autumn and winter of 1901/02, so that by the 1902 season they had a better glider to fly at Kitty Hawk. After devising a moveable tail linked to warping wires operating on the wings the previous tendency to spin and crash was greatly reduced, and when Patrick Alexander came by appointment to Dayton, they were working on 'Flyer No. 1' that would have an engine and, before another year had elapsed, become the first powered airplane that would fly.

During August and September, 1902, they built their No. 3 glider, which they tested successfully at Kill Devil Hills, Kitty Hawk, during September and October, making nearly 1,000 glides.

Octave Chanute and his assistant Augustus M. Herring had arrived at Kitty Hawk on October 5th, 1902, to join the Wrights in gliding experiments, staying until October 14th. Their tests of a multi wing machine built by Charles Lamson for Chanute were unsuccessful.

The brothers Wright returned to Dayton for the winter of 1902/3, confident of overcoming their next problem - that of the engine and propellers. They expected to be able to use an automobile engine, but found none suitable, so they designed and built their own. Then they found all the published material about propellers to be of little use, - presumably including the Alexander and Walker material - so they conducted their own research, and built their propellers. It was December 24th, Christmas Eve, 1902, when Patrick Alexander reached Kitty Hawk and it is a matter of conjecture as to where he spent Christmas. If he had stayed with the Wrights, this would presumably be on record. It was mid January 1903 when he returned to England, nearly 12 months before the Wrights' 'Flyer No. 1' was to make its epic first flight on 17th December, 1903, but when Patrick Alexander met the brothers, there may have been little evidence that success was relatively imminent.

The first thing Patrick Alexander did on his return to England was to write Major Baden-Powell a letter dated 21st January, 1903:

"Dear Major Baden-Powell,

I have returned from America and met and saw most of the machines and inventors worth seeing.
As I should like to meet you to have a chat on aerial matters can you let me know when and where it would be convenient to meet.
Langley, Graham Bell, Chanute and others send their congratulations and regards.

With best wishes for the new year,
Believe me
Very sincerely yours
Patrick Y. Alexander"

The congratulations were, no doubt, in respect of Major Baden-Powell's fine record in the South African (Boer) War, and because he had become President of the Aeronautical Society of Great Britain. He had arrived back at Victoria Barracks, Windsor on Monday July 21st, 1902, in command of the time expired men and reservists of the Scots Guards. The Council of the Aeronautical Society met him with an illuminated address of congratulations on his safe return, and said that they were much gratified to learn that he had carried out useful and successful experiments with his military kites.

When Patrick Alexander met the Major, he told the story of Mr. Pennington of New York. This gentleman had planned an extremely large balloon for the purpose of carrying fruit from Chicago to New York. He was also going to bring coal and bricks down to New York City. Mr. Pennington's balloon was to have a smoking room, marble staircase, ladies room, library, piano and so forth. When asked how he got the lifting effect, he said all the machinery and furniture would be hollow. When it did not work, he attempted to get over that little difficulty by pumping in more hydrogen, in the lifting effect of which he had great faith. Unfortunately, it still would not work.

There were many ill conceived schemes, which tended to give aeronautics a bad name. All the same, it was confidentally expected by Patrick Alexander and other optimistic aeronauts that someone, somewhere, would soon fly a heavier than air machine.

In March 1903, Octave Chanute came to England and was entertained to dinner at the Carlton Hotel by the Aeronautical Club. The "Top Table" to meet and honour Chanute included Patrick Alexander and Major Baden-Powell. The occasion was less brilliant than the banquet held on 25th November, 1901, held in honour of Santos Dumont, possibly the theories and practise of Chanute were not appreciated as much as the unique and remarkable feat of Dumont in flying his airship around the Eiffel Tower in Paris and actually back to his starting point. But the work of Octave Chanute was contributing to the successes of the Wright brothers, and in due course these would stun the aeronautical world.

After the reception in London, Chanute went to Paris on April 2nd, 1903, where he gave an illustrated lecture which was attended by Patrick Alexander. He described in detail not only his own (1896) gliders, but also the 1902 model of the Wright brothers. The latter was seized upon as a step in the direction of aviation progress, and several Frenchmen formed an Aviation Committee to beat the Wright brothers, and build a powered aeroplane. They made haste so slowly that it was to be March 1904 before their leading designer, Archdeacon, had a glider built but this was not successful. Other attempts also failed, until some Frenchmen contended that the Wrights' designs were falsely claimed to be satisfactory. This was because despite details being available, they failed to make even a reasonably accurate copy, nor to appreciate the need for pilot control, and were more concerned to avoid what was termed slavish copying of the American gliders.

Being French born, Chanute had no difficulty in addressing his compatriots. The chief object of Octave's talks were to benefit the St. Louis Exposition of 1904, of which he was Honorary Commissioner. He wrote to the Council of the Aeronautical Society, who invited their members to comment upon the published rules of the aeronautical contests to be held in connection with the Exposition.

He returned to the U.S.A. via England on the German liner 'Kronprinz Wilhelm' which left Southampton on 29th April, 1903. The French journal l'Aerophile were pressing him for photographs of himself and the Wright brothers, to be published

118

with an article that he had agreed to prepare. Many other people wanted copies of the photographs, - he wrote "On receipt of this go to the photographer and be 'took' and send me two copies of each at Chicago, where I expect to be on May 8th to 10th. You might get the photographer to print at my expense a lot of pictures . . .there is a run on them. I know you to be so modest as to demur, but the thing is not to be avoided, as the editor was very particular. I wish to please him because he has now apologised for having allowed a correspondent (some years ago) to call me a thief in his columns, and as a token that I bear no ill will, I have agreed to have my own picture taken and to "look pleasant".

"It seems queer," he continued, "that after having ignored all this series of gliding experiments for several years, the French should now be over-enthusiastic about them. The Germans and English have taken more notice, and it does not come as a surprise to them that men actually take toboggan rides on the air. Our friend Mr. Patrick Alexander came over from London to hear me spout, and sends his best respects to you. He says that when I get to London (which I expect to do on the 10th) I may effect considerable good for the St. Louis exposition, which is the chief subject of my talks, and the main object of my present stop in the French capital.

I have just ordered an Anemometer Richard which I will bring back with me and send you with my compliments.

With best respects to you and Orville.

Octave Chanute"

Early in 1903, Patrick Alexander was being increasingly troubled by his leg, the one broken on the voyage to Fremantle in 1885. He had three other matters on his mind; there was his ambition to be the first Englishman to fly in a heavier than air machine; he was endeavouring to keep in touch with every aeronautical designer whose work seemed to show promise and to visit the most interesting such as the Wright brothers, and thirdly, there were the products of his Experimental Works. One of these was his "Aerosac", and this new invention he gave a talk upon to the Aeronautical Society spring meeting in April, 1903.

The Aeronautical Journal - April 1903

THE CHAIRMAN : Mr. Alexander will now describe his new invention, "The Aerosac".

"It has been the custom in Japan for the last 500 years to hang these object, shaped like fish (referring to diagram on screen) over certain houses during the month of May. They are from 30 feet long and about 6 feet in diameter. There are several curious points about them worthy of notice. First, one observes the fine threads that are holding the fish. This gives rise to the thought that the head resistance is small. In fact this is the case, there are three threads and they are very fine, indeed. The fresh air blows in at the mouth. Several of these have been made up in very simple form, being merely bags with the end drawn in something like a pillow. The name "Aerosac" has been suggested by Mr. Groombridge, and I consider it a good name. As kites, they do not fly high, but possess remarkable stability. They are cheap to make, and have very little pull, in fact, at times, they have been observed to float almost by themselves. They are also extremely portable, and are almost instantly extended by

119

the wind. They are easily packed, and may be stowed away in a small compass."

THE CHAIRMAN: "Mr. Alexander is very modest, and he won't tell as much as he could about these things. Now, I happen to know something about them, because I have been down to see Mr. Alexander experiment with the Aerosac, and I have seen what he can do. I know he has gone into the matter very scientifically, and he has had some big - I don't know whether we can call them machines - but big pieces of apparatus somewhat similar to the fish which you have seen on the screen, and he has made careful tests with these in order to find out the amount of resistance that the air blowing against the opening at the end presents. And there seems to be no doubt that for some reason which I do not think Mr. Alexander can explain very accurately, the wind has a peculiar action. It blows into the hollow, and then it seems to come out again round the edges and in some way lessens the resistance, which one would otherwise have thought would have occurred in a large box inflated with the wind. Mr. Alexander has one of these machines, which I suppose is about 6 feet in diameter, and we made rather a peculiar experiment with it. This sack, is perhaps, about 20 feet or 30 feet long and 6 feet in diameter with a big hole at the front distended by a hoop, and we put its head to the wind. The wind blew it out tight and we all got inside. However, we tested with an anemometer to find which way the wind blew, because when you are inside you cannot feel any wind. We found, in testing it with the anemometer, that the wind blew straight in at the front aperture, but anywhere else it blew in the opposite direction. The result was that just close to the surface apparatus the wind was blowing along its surface, first of all practically at right angles to the wind, and then in the same direction as the wind. I think it is a most interesting subject, and one that requires a good deal of investigation. I am not convinced that it can be applied to any very practical purpose, but Mr. Alexander thinks it can, and I hope he will show us how it can very shortly."

In 1904, Major Moedebeck published in Germany a "Pocket Book of Aeronautics", and credited "Flugtechnikern Mr. Patrick Y. Alexander of Southsea, England", as well as Octave Chanute of U.S.A., with helping.

In 1907, the pocket-book was translated from the German version into English by W. Mansergh Varley B.A., DSc, PhD., whose name occurs in connection with Patrick Alexander's sonde balloon work. Varley states in the translator's preface "Mr. Alexander, the well known authority on aeronautics", suggested that he should undertake the translation. Moedebeck was a "Major und Bataillons Kommandeur im Badischen Fussartilliere Regiment Nr. 14", at Strasburg. The small book records the history and development of aerial navigation and presents a summary of the state of the science at that time, with chapters "on the physics of the atmosphere, and other branches of aeronautics from earliest times to the present day". It contains in meticulous and practical detail with illustrations what anyone making a balloon ascent needed to know, and how to take meteorological readings from a balloon equipped for such work.

While Patrick Alexander and Octave Chanute were in Paris, Mr. Groombridge had an exhibition of his aeronautical inventions with a Mr. South at 69, Regent Street, London, from April 27th to May 2nd, 1903. These included the Groombridge propeller first exhibited at The Mount the previous September, and a sectional model subsequently constructed at Alexander's Experimental Works which he presented to Mr. Groombridge. The original model was mounted on a

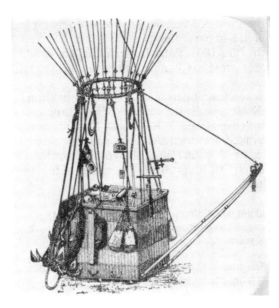

Balloon basket equipped for meteorological work

stand, with a handle the turning of which showed the action of the propeller vanes. The action was described in the Aeronautical Journal dated July 1903:

"The general construction of the new propeller consists of a main or driven central shaft, which forms an axis within a rectangle, the two vertical sides of which form the axes carrying the vanes. In the driving stroke the vanes extend outwards, beyond the rectangle, while they return edgewise or feathered within it. During the propelling stroke, the vanes become strained backwards, against the resistance of springs, and as the vanes yield to the air, the air remains practically unmoved, and thus becomes an inert or solid fulcrum against which the vanes press. As the vanes come into action they assume a vertical position, while at the completion of the stroke they automatically feather. The propelling stroke is effected upon a long or extending radius, the feathering upon a shorter one. The main central shaft carries opposite to each other two sets of vanes, so that one set is propelling, while the other is feathered, propulsion being continuous."

Mr. Groombridge also showed another propeller based upon the same principle of vanes, springs and feathering, but worked by "very different mechanism:, and a "Proposed Aerial Navigator". The latter was for an aeroplane 80 feet in length and 60 feet breadth having wings in front of, and behind the six propellers which were to be driven by three engines each of 20 horse power, the machine having four wheels. There was also a "new method of steering", which was "by a guiding vane changed with rapidity and ease from a passive to an active state." The object appears to have been to minimise the effect of the wind when the machine was on the ground. These designs are no doubt typical of the many that were being produced and never flew.

The next month, June 1903, Patrick Alexander was ill and suffering severely from his bad leg. He wrote to Chanute that he intended to return to America by the autumn.

In June 1903, there was an International Kite Competition for the Highest Kite Flight at Findon, Sussex, under the auspices of the Aeronautical Society. Patrick Alexander had wanted to attend, as his friends Major Baden-Powell and Samuel Cody were among the competitors, and their rivalry should be interesting to watch. The judges included Dr. William Napier Shaw of the Royal Meteorological Society, Sir Hiram Maxim and Eric Stuart Bruce, Secretary of the Aeronautical Society. He wrote to the latter:

"Sorry I could not come, thanks for the programme. My poor old broken leg is a great grief to me and has given more than my share of pain with all the bad weather we have had this year."

In September, 1903, one of the last sonde balloon experimental ascents made by Patrick Alexander from Batheaston reached a height of 20,000 metres, the highest ever made in England at that time.

Chapter 18

The Wright Brothers make the First Powered, Man Carrying Flight December 17th, 1903

Early in September, 1903, the Wrights were shipping their goods to Kitty Hawk from Dayton, they expected to travel themselves on the 20th September, and to take a week erecting a building, so trials were unlikely to start before October 25th.

On September 12th, 1903, Chanute wrote to Wilbur Wright ''. . . I have a letter from Mr. Alexander saying he expects to be in this country the last week in October. He told me in London that he might go on to Japan. Have you heard from him? I have not led him to believe that he would be welcome to see your experiments, and nobody knows, from me, what you propose to do this year. . . I am really sorry for Langley, he has had more than his share of mishaps, and the pesky reporters are giving him the reputation of a bungler. . ''

Wilbur Wright replied to Octave Chanute on 23rd September, 1903; ''. . . We were glad to learn that Mr. Alexander is thinking of visiting this country again. Orville and I made a firm resolve that Dr. Spratt and yourself should be the only visitors in camp this year up to the moment of actual trial. We have so much to do, and so little time to do it in. However, if Mr. Alexander's trip should occur at a time that would make it at all practicable to invite him to camp we shall certainly do so, as we were much pleased with him so far as his brief visit last year enabled us to make his acquaintance. We both liked him very much. We will consider the matter further when we see how things progress in camp.''

Visits by anyone who might delay their work, or benefit from their research were becoming less popular with the Wrights, for reasons that Chanute knew well. Their secrets were not yet patented, - the patent was not granted until 1906, and a lot was at stake.

By 24th October, 1903, Octave Chanute was able to write to Wilbur Wright, ''it is with very pleasant excitement that I learn of your success and expect future developments . . .'' He addded that Mr. Alexander had written that he would sail from Cherbourg on the 'Kronprinz Wilhelm', which was due in New York on 27th October. Octave Chanute would stay at the New Willards Hotel, Washington, after leaving Chicago on 1st November, and he wrote Patrick Alexander to meet him in Washington, not telling him that the Wrights were at Kitty Hawk, nor hinting at their plans, ''so he would not be aggrieved if he is not invited. It is a marvel to me that the newspapers have not spotted you . . ."

Alexander did not receive Chanute's letter, so he did not go to Washington, and was unaware that a telegram from the Wrights awaited him at the New Willards Hotel.

Octave Chanute wrote to Patrick Alexander on January 18th, 1904:

> "I was very sorry not to find you in Washington . . where I found a telegram inviting YOU to the camp. . . I got to the camp on the 6th November. . . Finally on the 17th December (I could not stay so long) the first dynamic flight in history took place. The Wrights are immensely elated. They have grown very secretive, and nobody is to be allowed to see the machine at present, so you have lost your chance. They talked when I was in camp of bringing the machine home and working it on a lake about 15 miles wide as soon as it froze over, but I do not know if this will be done as I have not seen them and letters are now very scarce . . ."

Patrick Alexander must have been extremely disappointed when he realised that the telegram he missed getting at Washington in November, 1903, might well have enabled him to witness a supreme historic event. First he was to read in the English press reports of the Wrights' success.

The world's press had long printed prophesies that a man would fly without the support of a gas bag. Yet when the Wright brothers succeeded, on 17th December, 1903, and the first dynamic flight took place, only these perfunctory reports were published:-

"BALLOONLESS AIRSHIP"

"(From our own correspondent)
New York. Friday, Dec. 18th, 1903.

Messrs. Wilbur and Orville Wright of Ohio, yesterday successfully experimented with a flying machine at Kitty Hawk, North Carolina. The machine had no balloon attachment and derives its force from propellers worked by a small engine.

In the face of a wind blowing twenty-one miles per hour the machine flew three miles at the rate of eight miles per hour, and descended at a point selected in advance. The construction of a box kite was used in the construction of the air ship."

(DAILY MAIL 19/12/1903)

"THE LATEST AIRSHIP"

"According to the 'American' (New York), Messrs. Wright Brothers have successfully experimented with a balloonless airship at Kitty Hawk in Virginia.

The machine, which is really an immense kite with propellers and steering apparatus, is said to have made eight miles an hour against a twenty-one mile wind"

(DAILY MIRROR 19/12/1903)

The first flight was made by Orville Wright and lasted 12 seconds, while the aeroplane flew 100 feet. Four flights were made that day, 17th December, 1903, the best was made by Wilbur Wright lasting 59 seconds, the machine flying 852 feet - over ½ mile through the air, in a twenty-one mile an hour wind.

The reports of the Wrights' powered flights that appeared in the British press were also reported in some European journals, but they were given little prominence, and only a few believed them. Alexander and Colonel Capper were believers, but in France, experimenters tended to fail to apply correctly even Chanute's reports of the brothers' gliders. The powered flights were seldom referred to again in 1904, and were even ignored.

Throughout 1904/05, while the Aeronautical Society members were flying kites and examining birds for the secrets of flight or harking back to the early balloons and attempts to make them navigable, the Wright brothers were pressing on with improvements to their "Flyer". This had almost been forgotten except at Kitty Hawk, and there the farmer above whose land the flights were being made grew so accustomed that he scarcely looked up from his work, and would only observe to his employees that "the Wright boys were at it again". The Wrights planned to make a flight of one hour duration, but at one time they found their trials were attracting undesired attention, so they stopped flying and concentrated upon technical improvements.

They offered their invention to the U.S. government, and when they were turned down without even an attempt at an investigation, they approached the British government, without making progress.

In November, 1905, they sent letters describing their triumphant season from June 23rd to October 16th, 1905, at Huffman Prairie. One of these letters was addressed to Patrick Alexander.

At the General Meeting of the Aeronautical Society on December 15th, 1905, Patrick Alexander read the following letter from Orville Wright. His news was received with polite scepticism. Their President, Major Baden-Powell, was in the chair, and his subsequent comments show that he was extremely interested. He had, of course, the benefit of Patrick Alexander's previous reports after his visit of Christmas 1902.

Extract from the Aeronautical Journal Vol. X, January 1906

GENERAL MEETING

"The opening meeting of the Forty-First Session of the Aeronautical Society of Great Britain was held at the Soceity of Arts, John Street, Adelphi, on Friday, December 15th 1905. the President, Major B.F.S. Baden-Powell, was in the chair."

RECENT EXPERIMENTS OF THE BROTHERS WRIGHT

Mr. Alexander then read the following letter from the Wright Brothers, dated November 17, 1905:

"We have finished our experiments for this year after a season of gratifying success. Our field of experiment, which is situated eight miles east of Dayton, has been very unfavourable for experiment a great part of the time, owing to the nature of the soil, and the frequent rains of the past summer. Up to September 6, we had the machine on but eight different days, testing a number of changes which we had made since 1904, and as a result the flights on these days were not so long as our ones of last year. During the month of September we gradually improved in our practise, and on the 26th made a flight of a little over 11 miles.

On the 30th we increased this to twelve and one-fifth miles, on October 3 to fifteen and one-third miles, on October 4 to twenty and three-fourth miles, and on the 5th to twenty-four and one fourth miles. All of these flights were made at about thirty-eight miles an hour, the flight of the 5th occupying thirty minutes three seconds. Landings were caused by the exhaustion of the supply of fuel in the flights of September 26 and 30, and October 8, and those of October 3 and 4 by the heating of bearings in the transmission of which oil cups had never been fitted. But before the flight on October 5 oil cups had been fitted to all the bearings, and the small gasolene can had been replaced with one that carried enough fuel for an hour's flight. Unfortunately, we neglected to refill the reservoir just before starting, and as a result the flight was limited to 38 minutes. We had intended to place the record above the hour, but the attention these flights were beginning to attract compelled us to suddenly discontinue our experiments in order to prevent the construction of the machine from becoming public.

The machine passed through all of these flights without the slightest damage. In each of these flights we returned frequently to the starting point, passing high over the heads of the spectators."

ORVILLE WRIGHT

THE PRESIDENT: "I think that sounds like a remarkable statement. We have not heard much of what the Brothers Wright have been doing recently. We heard a year or two ago that they had made some successful flights, but this sounds a very successful result. I shall certainly be longing to hear more of the details of these flights. To remain half an hour in the air seems extraordinary."

The first flight of the 1903 Flyer photographed at Kill Devil Hill near Kitty Hawk by J.T. Daniels, using the Wright's camera, on December 17th, 1903. Orville is the pilot and Wilbur is running alongside.

The first powered flight by the Wright brothers in the 1903 "Flyer" was photographed at Kill Devil Hills near Kitty Hawk by John T. Daniels of the Kill Devil Life Saving Station using the Wrights' own camera on December 17th, 1903. Orville Wright is the pilot, and Wilbur is running alongside. The machine made four flights that day, the first covered 120 feet at an average speed of eight miles an hour. Wilbur made the fourth and longest flight of the day, covering 852 feet, and staying in the air for 59 seconds. The air speed was about 30mph as there was a wind of about 21mph.

The total flying time that historic day was 98 seconds, and the machine was never flown again. It was conserved in the Science Museum, South Kensington from 1928 to 1948, and was then transferred to the National Air and Space Museum, Smithsonian Institution, Washington D.C., where it remains.

Chapter 19

Alexander and the
Wright Brothers, 1904 – 1908

Having learned of the Wrights' first historic flight from the newspaper cuttings now in his collection, then getting Chanute's letter dated 18th January, 1904, Patrick Alexander realised that he had not only missed receiving his telegram at Washington, but also that he might have been a witness to the flights, or at least received a first hand report from the Wright brothers, and he left England for Austria. In Vienna, he met Mr. Nimfuhr, secretary of the Austrian Aeronautical Club in Europe. The Wright brothers were concerned to find that incorrect drawings alleged to be of their machine were being published in Europe having been taken from the New York Herald. "Relations were somewhat strained", wrote Wilbur Wright to Chanute, adding that their late assistant Mr. Herring "may have been working with Mr. Alexander, and possibly pulling his leg". There were wild rumours about, such as that a Russian captain had made successful flights reaching 60 miles per hour and mysterious news of great things in America.

1904 seems to have been a period of rumours. It was also the year of the Exposition at St. Louis, U.S.A., and Colonel Templer, Superintendant of the Balloon Factory at Aldershot, recommended to the War Office that Lieut. Col. Capper should be sent for a month or six weeks as "undoubtably there will be the latest things in aeronautics and an immense amount to be learnt there." Capper was to be Templer's successor as Superintendent of the British Government balloon factory at Farnborough, which was the forerunner of the Royal Aircraft Establishment. In the event, the aeronautical part of the Exposition was a failure. Help for Colonel Capper's visit to U.S.A. was given by the letters of introduction that Patrick Alexander was able to supply. These letters were to a number of inventors and experts including the Wright brothers, Graham Bell, then engaged upon experiments with his tetrahedron kites, and Professor Langley, whose steam powered flying machine "The Aerodrome", termed a "man lifting machine" had failed at trials on the Pontomac River on October 7th and December 8th, 1903, after which he gave up, as his Government grant was ended. Capper was enabled to meet:

Mr. W.J.H. Hammer   New York - who was considered a flying machine expert.

Professor Marvin	Washington - kites, air conditions and self registering meteorological instruments.
Professor C.M. Manley	Washington - flying machines and light motors, he made a radial engine for Professor Langley's unsuccessful machine.
Professor A.F. Zahm	Washington - air resistance and the friction of bodies moving through the air.

And many more who were engaged in aeronautical work.

Alexander wrote to the Wright brothers on August 20th, 1904:

> *"Dear Sirs,*
> *I am extremely sorry not to be able to get to St. Louis this year. I was looking forward to the pleasure of seeing you once more.*
> *My friend Lt. Col. Capper, C.B., R.E. is visiting America and will go to St. Louis and he would very much like to have a talk with you.*
> *Any assistance that he may stand in need of during his visit I shall take as a great favour.*
>
> *Wishing you all prosperity,*
> *Believe me,*
> *Very sincerely yours,*
> *Patrick Y. Alexander."*

Colonel and Mrs. Capper sailed from Liverpool in the R.M.S. 'Campania' on September 10th, 1904, and arrived in New York on 17th September. The day before reaching New York, Colonel Capper wrote a letter to Messrs. Wilbur and Orville Wright, Dayton, Ohio in which he mentioned his letter of introduction from Alexander, and that they would be staying from 17th to 25th September at Holland House, New York and for 3 or 4 weeks in St. Louis at the Washington Hotel. He wished to meet the Wrights at Dayton or St. Louis.

Colonel Capper had found that he could travel by various routes between New York and St. Louis for the same rail fare, and could return by a different route without extra cost, and this would assist him to include Dayton on his itinerary.

He was a very meticulous organiser, even getting in touch with the U.S. Consul-General in London, who was more than helpful.

The St. Louis Exposition from May to October 1904 had been chosen by President Theodore Roosevelt as a means of celebrating the Louisiana purchase from France. It included the International Aeronautics Congress, covered an area of over 1,200 acres and was mainly for machinery, but the aviation exhibits were intended to show the shape of things to come and what had been achieved.

Major Baden-Powell reported to the Aeronautical Society that the aeronautical exhibits had been very few and meagre, and what there were scattered and badly or inaccurately labelled. The exhibit of the Berlin Aeronautical Society included the famous balloon "Berson", inflated, and with the car used to make a record

129

ascent to 35,430 feet, also meteorological kites, balloons and instruments.

The United States exhibits included two of Professor Langley's 'Aerodrome' with their light engines. The Aeronautical Enclosure with its high windscreening fence, balloon house and hydrogen making apparatus was promising - but the hydrogen generator became defective. The largest of the three airships was never filled, and the others were far from satisfactory and no advance upon the earlier French and German airships. The gliding machine on which Mr. Avery conducted experiments for Chanute was beautifully made, light and rigid.

At St. Louis, Colonel Capper was able to renew his friendship with Octave Chanute who was a fine character, willing to tell anyone all he knew.

In those days of unsubstantiated claims to have solved the secret of flight, it says much for Chanute's reputation and character that Colonel Capper accepted his assurance that the Wrights had achieved powered flight.

Helped by Patrick Alexander's letter of introduction, Colonel Capper and his wife met the Wright brothers at St. Louis, where they had not exhibited. They were invited to Dayton, where the Wrights entertained them most hospitably on October 3rd, 1904, and showed photographs of the flights, and the Wright engine. They were not shown a machine - their latest one was under repair after a bad landing from their 71st flight. This was as near as anyone as technically minded as Colonel Capper was allowed to get to the Wright machines, which were not yet patented and the Wright brothers were naturally cautious. A man such as Colonel Capper could glean too much from merely seeing the machine. Even the farmers in the Dayton area were asked not to talk, especially to reporters, about the Wright machines that had been flying over their land for five years, first gliders, then the powered "flyer". Application for patent on their glider was made on March 23rd, 1903, but not issued until May 22nd, 1906.

Colonel Capper accepted the Wrights' claims when he visited them in Dayton, without even seeing the mysterious 'flyer' in its repair shed, let alone in the air. Patrick Alexander had, of course prepared him for the Wright brothers' achievements, though he would not have known that they had on September 20th, 1904, achieved a complete circle, and landed safely after crossing the starting point. The brothers described Mrs. Capper as an unusually bright woman, perhaps she also summed up the situation correctly and confirmed her husband's opinions. He took back to England a photograph of Chanute's glider taken at the St. Louis Exposition with its dart-like tail and fixed rudder. The aviator 'piloted' the machine by body-movements, as had Lilienthal and Pilcher. Moveable control surfaces - rudders and ailerons - had been envisaged by Caley in 1843, and then virtually forgotten. The Wright brothers had designed a machine that could be controlled by the pilot, (and not merely pulled into the air like a kite) by inherent stability and power from an engine - or even by a horse pulling a tow line.

Few understood how the Wright brothers had managed to devise a method of controlling their machines in the air - by what they termed "Wing Warping". This was described as their secret, yet the Wrights had in 1904, given enough details in their Patent No 6732, "Aerial Machines without Aerostats; Steering". (An aerostat was lighter than air, i.e. a balloon, and reporters referred to the "balloonless airship ...") Did Griffith Brewer, the patent agent, fail to realise the importance of the patent, nor draw Patrick Alexander's attention to it?

The Wright patent was discovered by the Illustrated London News, who in January 1908 printed an article which mentions Patrick Alexander's knowledge of the Wright brothers' subsequent flights in 1905.

In January 1905, the Aeronautical Society received the reports of Major Baden-Powell and Colonel Capper about the 1904 St. Louis Exposition and the meetings of the Aeronautical Conference in which the British representatives took a prominent part.

Large prizes - perhaps too large - had been offered but not awarded, no good reason being given, a complaint that applied to Baden-Powell's entries. "Startling novelties" had been publicised, but were not forthcoming; the leading aeronauts such as Santos Dumont and the Wright brothers had not entered exhibits, possibly because the expenses of transport alone were very heavy. The Wright brothers were in the middle of their period of secrecy, and many, including Major Baden-Powell, seem to have forgotten their flights of December 1903.

Baden-Powell said he would not be surprised if there was a report before long of a gliding machine being driven through the air by an engine, adding "I am not at liberty to give any details on the subject". Of the £30,000 prize money, plus £10,000 for expenses, only £100 for the kite competition had not been withdrawn. His own entry had suffered a broken line. The wind was too light for the minimum height of 1 mile to be reached. The only entry in the Gliding Machine class had been withdrawn, as provision for a downhill glide was not made. An exhibition flight by one of Chanute's gliders towed from an electric winch had been given but Mr. Avery, who manned it, suffered injury from a nasty fall. Three airships were present, one was never filled, as the hydrogen generator failed, another was more a balloon than an airship, being uncontrollable, and a third was underpowered and too heavy to rise properly, besides having paddle wheels instead of propellers, and did not move faster than 3 miles an hour. "At all events, we learnt some lessons as to what NOT to do," said the Major.

At least the St. Louis Exposition had been a success as a meeting of kindred spirits. On his return to England, Colonel Capper wrote a very favourable report to the War Office dated 30th January, 1905:-

"I wish to invite very special attention to the wonderful advance made in aviation by the Brothers Wright. I have every confidence in their uprightness, and in the correctness of their statements. It is a fact that they have flown and operated personally a flying machine for a distance of over three miles, at a speed of 35 m.p.h."

After getting the news of the first successful flights by the Wrights on 17th December, 1903, Patrick Alexander knew that his ambition to be the first Englishman to fly a heavier than air machine was no longer possible. Perhaps he could achieve his second ambition, to be the first Englishman to fly as a passenger.

The newspaper paragraphs about the flight of the "Balloonless Airship" published on 19th December, 1903, appeared to be forgotten. The flights or failures to fly of airships occupied pages of newsprint. Santos Dumont and his little one man airships were sometimes front page news, but the Wright brothers were reported on the inner pages or not at all. This was especially so in America, where their work and exploits attracted little attention for some months, except for irritation at their secrecy.

The brothers did invite the press to Dayton early in 1904, but there were minor engine troubles that precluded a take-off, and the pressmen left, never to return.

The Wrights made no flights between October 16th, 1905 and May 6th, 1908, during which time they were secretive in the face of attempts to obtain details of their designs.

The Wrights made another historic flight on September 20th, 1904, when Flyer II flew the first circle. This was witnessed by Mr. A. Root, whose account appeared in his apiarists' journal "Gleanings in Bee Culture", in which he described what he saw, heard and felt on this momentous occasion.:-

"God in His great mercy has permitted me to be, at least somewhat, instrumental in ushering in and introducing to the great wide world an invention that may outrank electric cars, the automobiles, and all other methods of travel, and one which may fairly take a place beside the telephone and wireless telegraphy . . . It was my privilege, on the 20th day of September 1904, to see the first successful trip of an airship, without a balloon to sustain it, that the world has ever made, that is, to turn the corners and come back to the starting-point . . . When it first turned that circle, and came near the starting-point, I was right in front of it; and I said then, and I believe still, it was one of the grandest sights, if not the grandest sight, of my life. Imagine a locomotive that has left its track and is climbing up in the air right toward you - a locomotive without any wheels, we will say, but with white wings instead. Well, now, imagine this white locomotive, with wings that spread 20 feet each way, coming right toward you with a tremendous flap of its propellers, and you will have something like what I saw. The younger brother bade me move to one side for fear it might come down suddenly; but I tell you, friends, the sensation that one feels in such a crisis is something hard to describe . . . When Columbus discovered America he did not know what the outcome would be, and no one at that time knew. In a like manner these two brothers have probably not a faint glimpse of what their discovery is going to bring to the children of men. No one living can give a guess of what is coming along this line . . . Possibly we may be able to fly over the north pole, even if we should not succeed in tacking the 'stars and stripes' to its uppermost end."

The Russo-Japanese war of 1904/5 undoubtably attracted Patrick Alexander's attention, and he certainly collected a quantity of newspaper reports. Balloons and kites were used by both sides, but more effectively by the Japanese.

The New York Herald later contained a note that Patrick Alexander had been attache to both the Russian and Japanese armies, but no records to this effect have been found - but there is a gap in his records during 1904. The statement that he went to the Far East and Japan was repeated several times subsequently.

He attended the Congress D'Aerostation Scientifique at St. Petersburg from 29th August to 3rd September, 1904. A.L. Rotch, Director of Blue Hills Meteorological Observatory at Boston, U.S.A., read a paper on "The Exploration of the Atmosphere - The Use of Kites to obtain Meteorological Observations", and sent Patrick Alexander an autographed copy with his compliments. At that time Alexander had left Batheaston and was living at 'Pinehurst', Mytchett, Farnborough.

Patrick Alexander was not present at the January, 1905, meeting of the

Aeronautical Society - this coincided with the period of the Russo-Japanese War, so perhaps he was busy there - but his work was applauded by Dr. Hergesell in connection with the work of the International Commission for Scientific Aeronautics. Dr. Hergesell's report had been translated by Helen Bruce and was read by her father, the secretary. It included that "the English Balloon-sondes ascents are the work of Mr. Patrick Alexander, and it was Mr. Alexander who not only also facilitated Monsieur Teisserenc de Bort's balloon-sondes experiments, but ensured thoroughly valuable results by sending his assistant to Strasbourg to study in practice the technicalities of these ascents, and the method of reducing their results. (Again, Patrick Alexander would surely have done this himself if he had been available in Europe).

Colonel Trollope spoke of the great interest in meteorological work by both manned and unmanned balloons, the results of which were published by the Aeronautical Commission.

The meeting was impressed by a report on Captive Balloon Photography by Griffith Brewer and also by an illustrated report on man lifting kites by Samuel Cody, the highest ascent being 1,600 feet.

The report of the International Aeronautical Commission at St. Petersburg from 29th August to 3rd September, 1904, when Patrick Alexander was the British Secretary, included the remark that "At present it is the efforts of Mr. P.Y. Alexander alone - the only British observer - that redeems our country from the reproach of barrenness in balloon sondes research. Many more such observers are needed . . ."

By 8th January, 1905, Patrick Alexander was in Italy, where balloon ascents were being made by the Italian Aeronautical Society on Wednesday and Thursday, 8th and 9th January, 1905, outside Porta del Populo. The first ascent was to be the balloon "fides", directed by Lt. Puglieschi and accompanied by Mr. Patrick Alexander. After three hours of inflating the balloon, "Lt. Gianetti as pilot and Patrick Alexander climbed into the balloon and at 12.30p.m. they ascended over a kilometer into the air, taking an easterly course, and disappeared from sight". By 22nd January, 1905, he was back at Mytchett.

At the next meeting of the Aeronautical Society in London, Patrick Alexander read the following paper entitled "Notes on Some Recent Experiments in Aerodynamics":-

General Meeting
The second meeting of the 40th Session of the Aeronautical Society of Great Britain was held at the Society of Arts, John Street, Adelphi, on Tuesday, March 14th, 1905. The President, Major B. Baden-Powell, occupied the chair.

Notes on some recent experiments
in aerodynamics

By P.Y. Alexander, M.Aer.Soc.

"On the occasion of the launching of the first balloon in Italy, a very interesting discussion was raised with regard to raising surfaces in the atmosphere and propelling them downwards - as to whether we experienced the same resistance. Professor Hergesell, of Strassburg, very kindly arranged for some experiments to be carried out. The apparatus was rigged up, and we tried spheres and discs of varying diameters; but with the spheres we were very much bothered, and I may say our chief trouble was with the vertical currents in the tower of the Cathedral. However, the experiments are still going on, and so far we have found that the spheres rise vertically quicker than they descend. It is rather difficult to understand this. It may be because as the sphere, which was a skin balloon, was rising, the air inside was expanding and blowing the balloon out very tight, and possibly took out wrinkles and other obstructions, the air passing over the surface; but with the discs themselves, as far as we went, we found they practically rose and fell at the same speed. I have not noticed any experiments of this description, and I thought the matter was worth bringing before the Society.''

"THE PRESIDENT: Though this is an interesting fact which Mr. Alexander has brought forward, from the title of the paper, I was very much in hopes that we were going to hear a few more remarks about Aerodynamics, and I thought, perhaps, this would be a good opportunity of announcing a little result that I obtained from experiments, which, I may as well say at once has nothing very much to do with what Mr. Alexander has said. It is as regards the general forms of aeroplanes as used in gliding machines. I have found from repeated experiments that the ordinary form of aero-curve, such as that used by Langley, Chanute, and others, concave underneath and convex above, always has a tendency to turn over. It is always liable to dive forward. I believe this may account for a good many of the mishaps and non-success of this form of apparatus. Now if the front or anterior edge be curved downwards, and the after or posterior edge be turned upwards, a very steady and stable glider results. The fore and aft section is like a flattened 'S', or Hogarth's "line of beauty".
The extent to which the posterior edge can be turned up without detriment is somewhat surprising. I have sometimes so turned it round as to form a distinct concavity to the line of advance, and yet the model had glided forward at a considerable speed, and with great steadiness (models exhibited). I will not now go into the aerodynamical priciples involved. I have not investigated that subject very carefully, but I hope on some future occasion to do so.
P.Y. Alexander's paper was followed by one by the Secretary, Eric Stuart Bruce, entitled, "The Shape of Navigable Balloons".
He commenced with the question, "Is the navigable balloon worth improving?", and gave a long and detailed talk regarding successful and unsuccessful navigable balloons, including the Zeppelin on the occasion of its first ascent on July 1903. He said that Count Zeppelin seemed to think more of safely balancing his machine than of quickly maneuvering it. (He used his Aerial Graphoscope to throw a picture of the airship in space, and not on a screen).
Afterwards, Patrick Alexander said he was pleased to say something about the Zeppelin airship as he was one of the assistants there. "Unfortunately, the steering gear broke down very shortly after the airship started, and they could not get any reliable results with the screw propeller. The screw propeller has everything to do with a navigable balloon. If you used large propellers revolving at high speed you do not get the same thrust, the reason being that the wind blowing into the propeller causes a small one to lose its grip of the air, whereas a large one does not. That seems to be a very important point with regard to navigable balloons."
Mr. Alderson thought that Count Zeppelin's estimate of the speed of the Zeppelin as 18 miles an hour a considerable exaggeration, and he thought Mr. Alexander would be able to confirm that the speed was 3.5 miles an hour.

134

Patrick Alexander replied that "there was no doubt that for a few seconds its speed was 18 miles an hour". There was nothing more to be said.

On March 1st, 1905, the Wrights wrote to the War Office and in April, 1905 Patrick Alexander went again to America. Coincidence?"

Chapter 20

Was Patrick Alexander a Spy or a British Government Agent?

As an entrepreneur able to travel anywhere in the world, and possibly more knowledgeable than anyone about aeronautical progress everywhere in the world, by reason of his visits and worldwide press cuttings arrangements, anyone not desiring publicity might regard him as a spy. Certainly he was well informed upon occasions.

The first reliable account of the Wrights' experiments did not appear until 21st February, 1906, when the journal "Car" printed a statement by Octave Chanute, possibly the one person whose knowledge of aeronautics, and whose reputation for accuracy was such as to command complete respect. He recounted the early history of the Wright gliders and the successful flights of their first powered machine in December 1903, and how this stirred French aviators to say that "the native land of Montgolfier could not incur the shame of allowing foreigners to compass the final invention of a true flying machine." The French urged that they should hasten to beat the Wrights. Some tried to copy the Wright design, but failed, not only because of inaccuracies in design, but because - as the Wrights had learned - the art of flying a glider or a powered machine can only be learned slowly. The Wrights enjoined absolute secrecy upon all their friends, and worked on, making 105 landings in 1904, including curved and then circular flights.

In January, 1905, the Wrights offered their machine to the U.S. War Department but this was refused without any attempt at investigation. So, knowing that Colonel Capper had been favourably impressed by his visit to see them in October, 1904, the Wright brothers wrote a letter to the War Office dated March 1st, 1905, offering a flying machine for scouting purposes.

It may be a coincidence that Patrick Alexander went again to see the Wrights in April, 1905. The Wrights waited for several months without a reply from the War Office, and were then persuaded by Octave Chanute in October, 1905, to offer their machine to the U.S. War Department again, and again it was refused, apparently the Department thought that the Wrights were asking for financial assistance.

The War Office in London had not completely ignored the Wrights' letter - in May, 1905, all the papers regarding the Wrights' aeroplanes had been sent to their military attache in Washington, Colonel Hubert J. Foster asking him to visit Dayton and see the machine in action. The War Office wrote accordingly to the Wright brothers and the letter duly reached Dayton, but Colonel Foster did not contact them because he was also attache in Mexico, and was away in Mexico on a visit. War Office protocol precluded early action to remedy the situation, and it was November 22nd, 1905, before Colonel Foster's letter arrived asking to be received at Dayton. The delay had not worried the Wrights, who were glad to be able to get on with their work without interruption, but, as usual, they refused Colonel Foster's request for a demonstration flight. Their terms were "no demonstration flights in advance of an agreement as to terms of sale", and Colonel Foster only had instructions to witness a demonstration. When he wrote admitting that he was not authorised to do more than witness a flight, the Wrights replied that they were not prepared to risk a flight to satisfy what might be only curiosity.

The War Office was reputed to be more interested in what other Governments were doing about the Wrights' aeroplanes than in acquiring one themselves.

In October, 1905, Patrick Alexander met Frank S. Lahm, a fellow member of the Aero Club de France, and expressed his strong belief that the Wrights had been making more power flights in Dayton. Lahm was impressed, and wrote to one of his correspondents in America, M. Bierce, asking for information. Bierce replied that two young men named Wright had been carrying out experimental flights in a very remote spot (Dayton). His reply could apply to the original flights made there, and the "Balloonless Airship" flights of December 17th, 1903.

Lahm then telephoned his brother-in-law, Henry M. Weaver in Mansfield, Ohio, asking specific questions about the authenticity of flights at Dayton, and received the following reply "Dayton Ohio 3 Decembre 1905. Pretentions Completement Verifees . . . . . " "Claims Fully Verified, Particulars by Mail." Meanwhile, their secrecy breached, the Wights stopped all flights from October 16th, 1905, and did not resume until May 6th, 1908. They became even more secretive in the face of repeated attempts to view their flights and to obtain details of their designs.

Until October, 1905, their latest machine was flown near Dayton, using a meadow 100 acres in area eight miles from the city. On one side was a road and an electric tramway with a service every half hour. Flights were timed to avoid the trams, and farmers David Beard and Amos Stauffer were requested to keep silent upon what they saw. Even the local press complied with the request for secrecy - except once, and that article did not get into general circulation.

Forty-nine flights were made in 1905, when one day a longer flight overlapped the tram time and they were observed. People became enthusiastic, told their friends, visitors assembled—and the flights came to an abrupt end on 16th October, 1905. But the news continued to spread.

World wide, every journal concerned with aeronautics contained articles reviewing the known facts—and the rumours—which lost nothing in the telling—and the one article in the Dayton press which had escaped the Wrights' barrier of silence was published in "Les Sports". A translation appeared in 'The Autocar' January, 1906. In addition to descriptions of the flying machine and its engine, these descriptions appearing to be opinions rather than specification facts, the interviewer had a talk with a resident whose house was opposite the field where flights took place.

The flight on October 5th particularly impressed this witness, who said that one flight had been timed to last an hour. The farmer who owned the flying field said "I was at work, and saw the machine, which continued to go round and round, and I thought it would never stop." The interviewer being a local man, the talks were regarded as local gossip, not a press matter. And local gossip was not the public demonstration before credible witnesses that was being sought.

In 1905, the French Government was told by Captain Ferber through Colonel Bertrand that the Wrights would sell a practical airplane, to be accepted only after satisfactory trial trips of 40 kilometres—the price would be higher if flights of greater distances were specified. Even though it was a "no satisfaction, no cost" offer, the French would only send a commission. When they arrived in Dayton, the French concealed their identity by saying they were studying water supplies in Dayton, but a telegraph clerk was suspicious of the coded cables to France, and tipped off a reporter, who was taken in by the 'water suppliers' story, and nothing reached the press.

The Frenchmen left Dayton without their real mission being discovered, then a few days afterwards Patrick Alexander dropped in casually at Dayton, and after some general chatting, enquired innocently . ."Is the French Commission still here?". The Wrights were flabbergasted. Hardly anyone, even in the French Government, knew of the commission's journey to Dayton, so how did this mysterious Englishman know about the visit? The Wrights assumed that he must be in the British Secret Service, and that he had crossed the Atlantic for no other reason than to try to catch the French Commission at Dayton. Certainly after only one day in Dayton, Patrick Alexander returned the next day to New York and sailed for England on the first boat.

Another time, Patrick Alexander apparently quoted the names of the secret French Commission members. The Wrights knew Patrick Alexander well, and liked him, but they may well have thought "This man is dangerous, he knows too much."

In France, General Brugere was put under arrest for discussing confidential matters with newspaper men.

There was a superfluity of Press reports, both true and false, prejudiced and unprejudiced. Perhaps in attempt to clear the air, the Wrights sent letters giving details of their 1905 experiments to Carl Dienstbach, the New York representative of Illustrierte Aeronautische Mitteilungen, Berlin, George Besan, Editor of the French Aero Club Journal L'Aerophile, and to Patrick Alexander in London.

The letters, dated 17th November, 1905, were published widely in France by 3rd December, but not in the American press. Patrick Alexander read the letter to the Aeronautical Society in London on 15th December and it was published in the Aeronautical Journal.

The Wrights' letter became the paramount topic of conversation in aeronautical circles in England. Major Baden-Powell appeared to the Wrights to have been surprised rather than impressed, and Octave Chanute was annoyed that Patrick Alexander did not make a positive statement on behalf of the Wrights' achievements, but allowed what he considered to be rather luke warm remarks of Major Baden-Powell to pass unchallenged.

Requests for verification were cabled across America, and then because photographs were denied and details withheld, there was a spate of disbelief. Faked information was provided by newspaper men to satisfy their editors, and this the Wrights denied as false and inaccurate. Chanute was also being pressed for photographs and information. In the circumstances, he was not prepared to comply—the Wrights might still be robbed of the financial fruits of their wonderful achievement. But, as he wrote to Wilbur Wright, "the remarkable way in which Orville's letter was being received, as in London, with Alexander and Capper both present, changed my mind."

The French press started to show interest in the Wrights, as did the New York Herald, and in November, 1906, Sherman Morse had a cabled message from the owner of the paper, Mr James Gorden Bennett in Paris "Send one of your best reporters to Dayton. Get the truth about the Wright brothers flights." The reporter got the truth, and articles about the aeroplanes and the Wrights appeared in the New York Herald, which was printed in both America and paris. the Paris edition clouded the matter by adding that "curiosity in Europe was clouded with skepticism (sic) owing to the fact that information regarding the inventions is so small while the results that the inventors claim to have achieved are so colossal." Santos Dumont, the famous airship man, was reported as saying that "he did not find any evidence of the Wrights' having done anything."

Lahm went to Dayton on November 22nd, 1906 with his brother-in-law, Weaver, and not only spoke to the Wrights, but interviewed witnesses not previously seen; he later wrote a letter to the Paris New York Herald expressing his complete belief in the reports of the Wrights' flights, this was printed on February 10th 1907. In view of the editorial doubts of their own reporters' evidence, it is not surprising that they headed the column "Flyers or liars... It is easy to say 'We have flown', it is difficult to fly..."

There had been too many claimants of actual or imminent flight perhaps, but no-one else had at least two governments showing interest, as the Wrights had. Public and reporters dismissed the reports of powered flight by the Wrights with the result that they were not besieged, and when H.G. Wells wrote in 'Tono-Bungay' of his character building a gliding machine "along the lines of the Wright brothers' airplane, and finally an airplane," American book reviewers chided Wells for putting such fantastic material into a story otherwise quite plausible.

It was a long period from October 16th, 1905, until May 6th, 1908, when the Wrights neither flew, nor allowed any stranger to see their aeroplanes, and towards the end of the period, someone began to invent fantastic flights, such as one on 1st May, 1908; stated to be "10 miles out to sea". Flights before U.S. Government Commissions were also invented, and when one such tale reached London, Patrick Alexander sent a telegram of congratulations to the Wrights.

It is probable that Patrick Alexander exchanged information with Colonel Capper, but it is possible that he knew a 'mole' in the War Office.

The Wrights' flights in October, 1905, - over 24 miles, greatly exceeded the short 'hops' being made in France in 1906/7 by Voisin, Santos Dumont, Delagrange and Henry Farman, which were regarded there as world records, yet none exceeded ½ kilometre.

After the long period of not reporting flights actually made by the Wrights, the world's press started to report what they were alleged to have done, with their considerable inaccuracies distorting the progress that was being made.

In the spring of 1906, Alexander went to see the Wrights again, but was received guardedly because Wilbur thought that the trip was to discover whether they had signed contracts to build for the French. He might, Wilbur thought, be a spy for Colonel Capper who had followed Colonel Templer at Farnborough upon the latter's retirement.

In December 1906, Alexander made yet another visit to the Wright brothers, this time crossing on the Caronia, Wright Senior's diary records "Patrick Alexander of Windsor, England, dined and supped with us, and at 10p.m. he & Orville started for New York. They went to the Aeronautical Exhibition". A later letter to Chanute mentions "when Mr. Alexander was here he told us that the last l'Aerophile contained a full account of our French negotiations with the names of the Commissioners etc, also that he had talked with one of them in Milan. . .We suspected he was trying to draw us out, and were not very responsive."

Apparently Alexander expressed indifference at the negotiations of the Wrights' with the British Government.

He probably knew that Colonel Capper and the War Office were giving belated support to Captain John W. Dunne, who had been invalided from the South African War through enteric in 1900. Dunne's friend was the far sighted H.G. Wells, with whom he left his records of flying models. He recommended experiments when reports of the Wrights' flights of 1903 reached him. Wells advocated a 'fool-proof' machine, that could maintain its own equilibrium. He was held up by the lack of a suitable engine, as was Cody and his 'British Army Aeroplane No. 1' which could only fly when he could borrow the solitary Antoinette engine bought for the Army's airships. This lack of suitable British engines was to lead to Patrick Alexander's competition, for which he provided a prize of £1,000 in 1910.

PATRICK ALEXANDER THE SUPPORTER
OF INDUSTRIAL ARCHAEOLOGY, AERONAUTICAL EDUCATION AND
DESIGN

His obituary by Griffith Brewer includes: "Alexander was renowned for his generosity and he spent far more in encouraging flying endeavour than was warranted by the income he received from the money left to him by his father. He had however a theory that few men live beyond the age of fifty and consequently this gave him freedom, seeing that he had no dependants, to spend the money on prizes to encourage aviation and education with an aeronautical background. . . . . (etc, etc).

One complete letter of application to Patrick Alexander for money survives. It is in French, and the signature is not clear.

I am indebted to Mr Marson for the following translation:

ALEXANDRA PARK
AVIATION WORKS

Offices: 77 Duke's Avenue, Muswell Hill. Facing Alexandra Palace, London, N.
19th January, 1905.

"Sir,

Please permit me to call upon your love of the sciences and in particular all that concerns industrial air navigation to beg your acceptance of the transfer of my patents relating to aviation, for which I am disposed to offer on the most reasonable terms, patents which I guarantee to you absolutely cover the complete answer to the problem of flight.

At Alexandra Palace I have started the construction of a flying machine consisting of the following parameters:

The construction is 20 metres long, 4 metres wide and 6 metres high. It has 8 wings to climb with and to keep it in the air, 4 for the propulsion itself. These wings are 15 metres long and 2 metres wide. The assembly has 32 metres of spread. It is made in three layers and will be able to transport 200 people at 60 miles (100Km) per hour.

The engine is around 100HP. It will cost at the most £2,000 everything included. It is half built and all the pieces of the mechanism will be to hand.

For a man like yourself who is actively interested in the problems of commercial flight and who has the means to occupy himself seriously in them, I can assure you that this machine deserves all your attention. It would be an advantage to the whole world that you should take it under your high and powerful protection. I am too old (69) not to be worried about its outcome if it were to remain in my hands alone, especially as I have been unable to raise the capital to finish it.

Please take my offer, and render for your country and the whole world the service of endowing them in a word, commercial flight.

Briefly, you have nothing to risk, you will make millions of pounds in very little time. Take my science and you will have done a great and beautiful thing.

I am counting on an answer from you,
Yours faithfully
A.D."

The last few lines and signature of the Frenchman's letter

141

The letter is of interest, not only that he was considered a possible promoter for the project, but also because it was written in French, which may confirm that Alexander was fluent in that language. There is no record of Patrick Alexander taking the bait - but apart from the records of his gifts and benefactions to the United Service College at Windsor, and its successor, Imperial Services College, the full extent of his financial help to encourage aviation and education with an aeronautical background is unknown. Certainly he was virtually bankrupt by 1922, and almost penniless when he died in 1943.

Patrick Alexander was said, by some, to be a "soft touch", even the Wright brothers suggested approaching 'Pat' for money for steamer fares home to U.S.A. after overspending in Germany in October 1907. They wanted to get home for Christmas.

The records of the developers of the Wandsworth Balloon Filling area indicate that they hoped Patrick Alexander might put some money into their venture. The adjacent rows of railway arches were used by early aeroplane and balloon builders. It became the site of a great electricity generating station.

Professor Langley, the American aircraft designer had been the first to recognise the importance of Stringfellow's steam engine for aircraft which won the Aeronautical Society's prize of £100 at the Crystal Palace in 1868 and which in 1889 he bought for £100. Langley gave the engine and parts of Stringfellow's first flying machine "with superimposed planes" to the great Aeronautical Museum at Washington U.S.A. where they can still be seen.

In April 1903, the framework, propellers, tail and car of Stringfellow's historic machine of 1848 were exhibited at a meeting of the Aeronautical Institute and Club at the St. Bride's Institute. Octave Chanute was present. He was announced as the greatest living expert on the history of aeronautics and briefly described the intentions of the aeronautical section of the forthcoming St Louis Exposition. He also told of the experiments then being carried out in the United States, and particularly the successful efforts of the brothers Wright to secure gliding flight. He said that in U.S.A. they thought it premature to experiment with a power-driven machine until they had solved the problem of stability. The meeting came to the conclusion that little advance had been made since the time of Stringfellow, but "we now have better motors and lighter and better construction".

Patrick Alexander recognised the importance of industrial archaeology, and tried to acquire and have restored the Henson Stringfellow flying machine models of 1842/3, 1847 and 1848. In December 1905 he was in touch with V.B.T. Stringfellow of Crewkerne, Somerset, with a view to the purchase of the remains of the original models for restoration by H.M.A. Alderson of Cumberland Lodge, Farnborough. (Alderson' postal address was Farnborough R.S.O. Kent; R.S.O. signified Railway Sub. Office.) He was a florist, but his interest in aeronautics resulted in this spare time occupation becoming a full time one. From 1905 to 1909, Alderson helped dispose of the relics of John Stringfellow which are now in the Science Museum, with models and restoration work paid for by Alexander.

Chapter 21

Patrick Alexander gives the Army an Observatory

In 1891 Patrick Alexander had purchased a fine 8" f12 refractor telescope made by the Dublin firm of Sir Howard Grubb F.R.S., complete with all the usual fittings associated with this type of professional instrument. He used it at Bath, and in 1902 offered it to the city. He was prepared to build, at his own expense, an observatory to house the telescope. The offer was refused on the grounds that it would be a charge upon the rates.

Later he used the instrument at The Mount, Batheaston, until moving to Mytchett, Farnborough in 1904. He would show it to visitors with pride, but it was probably a scientific toy.

His house Pinehurst, at Mytchett, was conveniently situated for Alexander to visit the Balloon factory, and Ball Hill, where gliders were tested. Before moving to Pinehurst, he stayed at the Queens Hotel on the main Farnborough Road, as related in the following letter:

> *15 Southwood Road,*
> *Cove, Farnborough,*
> *Hants.*
> *(Undated, c. 1965).*

" *To Mr. J. Forsyth.*

Dear Sir,
   Reading your article in the local paper about Mr. Patrick Alexander brought back many childhood memories. We lived for many years at the Kennels Iveley Farm where my father was in charge of 2 packs of Hounds (I think the R.A.E. Police dogs are there now) I can't remember the year as I was only 7 or 8 then. It was when Cody was experimenting with his manlifting kites and Col. Capper (as he then was) was in charge of the R.E. Balloon Section. He lent Mr. Alexander an Experimental Section, they lived under canvas one summer just by our place on the slopes of Ball Hill, which was much steeper then before the Air Ministry levelled it a lot. Mr Alexander was wealthy and his ambition was to perfect a Bamboo Glider that would fly without a man in it. He used to buy clockwork toys from the London street vendors to try and

find a way, it wasn't a success, it was a huge contraption and never got far off the ground from the top of Ball Hill. As the soldiers did their cooking at our place we were always in on things and he had them make some box kites in fact he gave us one when they packed up. He lived at the Queens Hotel Farnborough all that time and he often used to say he saw us enjoying ourselves with his kites.

Yours sincerely,
Miss C.S. Cranston. "

In June, 1905, the Aeronautical Club commenced the issue of Aeronauts Certificates, the conditions to be complied with were onerous, but not for an experienced balloonist such as Alexander. The first certificate was issued to C.F. Pollock on 14th June, 1905. He was an ardent aeronaut, and a founder member of the Club, as was Alexander. The second certificate was issued to Professor A.R. Huntington on 14th July, 1905, but the third application from F.H. Butler was not at first accepted, but was granted in January 1906.

Patrick Alexander had been making ascents for over 15 years, and possibly he considered—as did other pioneers—that their experience rendered a certificate unnecessary. Anyway, he was not given a certificate as an aeronaut. It may have been that obtaining certification of his flights was no longer possible. His health was giving him trouble again and as a result he wrote to the War Office on 19th August, 1905, offering to give his great telescope to the military at Aldershot, and to build an observatory at his own expense. After an exchange of memorandums, the Army authorities accepted the offer, and the project was placed in the hands of Colonel Capper, who now was Commandant of the Balloon School. R.E.'s work did not commence until March 1906 when the site was pegged out after being agreed and approved by Alexander.

The revolving dome was being designed and manufactured by Sir Howard Grubb, and to ensure accuracy, it was found that "a steel straight edge, not less than 18ft. long is indispensable." It took more than a month of interdepartmental correspondence before a straight-edge 16 feet long could be provided.

The following report of the opening ceremony is included by permission of Mr J.I.M. Forsyth, F.R.A.S.:-

The project was completed in November - December 1906. The opening was arranged to take place on the 22nd December, 1906, Lt. Gen. Sir John French was to perform the ceremony. Mr. Alexander was invited and naturally he accepted. He wrote that on the 20th he was lecturing at Kings College on Propellers and the 21st he would be in Paris inspecting an aircraft but would be available on the 22nd. All was ready when on the 21st a signal arrived at Corps H.Q. saying "Sir John detained in London. Ask Gen. Grierson (Gen. Officer commanding 1st Div.) to open observatory." H.Q. of the 1st Division was contacted and replied "Gen. Grierson commanded to Windsor on the 22nd." The 1st Cavalry Brigade was contacted to ask Brigadier General Scobell if he would perform the honours, unfortunately he was on leave in Scotland. One can imagine the panic at the Army H.Q. as a frantic search was made for an officer of General rank to perform the opening ceremony. Eventually the Commander of the 4th Infantry Brigade, Gen. Belfield agreed to open the observatory. Today there seeems to be some doubt as to who in fact did eventually open the observatory.

Army records show that it was Gen. Belfield but the Aldershot News reports that Major Gen. Eustace, Chief of Artillery performed the ceremony.

The problem of who was to open the observatory was not the only one to confront the Army. Mr. Alexander wrote saying that the only suitable train arrived at Aldershot at 10.30a.m. and the opening ceremony was not scheduled until 12.30p.m. This evidently presented a major staff problem - what to do with a civilian for two hours. This problem was solved when Col. Capper, Commandant of the Balloon Factory (now the Royal Aircraft Establishment), offered to take Mr. Alexander on a tour of the factory and to take him to luncheon. He also arranged to lay on a car to collect the guest from the station - quite an honour in 1906.

On the day all went well, it was apparently a fine day for after the ceremony Mr. Alexander set the telescope so that those present could observe the spots on the sun. The observatory was then on Army charge and remains so to this day.

Patrick Alexander's telescope

The telescope and observatory still remains as a military charge and until it fell into disrepair, was used by Army Sappers (R.E.s), and amateur and professional astronomers. The famous white spot on Saturn was discovered by a Mr. John Pettley in early August, 1933, the same night as it was discovered by Will Hay, being reported in several issues of 'English Mechanic'. A key hung in the observatory to enable the user to switch off the nearby street lights, if these interfered with observations.

At one time, military regulations permitted the key to the observatory to be issued only between 9am and 5pm, which made only solar observations possible.

By 1979, the dome was in such disrepair that the weather had resulted in corrosion in the gearing. With no offical means of paying for maintenance except that arranged by the military who could usually manage to overcome such difficulties, eventually the observatory was closed until funds can be found for such non-essential services.

The observatory can still be seen opposite the Headquarters building, at the junction of Queens Avenue and Steeles Road, Aldershot. A circular red brick building with its distinctive domed roof, it bears a metal plaque:

PRESENTED TO THE ALDERSHOT ARMY CORPS
BY PATRICK Y. ALEXANDER ESQ. 1906.

On the map of the 'Aldershot Military Town Trail' published by the Southern Tourist Board, it appears as No. 8 ROYAL OBSERVATORY.

It is something of a mystery which 'flying machine' Patrick Alexander rushed to Paris to see on 21st December, 1906, after lecturing at Kings College on 20th December on "Aeroplanes and Propellers". In his letter accepting the invitation to attend the opening of the observatory on 22nd December he addded that the flying machine to be seen in Paris would prove to be "of no practical utility, I fear". He must have been right, as the only flying machine that made even a short 'hop' was the 14-bis of Santos Dumont, so called because its first airborne appearance was suspended from his airship No. 14. He managed to achieve a free flight of 60 metres on 23rd October, 1906, using a 50hp Antoinette engine and 220 metres in 21.2 seconds on 12th November, thus winning the Aero-Club of France prize of 1,500 francs for the first flight by a heavier than air machine over a greater distance than 100 metres. Such was the depth of progress in Europe that this effort was acclaimed as a sensation. It might have been enough to require Patrick Alexander's visit, but what a feeble effort it was compared with the Wright's flight of over 24 miles in 38 minutes on 5th November at Dayton the previous year.

His lecture at Kings College on 20th December, 1906, was published in the Aeronautical Club Journal "Flight" on October 28th, 1911.

The Observatory presented by Patrick Alexander
to the Aldershot Army Corps in 1906

Chapter 22

Aeronautics and Aviation in 1905/6

During 1905, Patrick Alexander opened offices at 73, Pearl Buildings, Portsmouth. His last letter with a Pinehurst, Mytchett address is dated 20th March, 1905, and in December the same year he was writing from the new Portsmouth address.

The next occupier of Pinehurst was to be Samuel Cody who brought his family there in 1906 when his previous 3 monthly engagement as Instructor to the Army was renewed for two years.

At first, Cody kept his gig and white horse "Vicky" there, but after having been taken for a ride in the Hon. C.S. Rolls' new model Silver Ghost Rolls-Royce automobile, he was instantly converted, and went to London and bought a Simms-Welbeck open tourer from a shop in the Edgware Road, which he proceeded to drive down to Aldershot with neither instruction nor accident. Colonel Capper was without a private car, and Cody would drive him and his family to Battersea Gas Works where Capper kept his balloon.

By 1910, Cody's expenditure on aviation was such that it became necessary to cut down expenses, and he removed to a smaller house at Ash Vale.

In January 1906, Patrick Alexander was using another adddress; 'Rothesay', Spencer Road, Southsea, when he wrote to Colonel Fullerton, secretary of the Aeronautical Society asking for a copy of the latest statement of accounts of the Society.

He used both addresses upon occasion for some months, as when he undertook to send a paper entitled "Aeroplanes Experimentally Demonstrated" in a letter dated 3rd February, 1906, from 'Rothesay' and he wrote to Fullerton on another occasion giving the impression that he was extremely busy and pressed for time (15th Feb. 1906).

His manuscript talk as follows, about the Wright brothers, is undated and with no heading, but is from about 1906:-

"In 1902 I had the pleasure of making the acquaintance of the Wrights who commenced in 1900 with a double decker gliding machine without any idea they were going to achieve their present success, in fact they took up gliding just for the fun of the thing and after prac-

tising several years with the glider they bought in 1902 a Toledo gasolene motor and attatched it to their aeroplanes.

During the last 4 years they have flown 160 miles in flights of 24 miles and less; the flights could have been longer had the fuel capacity been more. As the machine was an experimental one only enough fuel was carried to peform certain evolutions and tests.

During their preliminary experiences with the glider they gathered much valuable information necessary for control in winds as high as 35 miles an hour and finally with the power machine they were able in the Autumn of 1905 to attain a flight of 24 miles in half an hour. Soon afterwards they demolished the machine intending to make an entirely new one this year embodying their previous experience.

The weight of the machine is half a ton including the aeronaut and when flying at 30 miles an hour possesses to some extent considerable momentum which in itself contributes to the control and stability.

There is nothing new in the machine mechanically but scientifically they have gathered much that is of value in aerial navigation.

The greatest speed of wind that has ever been blowing while they have been flying with the motor machine has never exceeded 17 miles per hour.

500 sq. ft. of surface suitably disposed is enough to carry half a ton at 30 miles an hour. About 14 h.p. was used. I understand from 8 to 10 h.p. would be enough.

I do not say this machine is the type of the future, they do not say so themselves. Similar machines can be built for £1,000.

It seems to me the time is arriving when the Admiralty and the War Office must within the course of the next few years take more serious interest in Aeronautics than has hitherto been the case - With our wealth of facts and figures in Aerodynamics the difficulty is not how to build a machine but what type of machine is really wanted. Each nation will fashion their machines after their own ideas although main principles will govern the construction of all.

Whether we have to fight on the seas, on land, or in the air British brains and British blood is as good as ever it was and today Old England is well abreast with all other nations in the struggle for supremacy in Aerial Navigation.''

An example of Patrick Alexander's handwriting from
his Wright brothers manuscript

In the summer of 1905, W.H. Dines, F.R.S. was helping with naval trials and maneouvres on H.M.S. Seahorse, a destroyer, at Portsmouth, with kites and meteorological work - he seems to have taken over Alexander's work in this respect, and later Colonel Capper joined in.

Patrick Alexander's interests continued to be varied. In 1905, he noted that the Germans had set up a Telefunken radio station at Corunna, ostensibly for a local newspaper, but as signals intercepted between Gibraltar and Lands End were communicated to the German Consul, and thus to the German government, suspicion was aroused.

The Aeronautical Club started monthly dinners in February 1906 to honour feats such as the crossing of the Channel by Pollock and Dale, in the Club balloon, the menu being embellished with topical aeronautical cartoons. Patrick Alexander used to attend, and early in 1906 he was elected a member of the Meteorological Committee of the Club, together with Sir Norman Lockyer, the Hon. C.S. Rolls, Professor Huntington, Mr. Roger Wallace, and Messrs. Pollock and Dines, F.R.S.

They were to work with the Royal Meteorological Society on a series of balloon ascents of the higher atmosphere, in continuation of the pioneer work of James Glaisher F.R.S. - work that Alexander had been the sole British experimenter and observer of with his 'Sondes balloon' ascents from Batheaston.

Patrick Alexander was also elected a member of the technical committee of the Aeronautical Club, which included Sir Hiram Maxim, the Hon. C.S. Rolls, Sir H.E. Colville, Major Baden-Powell, Colonel J.E. Capper, Professor Huntington, Dr. Hutchinson, and Messrs. Frost, Pollock, Spencer, Simms, Wallace K.C. and Moore-Brabazon.

In March, 1906, he was busy in Paris, so much so that he had to write to the Secretary of the Aeronautical Club from the Hotel Continental,
"I am awfully sorry I will not be able to give or prepare a paper for the meeting - I have so much to do, under the circumstances would you kindly postpone my remarks until some future occasion. Trusting this will not incommode you,
Believe me,
Sincerely Yours,
Patrick Y. Alexander."

Most of the ballooning fraternity tended to be scornful of the attempts of the "heavier than air" theorists to take to the air. While admitting that a balloon was largely at the mercy of the winds, they contended that a knowledge of meteorological skill permitted pre-determined flights. Tests of these skills were arranged, such as the 'Concours d'Obidiene' in Paris. The competitors had to declare before their ascent the exact place of descent. Their decision was based upon the direction taken by small balloons released shortly before the starting time, the meteorological information available at the time, and of course their skill. Patrick Alexander went to Paris on 27th May, 1906, with Professor Huntington and the Hon. C.S. Rolls to watch eight balloons start one after the other from the grounds of the Aero Club of France.

The winner, Alfred le Blanc, came down within 100 metres of his target, his passengers being Monsieur Henri Martin and Mme. 'X', they aimed at "bifurcation de la route de Marcilly a Meaux et de Marcilly a Etrepilly". They won 600 francs.

The second prize was won by M. Rene Gasnier with Pierre Gasnier; they aimed at Juilly, "au sud de Dammartin", which they missed by 2 kilometres, and won 400 francs. The third prize went to M. Georges Le Brun, who with Georges Dubois missed their target Neufmoutiers by 4 kilometres, and won 200 francs.

The wind was from the south-west, so targets were selected about 40 kilometres to the north-east of Paris.

The wind was very light and the fun for the members with motor cars was to try to keep one of the balloons in view, as a quarry. The many bends in the Marne, and the number of cul de sacs encountered resulted in the winning balloons getting clear, but one motor car caught up with its balloon when it landed, and a motor cyclette rider caught his quarry, thus winning a bronze medal. The "Balloon Chase" game became popular subsequently in England.

At this time, no-one in Europe had managed to take off with a heavier than air machine for more than a short 'hop' but in Dayton, U.S.A., Orville Wright was within a short period of managing to fly 12 miles in under 20 minutes in Flyer III.

In July, 1906, the first balloon race ever held on British soil, or more correctly in British airs, was arranged at Ranelagh by the Aero Club, assisted by a fatigue party of Royal Engineers of the Aldershot Balloon Section, and the Band of the 21st Lancers. The War Office had become profuse in its civilities to the Aero Club, possibly with a view to potential usefulness in emergencies. It was a society occasion, sufficient to draw the members' cars and carriages from the final match of the Croquet tournament, and from Polo.

Princess Vittoria Caetani di Teano climbed lightly over the side of the huge Aero Club III Balloon, as if stepping into her brougham. She subsequently wrote with enthusiasm for the journal 'The World' about her flight, in which her balloon came second, landing half a mile from Horndon in Essex, about a mile from the target. Patrick Alexander is not mentioned, although he was usually reputed to attend such events, but a letter from Colonel Capper mentions that he was at Salisbury Plain, working with the Balloon Companies exercising there, after spending some time at the Balloon Factory, Aldershot on 5th June, 1906. (The Army Balloon Factory had recently moved from Aldershot to Farnborough, but the address was still given as Aldershot for a period, causing some confusion).

THE GORDON BENNETT BALLOON RACE OF 1906

All aeronauts were keenly interested in the Gordon Bennett long distance balloon race, which was to start on 30th September, 1906, from the Tuileries Gardens in Paris, adjoining the Place de la Concorde. Patrick Alexander did not compete and his balloon is not mentioned.

The world's press was at the start, and the arrangements were abysmal, the English supporters being allowed to enter the Tuileries Gardens ascent area only after the Hon. C.S Rolls had collected up the entry cards of the few that had managed to obtain them, and used these cards to facilitate the entry of his friends. Patrick Alexander, with Mr. H.E. Perrin, Secretary of the Aeronautical Club, helped the Daily Telegraph reporter to obtain information.

The reporter wrote of their help . . "to whom I am indebted for much assistance and many interesting particulars . . " The Hon. C.S. Rolls had made a special crossing to France from the Isle of Man, where he had been successful in the Tourist Trophy Race, in order to get to Paris in time. His mother, Lady Llangattock, managed to get in with her son's help, as were sufficient Englishmen to cheer the ascent of Rolls and Colonel Capper in the "Britannia".

Colonel Capper had his eye-glass firmly in place, and saluted the cheers gravely - they doubted whether it would be displaced whatever happened.

During conversation immediately before the race, Griffith Brewer was told by Alexander that the Wright brothers had flown—this news Brewer received with disbelief even though he regarded Alexander as trustworthy.

Rolls and Capper came third and landed at Sandringham - at first they were placed fourth, but later calculations confirmed Rolls' contention that this was incorrect. The wind had taken the balloons north eastwards to the French coast, where several of the 16 competitors landed. The remainder crossed the English coast near Hastings, after which the course took a north easterly direction. Those still airborn found themselves after a night crossing in the full moon, with a poor wind, and too near for safety to the North Sea.

The French were mortified to find themselves un-placed, the winner being the only American, Lieut. Lahm, who landed at Fylingdales near Whitby and who subsequently was able to advance aeronautics in the U.S.A., while continuing to meet Patrick Alexander and the Wright brothers when in Europe. The Italian entry was second, landing near Hull. The result of an American win was that the next race was in the hands of the Aeronautical Club of America, and therefore to be held in the U.S.A.

The Aero Club de France arranged a magnificent and expensive banquet for the winners in the Salons of the Automobile Club de France, Patrick Alexander was prominent amoug the 100 or so guests at what was an event "des plus elegant, et des plus animes," together with the Hon. C.S. Rolls, Major Baden-Powell, Colonel Capper, Huntington, Wallace, (President of the Aeronautical Club of the U.K.) and Griffith Brewer. They pulled Lieut. Lahm's leg about the two U.S. flags flown from his balloon, as one had been upside down - a signal of distress.

Cameras had been forbidden to the competitors by the security minded French who had not been amused to see that photographs of their fortifications had been taken from balloons.

A few days later the world's newspapers dated 14th October, 1906, were reporting the 25th anniversary of the founding of the Berlin Balloon Association, and Patrick Alexander went to Berlin, where his old friend Capt. Hildebrandt was the organiser. It was not the latter's day, as he was run over by a motor cab in front of the quarters of the Aeronautical Corps, crushing his foot. The Berlin Balloon Association, meeting in the magnificent halls of the Technical College at Charlottenburg with members and delegates from many countries, heard four lectures by world famous ballooning scientists and experts. Professor Hergesell, on 'The Exploration of the Atmosphere Over the Ocean by Balloons and Kites' was reported as being "especially exciting to his audience", mentioning that balloons with registering apparatus had attained a height of 16,000 metres, and kites sent up from Jutland had reached 5,000 metres. He also related his meteorological experiences on Spitzbergen.

Geheimrat Miethe, Rector of the College, and inventor of colour photography, described the apparatus for taking natural colour photographs from balloons. He showed what were described as the most beautiful photographs of Berlin taken from 800 metres, and said that coloured photographs of the earth from a height could be made with the rocket apparatus invented by Herr Maul, an engineer. A series of sunset and sunrise photographs in colour concluded this lecture.

Major Gross, who had just returned from Friedrichshafen and the trials of the latest Zeppelin, lectured on "the Development of Motor Ballooning in the twentieth Century" detailing the rigid, semi-rigid, and flexible types of Count Zeppelin, Major von Parseval and the Brothers Lebaudy, all of which Alexander had seen at some time. As a military man, Major Gross paid most attention to the Zeppelin.

Professor Assmann of the Lindenburg Observatory lectured on "Aims of the Scientific Exploration of the Atmosphere", with "a wealth of interesting data."

The Berlin Balloon Association had presented Patrick Alexander with a fine trophy, (now in the Windsor Collection) after he had helped them in September, 1898, and he was an honoured guest at the banquet held in the Exhibition buildings, sitting among the 500 guests with Count Zeppelin, Professor Berson, the holder of many ballooning records, Professor Hofmann and Lawrence Rotch, the Director of the Blue Hills Observatory, U.S.A. Professor Hofman and Patrick Alexander had co-operated with the design of the machine, and when reporting upon the 25th anniversary proceedings, the New York Herald, 14th November, 1906, featured the latest Hofman Flying Machine, "which was on new principles, and the Kaiser had ordered that a full and detailed report be prepared and submitted to him."

The Hofmann Flying Machine

The flying machine of Regierungsrath J. Hofmann, of Berlin, is novel in several features (says "Engineering"). It is fitted with wings, a propellor, and an engine. When on firm ground or on the water—for the machine is constructed for floating as well, with special regard to easy descent, possibly - it moves by its propellors; when in the air it is also driven by the propellor; when it starts, gravity has come into play. Thus the ascent begins with a slight fall on an oblique line, until the winds are displayed against the wind, and the air resistance and the propellor force prevail. The wings can be folded, but not moved, and serve only as planes. As the propellor is to be capable of turning when the machine is on the ground, it has been fixed sufficiently high, and the machine rests on legs - one does not quite know how many legs. There are four tubes, forming a skeleton support, which folds up after the manner of a camp stool. When spread, the front leg or pair of legs rests on one roller, and the hind pair on two rollers. When the machine starts the legs are, by springs, jerked upward, and would, or should, in real flight, stick out, the one in front, and the other behind. The flight is intended to resemble the stork's flight; the stork is a very graceful flyer, but his start looks comically clumsy.

We say "should", because Mr. Hofmann's machine has not carried him yet. His first machine was wrecked in transport just before its trial; his second was a small model, driven by a carbon dioxide motor; his third actual model has cost him more than two years to build, but it has only a fifth of the size he calculates for a machine that would carry a man. It is a working model, however, and weighs 7lbs, the wings span about 9ft. The motor is a real steam engine, heated by alcohol. The boiler consists of seventy-two copper tubes. When the pressure exceeds 142lb, the steam can pass into the superheater, and then into the compound engine. The exhaust carries part of the combustion with it, so that the cylinder and and valve chests can all be jacketed with hot gases and steam. The crankshaft drives the propellor at fifty revolutions a second. A propellor with two pairs of blades, placed behind one another, as with Walker and Alexander's experiments, answered better than a four-blade propellor; each pair resembles two oars in alignment. An attempt to divide the wings into several aeroplanes after Chanute's fashion, failed dismally. The skeleton legs, steel tubes, or wood weigh about one-sixth of the whole mass, which is undesirable. The ribs of the wings have also been made of steel tubes. But Mr. Hofmann is going to try nickel tubes, which are to serve as condensers for the steam, so that the small quantity of water which can be taken on board - at present 2oz. - can hold out for a longer time. The tubes would be exposed to the strong air currents, but the realisation of this idea does not look very easy. The inventor is convinced, however, in spite of the sad fate of Lilienthal and Pilcher, that the problem of flight will be solved some day by a machine of his type, and not by a balloon such as Mr. Dumont-Santos exercises in calm air. "Engineering."

"Airships and Submarines"
(Foreboding in 1906 - a cutting kept by Alexander)

"Will Santos Dumont have to try again? He fulfilled the essential conditions of M. Deutsch's prize scheme, on Saturday, by navigating his air-ship from St. Cloud, round the Eiffel Tower and back again, but according to reports exceeded the time allowance by forty-four seconds. The Aero Club Committee are to reconsider their decision, led thereto, perhaps, by M. Deutsch, who is said to favour an award to M. Santos Dumont. Whether he actually obtains the prize is a secondary matter, however, because he has proved that his craft is under perfect control, and can be navigated in the teeth of a strong breeze. He is so far ahead of any competitor that he will be able to make several more attempts, if necessary, in order to comply with the letter of of the rules attaching to the competition. Now that the principle of air-ship navigation has been established, nimble minds in the Old World and the New will fasten upon it, and in due course evolve a type of machine fit for commercial and other purposes.

We fear the day is far distant when every man will go on business or pleasure in his own air-ship, for, like the motor car, an air-ship must remain, for a time at least, the luxury of a few. Primarily, no doubt, the nations will endeavour to secure air-ships as weapons of warfare. Armies would be impotent if attacked by a flock of air-ships, just as a navy would be powerless for offence or defence against a shoal of submarines. A few air-ships soaring over London would imply annihilation for the Capital, but just as the French submarines are to be checkmated by British submarines, so French air-ships will be checkmated by British and German air-ships. Nevertheless, the nation that first has a fleet of air-ships may dictate to the world. Fortifications, fleets, armaments, all would go for nothing against a few craft moving slowly athwart the sky, wheeling over cities and dropping deadly explosives as they moved. We presume artillerists will at once revise their notion of the use of cannon and endeavour to produce guns capable of firing straight into the heavens, for if once an air-ship were hit, her career would be ended. The most obvious thought in connection with the newest development of navigation is that air-ships and submarines, but more especially the former, will go far to render war impossible. The risks will be too horribly tragic.''

The great news towards the end of 1906 was the Daily Mail prize of £10,000 offered for the first flight to be made from within 5 miles of their London offices to within 5 miles of their Manchester offices.

Hofman announced shortly afterwards that he wanted to enter for the Daily Mail £10,000 prize, and Patrick Alexander was enthusiastic. The prize arose from a jibe by Santos Dumont that no worthy prize for aeronautics had been offered by England. When he heard about the £10,000, he said, with a shrug, ''When England does a thing of this sort, they do it well. . .''

Aeronautical designers all over Europe and America were as enthusiastic as Patrick Alexander about the competition. but apart from the Daily Mail the press tended to jeer - Punch offered £100,000 for a flight to Mars, and The Star offered £10,000,000 to the flying machine that flies five miles from London and back to the starting point, adding ''One offer is as safe as the other.''

There was a large number of inventors each convinced that their invention for a flying machine could win the £10,000. If only finance was forthcoming. A group of English sportsmen formed a company to finance penniless inventors in the interests of aerial navigation. This was the sort of venture that would have had Patrick Alexander's help and sympathy, but there is no record of what actually resulted, except that no worthwhile invention was produced, nor did a penniless inventor come near to winning the prize.

Chapter 23

Patrick Alexander is confident that Britain will have the first Aerial Battleship

Patrick Alexander wrote a letter to the Secretary of the Aeronautical Society dated 22nd January, 1905:-

"I thank you for your letter and think we can all congratulate ourselves that the Science of Aerodynamics is on a broader foundation than five years ago . . ."

In Britain, some thought that practical aviation was being neglected to a deplorable extent. There was probably a wealth of technological talent in the country and Alexander could speak bravely to the Daily Mail on November 24th, 1906:-

"Air Conquered in Theory
British Empire Ready to Conquer it in Practice"

"In theory, the conquest of the air was accomplished by the end of the seventeenth century," said Mr. Patrick Alexander, the aeronautic expert, to a Daily Mail reporter yesterday. Mr. Alexander is passing through London on his way to America, where he goes to study the progress made there in the science of aerostatics.

Mr. Alexander explained that at the end of the seventeenth century the principles of aviation were known in their entirety. It had been reserved for the nineteenth and twentieth centuries to apply these principles. The maintenance of equilibrium while in the air was at present the one great difficulty which militated against success. As at present constructed, airships were so light that their equilibrium was easily disturbed. In time we should make them heavier, until a point in their development was reached when it would be as difficult to upset their balance as it was to overturn an ironclad.

"The greater the surface on which the currents of the air have to act," he went on, "the greater will be the stability of the ship. It is my opinion that when the supreme type of airship has been evolved we shall find that the aeroplanes have been dispensed with altogether; for the size of the planes will be necessarily in inverse proportions to the size of the ship. As the ship grows in size and weight, the utility of the planes will decrease."

Mr. Alexander spoke confidently of the position occupied by Great Britain in the aeronautic world.

"Great Britain and the British Empire stand easily in the van of progress. We know more about the science of aeronautics than any other country in the world. As yet

156

we have not attempted to apply our knowledge, but silently and quietly we have been studying the subject, exhausting every possible theory and fact, until to-day our scientists may lay claim to have conquered the air on paper. To achieve the victory in practice will not be a difficult matter. It is my firm conviction that the first great aerial battleship will be built by a citizen of the British Empire, and that Britain's aerial fleet will rule the air as her ironclads have ruled the seas.''

It is rumoured that Mr. Patrick Alexander is going to the United States for the purpose of visiting the mysterious Wright brothers with whom he has been acquainted for several years. Mr. Alexander enthusiastically welcomed the Daily Mail £10,000 prize. ''It is,'' he said, ''a wonderful and marvellous offer.''

In February, 1906, Chanute and Wilbur Wright had further correspondence, this time about Moedebeck's pocket book, which contained a chapter on Lilienthal, and ended with a mention of the Wrights' work, adding that they do not wish as yet to make their construction known, the reason being that they had spent a good deal of time and money in developing it to efficiency. They hoped to obtain lucrative contracts first, and negotiations were in hand with France. Their letter to Patrick Alexander was printed in the pocket book instead, including some errors in the Aeronautical Club reprint that were to cause irritation to the Wrights later.

Then came a letter from Patrick Alexander to Wilbur Wright announcing that he would reach U.S.A. by the S.S. 'Caronia', a big Cunard liner, on April 16th, 1906, and would return to England on 24th April. He wished to call on the Wrights at Dayton during this period, if they would be at home. On the 19th April, Patrick Alexander sent a telegram to Chanute ''Will arrive Dayton Friday morning. Must leave ten same evening for Washington.''

Orville telegraphed back that he had an engagement, and could not meet him. Chanute's comment was ''I hope this will result in placing your machine in the hands of the British, a result that has commended itself to me from the start. . ''

On Friday, 20th April, Bishop Wright, father of Orville and Wilbur, wrote in his diary ''Mr Patrick Alexander, an Englishman of wealth, sups with us.''

Wilbur wrote to Chanute on April 28th from Dayton, ''Mr. Alexander spent a day with us then started home by way of Washington and New York. As near as we can make out, his trip was for the purpose of learning whether or not there was any truth in the reports that we had a contract with the French. I think he has asked to get information on this point by the government authorities. He sends his respects to you.''

On April 30th, Chanute wrote back to Wilbur Wright, ''. . . it rather looks as if the British will be the first to buy and the French will have to take a back seat for a year . . . I suppose your movements are being watched.''

The Wrights wrote to the Secretary, War Office, London on May 8th in reply to a letter dated 8th February, 1906, setting out their standard offer to various governments of a Flyer capable of carrying a man and supplies for a long trip, with instructions, data and formulae for designing machines of other sizes and speeds, together with some confidential disclosures.

In April, the Wrights' agent, Flint, appeared to be negotiating with the Russians; their negotiations with the French had paused because the latter said that nothing in the Wrights' aeroplane was patentable. The Austrians and the German Emperor were negotiating secretly with them, and Octave Chanute wrote to Wilbur Wright ".. The Kaiser had probably made up his mind to a war with France. The taking over of your machine by the latter causes him to pause, as he may not know that the sale is not exclusive."

In April 1906, the U.S. patent was granted, after long delays, in respect of the original gliding machine.

Wilbur wrote a long letter to Chanute from Dayton dated October 28th, 1906, about their successes, adding that they would have by Spring 1907 four or five new engines giving 8 horsepower more than the original and weighing 15lbs less. Also that they had a letter from Alexander announcing that he was coming to America again, this time to attend the New York Aeronautical Show in December, 1906, and he would arrive in time to attend the Memorial meeting at the Smithsonian on 3rd December, 1906, in honour of the late Professor Langley, and would like to go to Dayton the next day (December 4th). The Wrights wrote to Octave Chanute asking him to accompany Patrick Alexander to Dayton, as they would welcome his making a visit, as "favourable conditions we have been waiting for have arrived."

Bishop Milton Wright's diary for Wednesday, December 5th, 1906: "Patrick Alexander, of England, dined and supped with us, and at 10p.m. he and Wilbur and Orville started to New York."

At the Second Annual Exhibition of the Aero Club of America in New York, December 1st-8th, the newest Wright four-cylinder vertical engine was exhibited. The show was held in connection with the 7th Annual Show of the Automobile Club of America at Grand Central Place. The Editor of the Cosmopolitan Magazine, John Brisben Walker, gave a dinner in honour of the Wrights at the Century Club. Octave Chanute, Augustus Post, and "other prominent individuals attended"; no doubt Alexander was there, as he was highly regarded among the members of the Aero Clubs of America.

This was the occasion when Patrick Alexander introduced the Hon. C.S. Rolls to the Wright brothers. At that time some American papers described Patrick Alexander as a Russian, states C.C. Turner. Rolls had been driving his 'Royce' car in U.S.A., which attracted much favourable comment. (New York Herald 29/9/06).

The Associated Press stated that negotiations between the French Government and the Wright brothers for the latters' aeroplane had been definitely broken off months before. They noted that Patrick Alexander had arrived in Dayton on 5th December, 1906, and that Wilbur Wright had accompanied him to New York. Wilbur admitted to the reporter that it was Alexander's fourth visit to Dayton, and said that they were only going to New York to attend the International Aero Club exhibition. An interview with Alexander was refused, and the latter refused to even meet the reporter. It was current in New York and Paris that Alexander was acting for the United States Government, and was negotiating for the acquisition of the flying machine. This was vigorously denied by Wilbur Wright who added that Patrick Alexander was a wealthy Englishman possessed of a fondness for travel heightened by a keen interest in aeronautics and airship progress. This induced him to visit Dayton several times. As to negotiations with the French or any other government, Wilbur Wright positively refused to speak, and would only say that he would be returning to Dayton in a week or ten days.

Patrick Alexander's opinions were receiving close attention in U.S.A., where the New York Herald printed his article praising the Wright brothers (22/12/1906). He noted that in France the military airship "Patrie" was flying over Paris, maneouvering so as to drop a letter squarely on the War Office, and was receiving enthusiastic attention from the Parisians.

After Alexander had left for England, Wilbur wrote to Chanute that he had alleged that the last edition of L'Aerophile in Paris had included a full account of the Wrights' negotiations with the French, naming the commissioners, and that he had also talked to the latter in Milan. "We suspected he was trying to draw us out, and were not very responsive. It is very strange that he should have made such statements to us."

The Wright brothers read the Aeronautical Society Journal, and commented in their letters upon the progress of their rivals. Santos Dumont, who apparently had abandoned airships for heavier than air machines, (which were being called Dynamic Flying Machines at that time, there was no standard terminology). Langley had called his machine an aerodrome, a tail first aeroplane was called a canard - French for a duck. There were many other examples - translation difficulties and misunderstandings were common.

Many designers were experimenting with "dynamic flying machines", including Cody in England, and Chanute advised the Wright brothers that "some of them may develop something", and suggested that "it would not be wise to be very stiff if a good offer came from the British War Office" - it was thought at the time that Patrick Alexander was the War Office agent.

The early designers' 'hops' of up to 250 feet were the sort of success that an uncontrollable machine could manage given sufficient speed, but as soon as its momentum was exhausted it sank back to the ground. None of the 'flights' in Europe in 1906 had reached the degree of success of the Wrights in 1903.

In January, 1907, the Secretary of the Aeronautical Society wrote to Patrick Alexander asking for money to assist the library. He replied, pointing out that when he had assisted the Society with a payment of £100 per annum for 5 years, he had received a dozen tickets for each quarterly meeting, and a dozen journals after each meeting. "Now I receive but one ticket and one copy of the Journal; why is this? It gave me pleasure to distribute the Journals and my friends now consider I am tired of sending any more. Please kindly send me a statement of the last accounts, 1903/04 is the last I have. ." However, he made a donation, and the publisher recommenced sending him a dozen journals each quarter.

He had left Southsea by April, 1907, and from 18th April he asked that communications be addressed to 82, Victoria Street, Westminster, where for the first time he was on the telephone, Westminster 5712, in addition to his telegrams and cables coding of "Utile" London, and "Observer" at Portsmouth.

An Exhibition of "Flying Machine Models" was held at the Agricultural Hall during the week ending 14th April, and many designs were shown by their inventors, each of whom was confident that the machine shown was the prototype of one that would solve the problem of heavier than air flight.

The proof of such claims was put to the test on April 15th, 1905, when Patrick

Patrick Alexander judging "Flying Machine Models"
at the "Aeroplane Trials", April, 1907

Alexander was one of the judges. Most of the 'flights' consisted of dives into the ground, or at best glides into the spectators, who, despite the efforts of the police, persisted in impeding the trials. There were a series of failures and two or three modest flights, with the result that Alexander and the other judges did not award the first prize, and gave the second prize to someone who was to become famous as an aeronaut - A.V. Roe, who flew his "double-decker", as the biplane was termed, as far as the safety net.

It was a time when it seemed possible that one of the many inventors would produce a flying machine that would fulfill the designers expectations, but each trial seemed to result only in disappointment.

Mr. A.V. Roe, who secured the second prize, launching his model aeroplane at the "Aeroplane Trials" (The first prize was not awarded, as the standard was not considered sufficiently high)

Chapter 24

Ballooning in 1907

Residents in the vicinity of balloon grounds had their problems. Patrick Alexander noted a bitter complaint from one lady who wrote to her local newspaper asking help in ascertaining the name of an aeronaut who dropped a bag of sand down her chimney, ruining a fruit tart. Road-hogs were already unpopular, but air-hogs were likely to be worse, especially if parsimonious persons ballasted with half bricks instead of fine sand, suggested Vanity Fair.

Balloonists were supposed to sieve and dry their sand and to discharge this in a fine stream clear of anywhere that the descending material might cause offence.

On 11th September, 1907, Patrick Alexander left for the Brussels International Aeronautical Federation Conference accompanied by Professor Huntington, C.S. Rolls, Griffith Brewer, Frank H. Butler, Roger Wallace K.C. and Harold Perrin. Alexander was recorded as the Vice President of the Aeronautical Club. The balloonists in the party were to take part in the International Balloon Race, while the Aerial Congress discussed Aeronautical Passports, and an International Register of balloons. Everyone enjoyed a magnificent banquet at the Hotel Mengelle, which was attended by most of the prominent aeronauts of Europe.

The Gordon Bennett balloon race of 1907 took place from St. Louis, Missouri, U.S.A. because the venue follows the nationality of the previous winner, and an American aeronaut Lieut. Lahm had won in 1905.

Four British competitors were entered. The Hon. C.S. Rolls, Mr. Griffith Brewer, Lord Royston and Mr. Moore-Brabazon. They would cross in the 'Lusitania' which was due to sail about October 5th, 1907, with Patrick Alexander who had been chosen to represent England at the Aeronautical Congress at Jamestown, U.S.A. The Observer stated on 18th August, "Mr. Alexander is well known as a keen experimenter with aeroplanes. He is a friend of the celebrated brothers Wright of Drayton (sic), U.S.A. and is one of the few people who has seen their mysterious flying machine, while he has made balloon ascents not only in Europe and America, but even in China . . ."

The strong challenge to the Americans and other competitors by the British quartet seems to have worried the Aeronautical Club of the United Kingdom, who would have to deal with arrangements for the next Gordon Bennett race, if the

British won. In the event, only Griffith Brewer went, his companion being Lieut. the Hon. Claud Brabazon, who was taken ill during the race, so that Griffith Brewer had to make an early landing. The Aeronautical Club may have made a collective sigh of relief. As to the Aeronautical Congress at Jamestown, Patrick Alexander announced that "he will not represent England at the Aeronautical Congress to be held at Jamestown." No reason was given but 1907 was the year that his health was unsatisfactory.

The Germans won the race with the balloon "Pommern", covering 849 miles. The French entry "Isle de France" was second, with 848.8 miles in 44 hours - a new world endurance record.

After the St. Louis Gordon Bennett Race, there was a meeting of the International Aeronautic Congress at the Aeronautical Club of America, 249 West Fifty Fourth Street, New York, a meeting that Patrick Alexander was due to attend. Rear Admiral C.N. Chester of the United States Navy advocated a corps of airships as an antidote to the submarine and as the eyes of the battleship. He said, "the Russians found the airship useful against the Japanese, and used balloons from the Vladivostock fleet which explored the Japanese coast unknown to the Japs and obtained valuable information for the Russian forces." (This may or may not be accurate, but the end product of the Russo-Japanese War was the sinking of almost every Russian warship, as well as defeat on land).

Chapter 25

The French jeer "Bluff, Bluff, Bluff" at the Wrights

The French press tended to deride the reports of the Wrights' flights, which seemed so impossibly extravagant compared with the best efforts of French aeronauts. A typical article appeared in 'Le Petit Parisien' dated 1st January 1907:

Les Wrights

More and more it seems that the Wright brothers, the famous American aeronauts are nothing but good bluffers. Every day, new information comes in to confirm this opinion. One of our colleagues recently received the illustrated prospectus of an aerial navigation company, the centre of which will be at Dayton. A lot of planes are reproduced, excepting the mysterious contrivance from the Wrights.

Quite recently, Mr Patrick Alexander who travels widely, and has seen everything, was denying formally having ever seen the machine, while the Wright brothers quote as a reference his being a witness.

Finally, there is nothing to confirm the news that the American Government could have been negotiating with the Wright brothers.

Decidedly, the only thing that remains for this aeroplane is an attempt which has misfired.

Bluff, Bluff, Bluff!!
Author's Note: I am grateful to Mr. Marson for the above and other translations.

In Le Havre, a Wright flyer lay crated, having been sent there in July, 1907, to await a decision regarding demonstration flights in Europe.
described in the 'Automotor' dated 30th March, 1907.

Patrick Alexander, accompanied by Miss Moore-Brabazon represented the Aeronautical Club at the Memorial Service to the two officers lost in the Army balloon "Thrasher" whose fate was a matter of conjecture, after they took off at Aldershot watched by King Edward and the Japanese Crown Prince. The balloon was found off Abbotsbury beach. The Service was held at the St. Georges Garrison Church, Aldershot on 8th June, 1907.

In 1907, Patrick Alexander was active in Aeronautical Club affairs, being on both the Technical and Meteorological Committees. The minutes of the

Aeronautical Club at that time included a note that the Aeronautical Club had completed arrangements for . . . important practical experiments with Aerial Navigation, including propellers, aeroplanes (wings), engines etc. Donations were desired, and for once Patrick Alexander's name does not appear.

In Europe the negotiations between the Wright brothers and the French were continuing, and Patrick Alexander's letters indicate that he was trying to keep in touch.

In June, 1907, Octave Chanute wrote to Orville Wright enclosing a letter he had received from Alexander, in which the latter urged them to make "everything public". Chanute did not agree, but suggested that it would be well to say more about "your performances", which so far he had refrained from doing, for fear he might say too much. This was during the period from 16th October, 1905, to 6th May, 1908 when the Wrights made no flights, and kept complete secrecy about their work, an attitude that was criticised widely at first, then they tended to be remembered less and less, and even their successful flights of 1903 were forgotten by some people. Alexander's letter was the subject of some comment by the Wrights. "Mr Alexander seems much better satisfied with the conditions of aeronautics in England than one would expect after reading the various articles on the subject in the recent English press. I am of the opinion that our delay in coming out with our machine has placed us in a better instead of a worse condition, as Mr Alexander thinks. The late telegrams from Wilbur seem to indicate that there is a very good prospect of doing business and at a better price than any of our former deals."

In Paris, Wilbur recorded that he had written "to K.W. and Alexander" besides having an automobile trip to Versailles. He was engaged in negotiations with the French authorities, when, just as the road to an early contract seemed clear, these negotiations were brought to a stop by "certain parties, who Wilbur does not care to mention in a letter, demanding that we raise the price by several hundred thousand francs in order to furnish them an opportunity for graft!!"

Wilbur told them that we would not consider such a proposition, "and if they insisted on standing in our way, we would take the matter out of the ordinary channel, and offer it direct to the Minister of War for his acceptance at once, we would proceed to Berlin." The bandits withdrew.

Negotiations dragged on in France and Germany, and Wilbur wrote to his sister Katherine from Berlin on October 22nd, 1907, . . . "Our negotiations here are not to the point of settlement yet. The technical department is in favour, but we expect trouble with the money end of the War Department".

The familiarity to be inferred by the reference to Jack - not even John - implies a more than casual friendship, Jack being Colonel Capper. "Pat" refers to Patrick Alexander, who was well known to the Wright family and a friend of many years.

Lieut. Lahm, a fellow American and aeronaut, is given his rank but no first name.

Colonel and Mrs. Capper had been guests at Dayton in October, 1904, and Orville spent a weekend with them in November, 1907 in England. He wrote to his sister Katherine, "Mrs. Capper wants to send you a climbing rose. I told Wilbur to get it if he goes out to see them on the way home".

I wonder if a plant from Mrs. Capper's garden did reach Dayton in Wilbur's luggage.

In November, 1907, Orville Wright came to France and watched Henry Farman trying to win the Deutsch-Archdeacon prize of 50,000 francs. All he had to do was take off and fly between two posts without landing en route. The flight - termed a "Kilometre Boucle" - was more than Henry Farman could manage until January 13th, 1908, and no other European flew the test course before him. The Wright brothers could have performed the feat with ease, and Orville said that he thought the prize would have been won months ago.

The incident led to a wager being entered into by Patrick Alexander and Griffith Brewer. At a dinner on 5th November, 1907, the two friends were advancing their own theories as to progress in aeronautics. It must have been a good dinner, because Patrick Alexander was not content merely to be a partisan for heavier than air machines, he brashly claimed that before another year had passed, he would fly a mile in a heavier than air machine, or pay Griffith Brewer £500. The wager was reported in the French journals, "Le Gil Blas", and "Soleil".

On the anniversary of the wager, the New York Herald reported "Mr. Patrick Alexander has just paid £500 to Mr. Griffith Brewer for a lost wager. Both men are enthusiastic aeronauts, and at a dinner on 5th November, 1907, Mr. Alexander undertook to travel a mile by means of mechanical flight within a year, or forfeit £500 to Mr. Griffith Brewer." "Mr. Alexander", says the Daily Express, "has made no attempt to win the money. Mr. Brewer says he will devote it to working out the problem of mechanical flight."

Patrick Alexander could have pleaded ill health, as he had given up his membership of several aeronautical societies during the year for that reason, but it was typical of the cheerful balloonist Griffith Brewer, that he should announce that he would spend the money on the problems of mechanical flight, which were very dear to Patrick Alexander's heart.

Griffith Brewer might have lost the bet if Patrick Alexander had enjoyed the luck that Brewer had in France, where Wilbur Wright had methodically and slowly assembled his flying machine behind closed doors, and under spartan conditions. On 6th October, 1908, Major Baden-Powell and Mr. Moore-Brabazon witnessed Wilbur Wright's flight - he had been making short flights since August 8th, having taken 5 months to build the machine. Many people hung about hoping that the taciturn Wilbur Wright would offer them a flight. He refused offers of money for the privilege, as accepting one would open the floodgates, and he wanted to be able to meet the terms of a French syndicate offer of £20,000 if within 6 months his machine made two flights of more than 30 miles. Unexpectedly, Griffith Brewer was offered a flight by Wilbur, as were Major Baden-Powell, F.M. Butler, and the Hon. C.S. Rolls. They were deeply impressed, but once again Patrick Alexander wasn't in the right place at the right time; he must subsequently have reflected upon the previous time, when by missing a telegram, he missed the first Wright flight in December, 1903. This time he missed winning his wager with Griffith Brewer for a flight of over a mile before 5th November, 1908. It was 30th October, 1908.

Chapter 26

Balloons and Airships

In August, 1907, the Daily Graphic was describing at length the attempt to break the world's long distance record in England's largest balloon. The "captain" was Auguste Gaudron, in whose company Patrick Alexander had made his first balloon ascent in 1891, and who made the Centenary celebration ascent for him at Bath in September, 1902. This time Gaudron was to be accompanied by J.L. Tanner, the owner of the balloon, and Charles C. Turner, who was an aeronautical correspondent. The aeronauts had to obtain the first passports taken out by balloonists, and get visas from Russian and other consulates. Newsmen anticipated that production of these in, say Russia, without evidence of having crossed a frontier might cause mystification.

Eventually they left the Crystal Palace on October 12th and 19 hours later found they had landed in Sweden, having flown 702 miles.

While Germany had built and flown a series of Zeppelins, and France had produced several that had made the headlines, no British airship had been built, except one that Dr. Barton built for the War Office and which was a failure. A small airship built by Mr. Willows of Cardiff had some minor successes, but nothing to compare with the German and French projects. The British public felt deprived. At last, in 1906 the building of a military airship was authorised. Colonel Templer got busy at Farnborough, working in secrecy, then handing over direct responsibility for the airship to Colonel Capper in a letter dated 5th November, 1906. Colonel Capper always regarded Colonel Templer as the designer of the airship.

On 6th September, 1907, the "Military Mail", an Aldershot journal, disclosed that the military airship being built, "with the greatest secrecy and security" at the Balloon factory at Aldershot was completed, and only awaited favourable weather for its trials.

The journal stated that King Edward and the Prince of Wales (later to be King George V) had inspected the airship, but very few others had been able to see it. A permit form the War Office had to be obtained, and "less than half a dozen outside Colonel Capper, Colonel Templer, Mr. Cody and Mr. Patrick Alexander have seen the airship other than the fitters and constructors; confidential men of proved character."

The article in "Military Mail" ended, "Colonel Capper has been assisted throughout by Mr. S.F. Cody, the inventor of the man-lifting kite, and Mr. Patrick Alexander, a gentleman well known in the sceintific world, who has followed as a hobby the study of aeronautics and astronomy. Only a few years ago he presented a magnificent astronomical telescope, mounted on a wonderful base, a gift that must have cost him a thousand pounds. He has had a good deal of experience in ballooning, having been attached to the Japanese Ballooning Staff during the late war in the Far East. Now he is devoting his time and wealth to the task of improving the aeroplane. He has made many improvements in aeronautics, and if he has solved the secret of the practical aeroplane, the British Army will be ahead of any other in its mastery of the air . . ."

Armed sentries guarded the Balloon factory day and night. It was possible that there was little to hide, except any differences due to Governmental niggardly policies, but a show of secrecy stimulated press interest wonderfully, and publicity

The first flight of "Nulli Secundus" on 10th September, 1907.

Propelled by the Army's solitary 50h.p. Antoinette engine - later to power the Army's first aeroplane. The enormous wings midships were intended to stop the airship rolling; being found to be unnecessary on the first flight, they were removed.

168

might lead to larger official funds. With little information about the air ship available, the Daily Mail added that "it was not advisable for anyone of foreign appearance to venture near the balloon factories". After giving credit for the design to Colonel Capper and Samuel Cody ("a United States subject") added "Another gentleman engaged in the airship has a quite unofficial position, but acts as superintending engineer," (this might be a reference to Colonel Templer), but the Bath Herald on 27th September, 1907, was mysterious, "I believe that I am right in saying that a distinguished gentleman aeronaut who formerly resided on the outskirts of Bath is the mysterious amateur who is believed to have solved the secret of a practical aeroplane. It is now being built for the Government under strict secrecy at Aldershot, and if it proves successful the British Army will be ahead of any other in the mastery of the air". To anyone who knew about Patrick Alexander the aeronaut of Bath and his 1902 celebrations of the 1802 balloon ascent, the allusion was clear.

On Friday, September 6th, 1907, the Daily Mail repeated some of the "Military Mail" article and stated, "besides Mr. Cody, Mr. Patrick Y. Alexander is advising Colonel Capper. Mr. Alexander was attached to the Japanese ballooning staff during the war in the Far East, and has made a study of practical aeronautics."

The next day, the Pall Mall Gazette said much the same. None of the information was subsequently withdrawn as incorrect, which is interesting, because when Patrick Alexander found that the Illustrated London News was describing him as "an Agent of the British Government" in an article dated 25th January, 1908, he successfully demanded a correction, which was published in I.L.N. on 25th February, 1908.

The British Military Airship story was repeated in the world's press, including the New York Herald. The "Observer" added that "Patrick Alexander had made many visits in connection with the work at Aldershot to France and Germany". Patrick Alexander was not the only one to go to Europe for information or materials. No suitable British engine being then available, Samuel Cody was sent to France by Colonel Capper to buy an Antoinette engine of 50 h.p. and as the War Office budget had been spent already, Colonel Capper met the expenditure out of his own pocket. Colonel Capper expressed his regret that no suitable British engine was available.

A series of trial flights began on 10th September, 1907, and were successful. The pressmen were slightly depressed by the apparent absence of anything revolutionary about the great sausage balloon, cruising around the countryside; soldiers rejected the name 'Nulli Secundus' in favour of "Saveloy". The official name was reputed to have been given by King Edward VII.

Cody was a constructional and mechanical genius, and dealt with the engine. Colonel Capper set out to gain experience as a balloonist, both as assistant to C.S Rolls, and with his own balloon. The third member of the crew of the 'Nulli Secundus' would be the Works Manager or the Chief Balloon Instructor at Farnborough.

The part played by Patrick Alexander does not seem clear, although by reason of his travels to inspect various flying machines he would be able to suggest means of overcoming some difficulties, and he was something of an expert on propellers, having been experimenting for years. He made journeys to Europe for unspecified reasons in connection with the project, and may have dealt with the press. Both the Daily Mail and the New York Herald seemed to be in touch with him periodically, and possibly the Military Mail.

Colonel Templer arrived in time to see the take off, and was joined by Patrick Alexander who spoke enthusiastically to the press.

On Saturday, 5th October, 1907, after only three hours total flying in the airship, Cody and Capper set off to fly around St Pauls Cathedral. By 10.50a.m. they were flying low over 'Pinehurst', where Patrick Alexander once lived, and Cody's family waved proudly from the lawn, while Cody shouted that he would be home for supper. Millions of people along the route watched their first airship and waved with delight as 'Nulli Secundus' flew over at some 800 feet, with Cody - always the showman - sounding a klaxon motor horn. They dipped over Buckingham Palace, not in salute as the press reported, but because Colonel Capper had promised the King that if such a flight was a success, he would bring the airship to the Palace and alight on the Palace lawns on October 14th for a royal inspection. The War Office was visited next, and the Army Council could be seen waving handkerchiefs and watching through field glasses. Then round the dome of St Pauls, with Cody taking photographs that failed to come out due to oil from the engine that smothered everything including the camera.

Cody's car containing seven sappers was trying to keep up with them, but the crowds were so dense that they could not get near Clapham Common, where Capper had first tried to land, as petrol was running short, they then made for the Crystal Palace, where they landed safely. There was just time for the press to be able to claim that England was Mistress of the Air as well as Mistress of the Sea, and that 'Nulli Secundus' was better than the French and German airships. Then came the anti-climax. At the Crystal Palace, the wind increased overnight, the seven sappers could not cope and the airship was broken up. But for one sapper, who released the gas and was promoted Sergeant on the spot, the result would have been worse. It was brought back to Farnborough in pieces, never to fly again. Some pieces were incorporated in the next airship, and the Antoinette engine became the power unit for Cody's aeroplane, whenever it was not required for other machines. Eventually one or two more engines were acquired by the British Army, but the clamour about War Office niggardlyness continued. The Royal Navy and the traditional British Army continued to take almost all of the money available for defence, much to the annoyance of Patrick Alexander and the air minded minority.

The accident to 'Nulli Secundus' was virtually repeated soon afterwards in the case of the French airship, 'La Patrie', which was not only damaged in high wind, but broke away from 15 men and took off without its crew. After being seen over Ireland, it disappeared for ever.

The French airship had previously made a flight of 3 hours, and the German "Gross" one of 3 hours, while the latest Zeppelin had flown 200 miles in just over 9 hours. Before it was wrecked, the 'Nulli Secundus' had flown for nearly three and a half hours, further and longer than any other airship, except for the Zeppelin, and was the only one constructed to retain hydrogen under pressure.

'Nulli Secundus II' was commenced a few months later, but there is no mention of Patrick Alexander taking any part.

The next flight by a British airship would be made on 14th August, 1908. Among the group of experts who met the crew as they climbed out of the airship was Patrick Alexander, ''who spoke in terms of the warmest praise of the whole trial,'' reported the Evening Standard.

In Germany on 6th August, 1908, the giant airship of Count Zeppelin - his fourth - had caught fire and been destroyed, to the grief of the Count. The Yorkshire Herald tartly remarked that he had spent his own fortune on one, and somebody else's fortune on another. The German nation was proud of the old man and his airships, and large sums were sent to him to help build yet another airship.

Three days later, on 8th August, Wilbur Wright would demonstrate the flying machine he had built at Le Mans using the parts sent over months before. The dramatic flight would be the greatest triumph yet, and be to the complete astonishment and chagrin of the disbelievers.

Chapter 27

The start of Aeronautics at Windsor in 1907

During 1907, Patrick Alexander's health was giving trouble again, and, during the year he began the connection with United Services College, Windsor (later to become Imperial Service College) that was to continue for the rest of his life. He was 40 years old, and convinced that he would not live beyond the age of 50. United Services College had been founded in 1874 at Westward Ho! in North Devon. Rudyard Kipling was a pupil during 1878 and 1881, and his stories of "Stalky & Co." are based upon the United Services College.

In 1906, the United Services College came to Windsor, joining with St. Marks School, Alma Road, Windsor. The amalgamation received publicity, and the aims of the new college - to give a public school education to the sons of men who had served the Crown or in the armed Services - attracted the attention of Patrick Alexander. It was not long before his address was United Services College, St. Marks, Windsor on 7th December, 1907.

Patrick Alexander went to Paris, where he met Orville Wright, who was not impressed by the French attempt to fly. Here, on a typical day such as November 19th, 1907, competitors for the Deutsch-Archdeacon prize were making repeated attempts to get their flying machines to fly more than short 'hops'.

The Wrights commented among themselves that it was not difficult to get an aeroplane to take off briefly, once sufficient momentum had been built up, but once this was exhausted, the machine would sink back to earth. The engines were underpowered and the aeroplanes generally had no means of flight control such as the 'wing-warping' that they had developed. The aeronauts of Issy worked on their aeroplanes to try and improve performance, and after each 'improvement', tried again and again, sometimes making brief hops. The length between wheel marks on take off and landing was eagerly measured and compared.

Alexander watched as Bleriot, Henri Farman and Santos Dumont repeatedly tried and failed. Eventually Alexander returned to London on 6th December, 1907. It was January 13th, 1908, before Henri Farman managed the "Kilometre Boucle" - the first circular kilometre flight in Europe, winning the 50,000 francs prize.

Patrick Alexander forecast how things were developing. On 7th December, 1907, he wrote to Major Baden-Powell:

PATRICK Y. ALEXANDER.

TELEGRAMS & CABLES.
"UTILE" LONDON.
"OBSERVER", PORTSMOUTH.
TELEPHONE 5712 WESTMINSTER.

82, Victoria Street,
Westminster,
London 7th. December 1907.
S. W.

My dear Major Baden-Powell,

What on earth are you up to in

Colman's Park?

May I come and see you?

I got back from Paris last night. I
think Bleriot with his new machine is now leading the way.

Farman has altered his, I think for
the worse. Dumont is still on with No.19.

You will be interested to hear that
I have resigned from The Aero Clubs of England, France America
and Germany. They are getting too prominent for me, so I am
clearing out and going to take up gardening.

Can you call round at this office
Monday afternoon next (9th.).

Believe me,

very sincerely yours,

Patrick Y. Alexander.

*A letter sent by Patrick Alexander to Major Baden-Powell,
dated 7th December, 1907*

173

THE TRANSATLANTIC AERO-'BUS OF 1950

"The Transatlantic Aero-bus of 1950", or "A Flight of the Future."
This cartoon is typical of many.
It appeared in 'The Graphic', 5th January, 1907

174

Alexander was right about Bleriot's new machine "now leading the way". The Bleriot VII flew for 45 seconds over 500 metres on 16th November, 1907, and his 'VIII' flew well later, making a celebrated cross country flight of 17 miles (with two landings en route) on 31st October, 1908.

Farman's 'Voisin Farman I' flew for 1 minute 14 seconds on 9th November, 1907, covering 1,030 metres, with similar flights on 11th and 13th January, 1908, the second including the first European circular flight, thus winning a prize of 20,000 francs. He was the guest of honour at L'Aero Club de France banquet. In July, 1908, he managed a 20 kilometre flight.

Santos Dumont's No. 19 was an ultra-light machine, the 'Demoiselle', which first flew for 200 metres on 17th November, 1907. It was barely successful as an aeroplane, until modified in November, 1908.

All these flights—and others—represented the best efforts of the European aviators, but on 8th August, 1908, Wilbur Wright was to demonstrate that those who called the brothers "humbugs and bluffers" were wrong, when he first demonstrated the superiority of the Wright aeroplanes before a critical audience at Le Mans, who immediately became convinced that the Wrights' claims were authentic.

The reference to Colmans Park meant the Norwich mustard magnate's estate at Gatton Park, Surrey, where Baden-Powell was experimenting since the previous summer with propellers driven by a 8 h.p. motor. Patrick Alexander had declined to assist financially, as he considered the power inadequate, and because others were experimenting with greater power. Baden-Powell left soon after, as he found the privacy inadequate, and took his experiments to deepest Hampshire.

Alexander wrote another letter early in February, 1908:

"Dear Sir,

Will you kindly publish in your next issue of the New York Herald Paris that I have resigned from the Aero Club of the United Kingdom, the Aero Club de France, the Deutscher Luftshiffer Verbandes Germany, and the Wiener-Flugtechnischen Vereins Austria, and the Aero Club of America U.S.A.
My health has been such as to preclude my taking such an active interest in aeronautics, as hitherto I have been unable to enjoy. The numberless communications I am now receiving are too numerous for me to give the attention that I should desire.
Thanking you in anticipation for the insertion of the above,

Very truly yours,

Patrick Y. Alexander."

Henri Farman was being deluged with begging letters from all over the world. The writers were convinced that they had the secret of perfect flight, and if Monsieur Farman would only send X thousand francs for materials, tickets to Europe and so on, the writer would make his-fortune and give, say, 25% to Henri

175

Farman. At this time (May, 1908) the proud boast was that Henri Farman was English and thus his successful flights in France were an English achievement. This was tartly rebutted by a Belgian who had found out that Farman was not only permanently living in Paris, (his father was a journalist there), but had become a naturalised Frenchman.

Similar begging letters were addressed to Patrick Alexander with his reputation for being a "soft touch".

Chapter 28

January 1908
The Illustrated London News find the "lost" Wright Patent

In March, 1903, the Wright brothers applied for a patent for their last glider which had proved so successful. This was granted in 1906 - but seems to have been generally overlooked, except for research carried out by the 'Illustrated London News':

AN UNSUSPECTED BRITISH PATENT:
THE WRIGHT BROTHERS' AEROPLANE.

During the frequent discussions which have been held during the last three years upon the aeroplane of the American brothers, Orville and Wilbur Wright, nobody suspected that their patent, with detailed plans and specifications, was lodged at this Majesty's Office of Patents. A few weeks ago a note in an obscure corner of a newspaper led The Illustrated London News to suspect that Messrs. Wright held a British patent, and a search of the office proved this to be the case. One of our Artists has accordingly made elaborate diagrams from the inventor's documents, and also shown the machine in flight. The air-ship is particularly interesting in view of Mr. Farman's successful experiment, and also in view of statistics which have just been published, giving the performances of the Wright machine. These were presented to the Aero Club of America. The most important flight of the aeroplane, with one of the brothers on board, was of 24 1/5 miles. The time was 38 min., 13 sec., or rather more than 38 miles an hour. The machine with its engine, gasolene fuel, and operator, weighed 925lb.

Some records of other flights are here given:-

Date	Miles (Metres)		Time		Cause of Stopping
Sept. 26	11-125	(17,961)	18 min.	9 sec.	Exhaustion of fuel.
Sept. 29	12-00	(19,570)	19 min.	55 sec.	Exhaustion of fuel.
Oct. 3	15-25	(24,535)	25 min.	05 sec.	Hot bearing.
Oct. 4	20-75	(33,456)	33 min.	17 sec.	Hot bearing.
Oct. 5	24-20	(38,956)	38 min.	13 sec.	Exhaustion of fuel.

There were seventeen witnesses of the flights. One witness was Mr. Theodore Waddell, of the United States Census department. Authentic testimony of the efficiency of the aeroplane has been given by Professor Alexander Graham Bell, Colonel

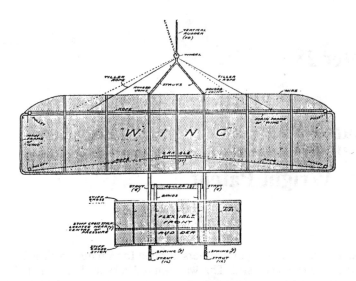

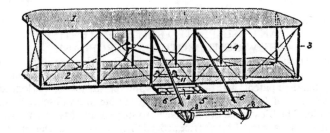

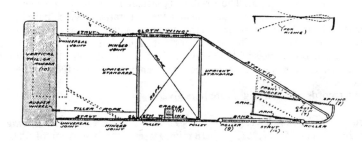

The Wright glider Patrick Alexander went to Dayton to inspect in 1902/3

Many illustrations of the Wright Flying machines were inaccurate, but these draw-
ings by W.B. Robinson for the "Illustrated London News' were made from the
Wright brothers' specifications in the Patent office.

1,2. *Wing surfaces of cloth cut on the bias attached to frames of wood and wire.*
  3. *Upright standards with ball-and-socket joints.*
  4. *Stay wires.*
  5. *Front horizontal rudder covered with cloth.*
  6. *Rudder struts.*
  8. *Springs.*
  9. *Operator's roller actuating front rudder.*
  10. *Rear vertical rudder or tail.*
  11. *Operator's cradle.*

Capper of the British Military Balloon Corps, and Mr. Patrick Alexander, an agent of the British Government. All the flights of which details are given here were made over a circular course of about three-quarters of a mile to the lap, which reduced the speed somewhat. In the straight the machine increased its speed; at the curves it slowed down. It is believed that on the straight the normal speed exceeded forty miles an hour. The flights of 1904 were at a height of about 50ft.; that of Oct. 5, 1905, when the machine travelled twenty-four miles in 38 min., was at a height from 75 to 100 feet. No higher flight was attempted, and the engine had never been driven at its utmost speed.

The experiments were held in a large, level field of eighty-seven acres, situated about eight miles east of Dayton, Ohio. The straight course measured nearly half a mile. The machine of 1903 flew at first with a wave-like movement until it was ballasted with 50lb. of iron attached to its nose. The 1904 machine needed 70lb. of ballast, but in the great flight of October, 1905, only 40lb. of ballast was used.

The circular flight of Dec. 1st. 1904 could have been continued, but the aeronaut's hand cramped on the steering-gear. When the aeroplane rounds a curve it leans forward just like a bird. The brothers Wright are the sons of a clergyman of Dayton, Ohio. They have devoted years to the scientific study of flying, and have collected a library upon the subject. It is rather interesting, in view of the source of our Illustrations, to see in the Times Engineering Supplement of last Wednesday, a statement that the Messrs. Wright had never patented their machine.''

The statement that Patrick Alexander was an agent of the British Government was one to which he took exception. He instructed his solicitors to take up the matter with the 'Illustrated London News', who duly published on 22nd February, 1908: "In a recent article on the Wright aeroplane, we described Mr. Patrick Alexander as 'an agent of the British Government.' This was incorrect, and we regret the error, into which we were led by an informant upon whose accuracy we relied . . ." In February, 1908, the Wrights were negotiating contracts with the United States Government—at a figure of about a quarter of that they had asked from the War Office; £5,000 instead of £20,000, the latter being similar to the figure of the terms with the French.

Chapter 29

The Wrights fly in U.S.A. and France

Outrageous statements insulting to the Wrights had been made by Archdeacon, the failed French aviator, at the monthly meeting of the Aero Club de France after Farman's flight of 26th October, 1907, when he won the Archdeacon Cup with a flight of 771 metres in 52.6 seconds. This was the first European flight comparable with the Wrights' flight lasting 59 seconds in 1903. Archdeacon said "Today the Wright brothers may claim all they wish. If it is true, (which I more and more doubt), that they were the first to fly through the air, they will not have the glory of it. . . "

In America, the Wright brothers had at last made a series of 10 ascents before the press, the longest one and a half miles and lasting 2 minutes. They had also solved a landing problem. It was May, 1908, and a project to fly a Wright aeroplane in Europe for demonstration purposes was under consideration. Reports of flights never made by the Wrights were sent worldwide, including one that a Wright aeroplane had flown 8 miles out to sea, another claimed that a Wright aeroplane had flown to a height of 100 feet. Patrick Alexander read the reports and sent a telegram of congratulation. Another report stated that both brothers had flown together - this was something they never ever did, except for one short flight.

The French stated with confidence that the Wright brothers had ordered 7 motors in France for their flying machines from Barrequand and Marr, a story that the Wrights were later to deny. The French object seemed to be to share in any glory that the Wrights won.

Wilbur Wright's diary dated Monday, May 4th, 1908, includes: "A telegram from Mr. Alexander congratulates us - we suppose on the fake report of a flight. This would indicate that the report has been cabled abroad. We have not yet seen the report." Katherine Wright had telegraphed that the newspapers had published a report of a flight by the Wrights - but they were not even ready for the season's test flights. It was later that someone had reported a sensational flight by the Wrights, 10 miles out to sea. No such flight had taken place - in fact they did not fly at all until 6th May, 1908.

Wilbur Wright wrote to Octave Chanute from Le Mans on July 10th, 1908:

"I have expected to have the pleasure of meeting you in person ere this, instead of having to write, as Mr. Alexander sent me word soon after I came to Europe that you were also on this side. But I have had no confirmation of it from any other source, and presume the information to be one of Mr. Alexander's peculiar vagaries. He is certainly the strangest man I have ever known.

I have been at Le Mans for some three weeks setting up one of our machines, but by mischance and insufficient carefulness I scalded my side and left arm pretty badly. Fortunately the injuries have healed without any complications and I will be all right in a day or two more. It will probably be near the end of the month before I am ready to begin practice, as the machine was less completely finished when shipped than I supposed it would be and I have no real assistant. The helper I have seems to be a rather nice young fellow, but his knowledge of English and mechanics is rather more limited than I had hoped to find it. If I had known there was so much work to be done, I would have brought a helper from America. Le Mans is an old-fashioned town of some 75,000 inhabitants, almost as much out of the world in some respects as Kitty Hawk.

P.S. My address remains care H.O. Berg, 11d, Regent St., London, S.W.5.''

On December 23rd 1907 the United States Signal Corps issued invitations for tenders which produced amazement. The aeronautical journals stated that the specifications were worded as though flying machines were a usual form of transportation and so exacting as to be unreasonable. The Signal Corps answer was that the specifications were drawn up after noting the statements of inventors as to what they could perform. Some clauses had been added to prevent the U.S. Government being trifled with, and "tests would be conducted with judicious reason and liberality."

Patrick Alexander was in New York at this time, and met Wilbur Wright, but nothing of note is on record. He seemed to choose to spend Christmas in the United States.

Of 41 proposals received, only three complied with the specification requirements, and awards were made on February 8th, 1908:

1. J.F. Scott, Chicago, £200, delivery in 185 days. (Mr Scott withdrew).
2. A.M. Herring, New York, price £4,000, delivery in 180 days.
    Herring had been Octave Chanute's assistant. He had produced models that flew, and gliders, but no powered man carrying aeroplane. Chanute said "Mr. Herring has been working for 15 years towards a solution of the problem of aviation. The present undertaking will bring the fruition of his endeavours or the defeat of all his hopes." He failed.
3. Wright brothers, Dayton, price £5,000, delivery in 200 days. (By August 27th, 1908).

On June 1st, 1908, the Bombay Gazette reported that "Patrick Alexander, the British Engineer, who is regarded as the representative of the British Government arrived in New York to investigate the Wrights' machine on 30th May, 1908." This was the machine that the Wright brothers were making to meet the requirements of the United States Government.

The report continues - "The fact that the coveted information for which newspapers recently have been willing to pay thousands lay unheeded under Patent

181

Application No. 121,303 for two years and could be had for two and a halfpence by anyone interested illustrates the minimum of attention paid to aeronautics in this country until the Wrights' six-mile flight, which was observed by your Special Correspondent at Manteo, North Carolina.''

Wilbur first flew publicly in France near Le Mans on 8th August, 1908. Orville made the test flights for the U.S. Army in a similar aeroplane which had been adapted to take a passenger, both pilot and passenger sitting upright for the first time. On September 3rd, 1908, Orville started the tests at Fort Myer, Washington, D.C. He made ten flights, and was airborne for nearly 6 hours. Then came an accident on 17th September 1908. He crashed, killing his passenger, Lieut. T.E. Selfridge. There was a crack in the propeller which flattened, setting up an unbalanced movement so that wires were torn loose and the machine went out of control. Orville was seriously injured.

Despite the accident, the Wrights became internationally famous. They had startled the world, and the U.S. Army was convinced that it needed the Wright aeroplanes.

Patrick Alexander now devoted his life to encouraging young men to become air minded, especially at United Services College, Windsor. According to J.I.M. Forsyth, in 1908 he went from U.S.A. to China, Russia and Japan before settling in Windsor.

Wilbur went to France in May, 1908, and built the flying machine in a secluded part of his friend Leon Bollee's factory at Le Mans under conditions that precluded anyone being able to repeat the detailed construction. He announced that he would fly the machine on August 8th, 1908 at Hunaudieres, about 5 miles away, without a preliminary test flight, and in front of an audience that came to be hyper-critical, and expecting to witness a failure. Wilbur took off, circled twice, and landed smoothly. The spectators were stunned and amazed at the effortless demonstration of control, far beyond anything achieved in France. The press was repentant and enthusiastic. The French pioneer aviator, Delagrange, exclaimed "We are beaten. We just don't exist!"

Patrick Alexander must have been amused to hear how his French aviator friends now admitted that the Wrights had revolutionised their world, and that his reports of previous flights had been no more than the truth.

It was still possible to denigrate the Wrights, by being critical of their "rail and derrick" aided take-off system, and by comparing the time required to learn to fly a Wright aeroplane, with the few minutes to learn how to take-off in a French 'Voisin' - but the latter could only manage 'hops', and had no means of turning safely.

The second period of negotiations with the British Government had ended mainly on the question of excessive price.

Octave Chanute was vexed by the Wrights' intransigence with the British, who he considered the best guardians of the aeroplane and its capabilities. He was critical of their policy of refusing a demonstration flight in advance of an agreement as to terms of sale. The Wrights refused to make demonstration flights purely to satisfy curiosity.

At Farnborough the British airship 'Dirigible No. 2' was being moved out of the hangar with its engines covered - security was strong, and cameras were strongly discouraged in the vicinity. Eventually it was to fly on 14th August, 1908, and Patrick Alexander was one of the crowd who watched and applauded, "with well deserved praise" stated the Morning Standard (and the Evening Standard).

There was rivalry - and a certain amount of acrimony - both at home and abroad, an example of the latter was the fantastic story accepted by the German Aero Club so that the Swiss 'Helvetia' won the 1908 Gordon Bennett race instead of J. Dunville of England in 'Banshee'. 'Helvetia' was thought in England to have been disqualified, as it had landed in the sea and had been towed into port by fishermen, but one of the passengers remained in the basket and claimed to have alighted on land. When this story was accepted by the Germans - who appear to have been engaged in a 'Hate England' periodic lunacy, led by the Kaiser - the Aero Club lodged an official protest by telegrams and letters to Berlin. None were answered. Later the Germans made a rule that landing in the sea meant disqualification - and said that this could not be legally retrospective. The Times commented "this incessant shuffling and despicable quibbling can convey only one idea - that of a desire to oust England from the race on the 'win, tie or wrangle' method . ." The Aero Club Committee's thoughts on this decision, which was universally pilloried - except in Germany - are not in the records, which appear to have been destroyed or not entered. One has to accept the decision of the governing body.

Chapter 30

Patrick Alexander and Motorless Flight

In December, 1908, he wrote to the Secretary of the Royal Meteorological Society resigning his Fellowship from the end of the year. He would apply for reinstatement in 1917, when he was given war work in Falmouth as a Meteorological Officer by the Ministry.

By Christmas Eve, 1908, he was again in U.S., and staying at the Albemarle Hotel having crossed on the luxurious Lucania. The American press noted that on Founders Day at the United Services College he was making another 3 day visit, and that he expected to be over again in a month.

The New York Tribune printed everything he said, and wanted more.

FOR MOTORLESS FLIGHT

P.Y. Alexander Predicts Aeroplane Triumph of Future.

"Patrick Y. Alexander, an Englishman of wealth, who keeps himself constantly employed in following from one country to another his hobby, the making of aeronautical experiments, has again just glided into the quietness of the Albemarle Hotel. He sent word to a few aeronautical friends in this city that he had arrived, after which he instructed the hotel clerk to show danger signals to any reporters who appeared hungry for news of the aeroplane or dirigible, and asked that his telephone be taken out. Then a reporter being sighted on the horizon, Mr. Alexander at once made a successful flight to his room. He broke all duration records for remaining above ground, and was, so far as could be learned, under perfect control the entire time - nine hours.

The English aeronaut crossed the Atlantic in a bad storm to chat for three days with close friends engaged in experimenting in aeronautics, which he referred to yesterday as the biggest thing in the Christian era. He will return to London on Wednesday on the Lucania, which brought him over. He was here last spring for seventy-two hours. He says he may be here again next month. It depends on whether he then wants to ask a question about aeronautics of some one in this country.

His contention is that man must learn to fly without a motor. He is able, he has found out by numerous experiments abroad, to lift himself off the ground for an instant. He says that in the experiments made with gliders by Lilienthal with 120 square

184

feet of surface to lift themselves against a 20 mile wind with 50 to 60 pounds pull.
"Why should we have such powerful motors as we now use to move us at that speed?" asked Mr. Alexander yesterday. He suggests that out of the air itself means will be found before long to utilise the latent electrical energy to produce artificial currents of sufficient strength to support a man in a flying machine - the same energy to be used to drive the apparatus.

There are now one hundred aeroplanes in England, he said, and £1,000,000 invested in the flying machines industry. Before the close of another year he predicts there will be at least fifty practical flying machines capable of sailing over Europe, with stops not more frequent than each thirty or forty miles. He added that there would be invested in the aeronautical industry in Europe in another year £10,000,000. The Russian government alone will spend £5,000,000 next year in aeronautical experiments, he declared.

Speaking of the Wright brothers, he said it was difficult to express the degree of sensation throughout Europe which was the result of their splendid work, and added that he knew of twenty-five sportsmen who had ordered Wright aeroplanes.

"The automobile clubs have been the backbone of all aero clubs," said Mr. Alexander when asked about a probable international coalition of automobile clubs having aviation sections, "and as long as gasolene motors are used in flying machines so long will the automobile men control aviation. They realise that the motor industry is closely allied with the flying machine, and they are going to control aviation as long as they can. The result is that automobile clubs abroad have taken up the subject officially, and the outcome will be that the aero clubs will lose their identity."

He surprised members of the Aero Club of America by informing them that the Aero Club of France had a short time ago been taken under the wing of the Automobile Club."

To the end of his life, Patrick Alexander maintained a belief in self-levitation.

On 31st December, 1908, Patrick Alexander was back in England and writing letters from United Services College, Windsor. It had been another busy year.

Patrick Alexander and the Dagenham Flying Ground

The Aeronautical Society decided at a meeting on 15th July, 1908, to form a Committee to consider the proposal of Major Baden-Powell that an Experimental Flying Ground should be obtained for the use of members. The criteria were to be accessibility from London, open country, slopes for gliding and model experiments, an expanse of water for floating tests, shelter for aeroplanes, and privacy.

Baden-Powell found a site that he considered met the criteria, a sub-Committee concurred, one guinea subscriptions were invited towards the cost of the ground, and donations towards a building fund. Members donated £200, of which Patrick Alexander with his usual generosity sent £100. The site was an area of reclaimed ground, east of Dagenham Dock, and almost completely enclosed by water, with the Thames on the south, Dagenham Breach to the left and north, and a canal and River Breach to the north. The area was flat and marshy, with few obstructions to flight. A two or three hundred yard long cinder track was planned as a "starting strip", landing would come later, practical flight was not yet a reality in England, whatever the Wrights and possibly the French were doing. Alexander was enthusiastic about progress, at first he visited the site several times, and in January, 1909, was full of praise, but only 18 members joined the experimental section. A lease for the ground at £50 p.a. was entered into by Baden-Powell who finalised the matter against the wishes of the Hon. Secretary who wanted more money to become available before expenditure was incurred.

The acquisition of a flying ground was to become contentious. Patrick Alexander visited the ground with Baden-Powell and was unstinting in his praise. He offered a "Whirling Table and a saddle back" which was a sort of experimental apparatus for testing wing sections and propellers.

Very few members commenced any work on machines. Visitors were uncomplimentary about the heavy growth of weeds - no grass being visible, and the proposed track for running machines was never completed although a quarter of a mile length, forty feet wide was built, the first of its kind. None of the sections to enable different directions of wind to be coped with were completed. Several other grounds had had similar difficulties, and did not meet the needs of a flying ground. There was not enough money to prepare such an area, and most areas were unsuitable to some extent. Experimenters used any area to which they could gain access and these had rough patches and ditches that were the undoing of many machines.

Publicity of the acquisition brought in some other people interested in the scheme. Badges and tickets were made available, an iron house erected, and sheds for aeroplanes to be built under cover. Baden-Powell's own 'Quadruplane' was completed about July, 1909, and was described as an amazingly crude affair, particularly when compared with the Wright flying machine in which Wilbur Wright had taken him up for the first time at Le Mans the previous year. It showed up Baden-Powell's lack of technical knowledge and ability, and may have made a jump or two, but having only a forward elevator as a control, it was probably a good thing that it never really flew.

There was a 'Special Day' for members and their visitors to view progress, which was not impressive, and the aeronautical journals were critical. The site was substandard and fell into disuse, the assets - such as they were - being sold.

In an optimistic moment, Patrick Alexander once described the Dagenham ground to a journalist, Harry Harper as "a breeding ground for flying machines", but it became a breeding ground for discontent among other members.

There was criticism, especially by Charles C. Turner, but no one really knew what was required to make an experimental flying ground. It was all experience, and hindsight, was as usual, better than the foresight of those who had taken the responsibility of the scheme.

Objectors were scathing, as the proper procedures had not been followed in respect of choosing the ground, authorising expense, or the legal functions. The dream of an Experimental Ground of the Aeronautical Society of Great Britain collapsed.

This attempt to make the Aeronautical Society with its scientists and theorists into a practical flying society had failed. On 18th March, 1910, within another year, Patrick Alexander had resigned and withdrawn his financial support. Colonel Fullerton, the secretary, also resigned. The site is now owned by Ford Motor

Company Limited.

Visiting England early in 1909, Henry Farman found very little help extended to him, and he returned to France, where the French were showing more sympathy and extending a greater welcome to inventors.

In January, 1909, Wilbur Wright was receiving both help and money in France - he had flown 77 miles over a triangular course, yet in England the subject was only of theoretical interest, and almost a joke. British Army Aeroplane No. 1 built by Cody, was being run along the ground "just to get acclimatised to the weather", sneered the Bystander, "and not to attempt anything so risky as flight", adding that "by watching the mistakes of others, the War Office is, no doubt, laying to heart much wisdom, and at very little cost."

The lack of a British aeroplane engine that would develop a horse power for each 3 or 4 pounds weight, was raised again, this time by Petrolius in The Standard. Motorcar engines weighed 10 to 12 pounds per horse power, and reliability was suspect, to say the least, when run under conditions of flight. Patrick Alexander gave thought to the problem. Perhaps a prize for a reliable British engine would help.

Chapter 31

1909 – The Wright Brothers are awarded a Gold Medal

1908 had ended with the President of the Aeronautical Society of Great Britain in his address to members saying that they met under auspicious and encouraging circumstances, and although much had still to be done to improve the aeroplane, great progress had been made, and mechanical flight had been accomplished. They had asked Wilbur and Orville Wright to accept the gold medal of the Society in recognition of their distinguished services to Aeronautical Science and elected them honorary members. Wilbur Wright had replied from Le Mans where the Society's letter had reached him, expressing thanks for the honours bestowed, and hoping to visit England before the end of the winter.

The letter Orville Wright had sent to Patrick Alexander dated November 17th, 1905, was re-printed in the Journal as it explained clearly what had been accomplished at that early date:

Wright Cycle Co.,
1127, West Third Street,
Dayton, Ohio.
November 17, 1905.

"Dear Mr. Alexander,
We have finished our experiments for this year, after a season of gratifying success. Our field of experiment, which is situated 8 miles east of Dayton, has been very unfavourable for experiment a great part of the time owing to the nature of the soil and the frequent rains of the past summer. Up to the 6th September we had flown the machine on but eight different days, testing a number of changes which we had made since 1904, and as a result, the flights on these days were not as long as our best ones of last year. During the month of September, we gradually improved in our practice, and on the 26th made a flight of a little over 11 miles. On the 30th we increased this to 12 and one-fifth miles, on October 3, to fifteen and one-third miles, on October 4, to twenty and three-fourth miles, and on October 5, to twenty four and one-fourth miles. All these flights were made at about thirty-eight miles an hour, the flight of the 5th occupying 38 minutes and 3 seconds. Landings were caused by the exhaustion of the supply of fuel in the flights of the 26th and 30th of September, and 5th

October, and in those of October 3 and 4, by the heating of bearings in the transmission on which oil cups had never been fitted. But before the flight on the 5th October, oil cups had been fitted to all of the bearings and the small gasolene can had been replaced with one that carried enough fuel for an hour's flight. Unfortunately, we neglected to refill the reservoir just before starting, and as a result the flight was limited to thirty-eight minutes. We had intended to place the record above the hour, but the attention these flights were beginning to attract compelled us to suddenly discontinue our experiments in order to prevent the construction of the machine from becoming public.

The machine passed through all of these flights without the slightest damage. In each of these flights we returned frequently to the starting point, passing high above the heads of the spectators.

If you think the contents of this letter would be of interest to the members of the Aeronautical Society of Great Britain, you are at liberty to communicate as much of it to them as you please.

Hoping that we may have the pleasure of seeing you on your next visit to America,

I beg to remain,

Very respectfully yours,

(signed) ORVILLE WRIGHT"

At a General Meeting of the Society held at the Institution of Civil Engineers, Great George Street, S.W. on Monday, May 3rd, 1909, the gold medal of the Society was presented to Wilbur and Orville Wright by the President, E.P. Frost J.P supported by eminent members of the Society including Major Baden-Powell who said "a few words" outlining the history of their epic flights, their struggles and successes. They were the first men to fly and some of those present including himself were among the first score or so of human beings to travel through the air in a flying machine. His remarks were illustrated by cinematograph pictures and lantern slides. The best item in the remarkable agenda was an illustrated talk by Colonel S.F. Cody who described his kites, both his "power kite", and his man carrying kite, and its use for taking photographs and for military observations. The "power kite", which had an engine, was flown on a wire without a pilot in 1907, and this was followed by the "Nulli Secundus" airship, which flew in September and October, 1907, and his "British Army Aeroplane No. 1" first flown on October 16th, 1908.

The third item on the agenda was the report of the Wings Committee, and their experiments with flapping wings, which had been modelled on the wings of a flying fox. As an example of the practical work of members, it was a classic.

PATRICK ALEXANDER'S LIBRARY AND "AERONAUTICS" 1909

The Aeronautical Club adopted the new journal 'Flight' as their official organ. The first number came out on 5th January, 1909, and contained a letter of welcome from Patrick Alexander enclosing a long list of the books and papers in his aeronautical library, which he was giving to the Victoria and Albert Museum Library. This unique collection is now in the Science Museum Library and Archives. The first item he listed was his 60 volumes of cuttings of aeronautical interest, which dated from 1892. Each volume had 200 pages, and much of the material in this book came from this source. He continued the collection until September 20th, 1913, by which time it amounted to another 60 volumes, most having 400 pages. There is no index, and the volumes form a formidable source of the aeronautical history of the world from earliest times until 1913, complete with what appears to be every published illustration and drawing. Patrick Alexander arranged for newspapers and journals from many parts of he world to be sent to him by cuttings agencies. There are also what appear to be souvenir papers which he collected personally during his extensive travels. Among articles in almost every language, those in English, French and German predominate. Some of the newspaper cuttings suffer from fragility due to acid in the paper, and access to the originals has therefore to be restricted. Most volumes are produced for inspection only in exceptional circumstances. Some pages are on art paper and are better preserved. The illustrations provide an interesting history of the work of the engraver and photographer.

After he had ceased to continue the series of books of cuttings, he still obtained and read as many journals and newspapers as he could acquire, and would return home bearing armfuls right up to the year of his death.

Whereas many records of research are of use subsequently, much early aeronautical material is only of archival interest and are of little or no practical value by reason of the futile methods advocated.

There were many proposals for manually operated flapping wings, and mechanical arrangements that were defective, sometimes dangerously so.

As an entrepreneur, he wanted to have a good intelligence service which could provide information regarding successful ideas and methods, while enabling defective developments to be avoided. The increasing momentum of aviation progress, and increasing secrecy and facilities for testing out of public view would make it an impossible task to manage single handed. By 1907, a volume of 400 pages was being filled every 3 weeks, and shelf space could have been a problem, besides finding the time taken in dealing with the cuttings, most of which bear dates in Alexander's writing, plus - in a very small minority of cases - his observations and criticisms.

From 1909 he was also collecting articles of interest to teachers of aeronautics, including the making of model aircraft which would be of value in his role of working with youths. He had been active in promoting the new technology, but this was advancing at such a rate that it is probable that he was being left behind.

An article by a newsman whose imagination exceeded his knowledge of history and the truth might be syndicated, so that inaccuracies became common among the cuttings, particularly regarding matters of popular interest, such as the Wright brothers latest achievement. If none was known, certain reporters were apt to invent flights that had never taken place, as in one instance when Patrick Alexander sent a telegram of congratulations to Dayton.

On more than one occasion, Patrick Alexander was not prepared to talk to the press. He may have aroused the newsmens' interest while in America by his obvious avoidance of reporters - rather like Greta Garbo - and this was also a ploy attributed to Colonel Capper when building Nulli Secundus I, with the object of arousing publicity to a financial advantage. It might be that he was able to sell copy, to the New York Herald for example, and there was no advantage in giving other reporters information for free.

As he was repeatedly reputed to be a British Government agent, - which he strongly denied - and even the agent of the United States Government in December, 1907, if true this would be a good reason for avoiding interviews.

While aeronautics were Alexander's greatest interest, he would sometimes have his attention caught by other matters. During an Antwerp Exhibition which he attended because of his interest at that time in deep sea diving, he put on a Siebe-Gorman diving dress and went down in the demonstration tank so as to make up his mind whether to follow up a project involving diving in the Greek Archipelago.

July, 1909 was the month that Patrick Alexander's booklet "Alexander's Aeronautics" was published for the Aeronautical Society. The editor was Major B.F.S. Baden-Powell, and Alexander arranged for it to be printed by the boys of the United Services College, Windsor where he had been since 1907. The reviews added:

> "This booklet . . . contains a series of tables bearing directly and indirectly on aerial navigation. Mr P.Y. Alexander and his pupils may be congratulated on the result of their labours. The tables include: Speeds and Pressures; Lift or Thrust of Screw Propellers; Specific Gravities and Weights; Metric Weights and Measures - these latter from the "Science Year Book" - and some concise data relating to balloons and balloon material. The booklet can be obtained from the Aeronautical Society on payment of 1d for postage."

The Aeronautical Society library was augmented by donations by members, and Patrick Alexander gave a copy of "Alexander's Aeronautics" in July, 1909, also a copy of "The Screw Propeller" by A.E. Seaton, and a complete barograph - a recording barometer. The Society purchased a number of books and models, together with lantern slides for loan to members for lecture purposes. They included "Aeronautics; an Abridgement of Aeronautical Specifications 1815-1891" by G. Brewer and P.Y. Alexander.

The Aero Clubs of America regarded Patrick Alexander with affection, and honoured him when they produced their book "Members of the Aero Clubs of America in Cartoon". Published by Aeronautics, 1908/09, each of the 32 cartoons depicts a member's character, aspirations and career, with verses underneath to supplement detail in the cartoon. He was the only Britisher included - unless Henry Farman qualifies, but he had French associations, and was French speaking. The series included eminent aviators led by the Wright brothers, and Glenn Curtis. There were financiers, politicians, balloonists - all Men of the Day with aeronautical connections.

The following four cartoons are from "Members of the Aero Clubs of America, 1908/09

PATRICK Y. ALEXANDER.

A MAN of great intelligence,
  And well supplied with brains,
Who, through his downright commonsense
  Unnumbered friends retains.
The homage of the great and small
  Is his in large degree,
Since in his genial manner all
  The true good fellows see.

The Art of flying well is blest,
  This patron *earns* his fame!
With a machine, his mind's obsessed,
  'Twill bust the motor game.
To fly by man-power is his plan—
  It'll come to that some day.
We must do honor to this man
  Is what the world doth say.

WRIGHT BROTHERS

THEY take a tumble now and then,
   These brothers brave and bold,
When something in the rudder breaks,
   And wires refuse to hold,
But after every swift descent
   They're always game, and say,
"O, that was just because we much
   Preferred to land that way."

If they should lose their legs and arms,
   These aviators true
Would still continue their attempts
   To navigate the blue.
They love to soar aloft and watch
   The swallow in his flight,
Their names are Wright because you see
   They're nearly always right.

193

HENRY FARMAN

THE balloon by Henry Farman
   Is regarded as a toy,
It's as an aeroplanist
   That he finds his greatest joy.
He's built the strangest airship
   We can ever hope to view,
Fitted up with wheels and rudders,
   And a big propeller too.

Judging from the tires and pulleys
   That upon the craft we spy,
It can run around the highway,
   It can travel in the sky,
And if once he gets it started
   On a steady upward flight,
Like the boy that played with powder,
   It will then be "out of sight."

194

DR. A. GRAHAM BELL

HELLO! hello! we're ringing up
   Across Canadian snows
The dean of scientific men,
   Whom everybody knows.
The Aero Club is calling you
   Upon the 'phone, to tell,
How very much we owe to you,
   O, Dr. Graham Bell!

Your fame is of the solid kind
   That don't evaporate,
Your busy brain is never still,
   But working long and late;
Inventor of the telephone,
   And wizard of the kite,
And master of the wireless, too,
   Good wishes, and good-night.

195

At last progress was being made with heavier than air flying machines, and could be shown to members at the Aeronautical Society meeting in January, 1909. Cinematograph pictures of the Wright flying machine were described by Baden-Powell. The machine was shown being brought sideways out of its shed, put on its trolley and attached to the launching apparatus at the pylon; the engine started and run for a few minutes. The launching chain, ropes and weight are made ready, caps are adjusted and coats buttoned tightly, the engine run up to full speed; Mr Wright released the trigger, the launch is made and the machine rises, turns, and flies back a few feet across the ground. More turns, then he lands. "And the cavalry men gallop across to keep the crowd back." They bring up the wheels, and a motor draws the machine back to the shed.

The members applauded long and loud. Then they watched films of birds in flight, at normal and slow motion speeds, the Gordon Bennett race of 1906, then the dirigible 'La Republique' which was the pride of France, followed by the German Zeppelin.

1909 has been called the Golden Age of Aviation in Europe, although it would take at least another year before practical flight became a reality in England. The need was felt for an efficient aeroplane, and a good flying ground. As the oldest Society engaged in aeronautics, the need was also for better premises, and 53 Victoria Street, London, was under consideration.

Patrick Alexander wrote to the Secretary, on 21st January, 1909, supporting the endeavour to obtain prestigious premises and increasing his annual donation of £100 per annum to £250 for each of the next three years. The ordinary subscription was one guinea (£1.05). In reply, he was asked whether he wished to become a member of the Council of the Aeronautical Society, but replied, "I do not care about my name being on the Council."

PATRICK Y. ALEXANDER,	*United Services College,*
Telegrams & Cables;	*St Marks,*
"Utile", London,	*Windsor.*
"Observer", Portsmouth.	*Thursday 21 1/9.*

To The Council
The Aeronautical Society of Great Britain
Westminster S.W.

"Gentlemen,
Some years ago, I had the honour of helping the Aeronautical Society of Great Britain to tide over one of the most crucial periods in its history.
At present more scientific interest in the Air and its uses for the service of mankind is being manifested throughout the World, than has hitherto been the case, and I am sure if the Council can see their way to acquire better accommodation and facilities at 53 Victoria St it will advance the influence of the Society.
Towards this end may I again assist to the extent of £250 (two hundred and fifty pounds) annually for the next three years the first donation to date from January the 1st this year 1909.

Believe me, Yours faithfully,
Patrick Y. Alexander"

Patrick Alexander had cheerfully supported the Aeronautical Society since becoming a member in 1901, and otherwise it would have collapsed for lack of money. He gave an annual donation of £100 and in reply to the secretary's first receipt, added, "I hope you have not blued the lot, drinking my health at the Buckingham Palace Hotel." The financial affairs of the Society were not always well kept, and he would ask from time to time for a statement of accounts. Members were not always sent receipts, a matter that upset Professor Hofmann of Berlin, and Alexander commenced paying his subscription and demanding a receipt to send to Germany.

There was competition to be the first to fly the Channel. One contender who seemed to have a good chance was Mr. Hubert Latham, in his Antoinette IV monoplane with its 8 cylinder 50 h.p. Antoinette engine, which unluckily failed when well out to sea, so that he had to be rescued by a French destroyer on 19th July, 1909. Six days later, Bleriot managed to coax his Bleriot XI with its 3 cylinder engine across to Dover, winning the Daily Mail prize of £1,000 and the Aero Club gold medal. Two years earlier Patrick Alexander had written that Bleriot was "leading the way" with his latest flying machine. Crossing the Channel with the unreliable engines of the day was a project that even the Wright brothers had not attempted.

Patrick Alexander repeatedly said that the Admiralty and War Office should take a more serious interest in aeronautics, but interest was weak. In April, 1909, the War Office ordered that experiments at Farnborough must cease, as the cost - £2,500 per annum - was too great. Within three months Bleriot had flown the Channel, making the flight that had foiled previous attempts.

Louis Bleriot was widely feted, and overnight became one of the world's popular heroes. He was courageous - and lucky.

The British press was stunned by the Bleriot cross Channel flight - although it had been obvious for some time that this would happen. The Wright brothers had flown greater distances, but crossing this 21 miles wide stretch of water had proved beyond the capabilities of other aeronauts.

M. & Mme. Bleriot were given a wonderful banquet at The Ritz, and 120,000 people went to Selfridges to see his monoplane during the four days the store had the machine on exhibition. The excitement was such that Selfridges stayed open until midnight, and some members of parliament spent four hours examining it in detail.

At that time the puny power of the engines available was such that a sudden tail gust of wind - or a severe down current - could cause the machine to stall and crash. Such accidents were not uncommon, and aeronauts learned by experience that some hills and local features resulted in these dangerous gusts.

But there were still many military commanders who could not see the aeroplane as more than a flying observation post.

The only pioneer likely to fly in England was Cody, who was criticised as incompetent by the ignorant, and others, including some Members of Parliament. Unable to get a reasonably good engine, restricted to the unsuitable ground at Farnborough, and with only £50 allotted to his machine, even his two year contract was not renewed by the War Office, who showed their opinion of the value of his

Louis Bleriot's monoplane after its epic flight
from Calais to Dover, 25th July, 1909
Taken from a postcard sold by the thousand at the time

machine by presenting it to him. Lord Northcliffe protested to the Government because the Wrights' flights at Pau were not observed by the War Office, only to be told that "aeroplanes are a long way off being the slightest practical use in war." So Lord Northcliffe put up another prize of £1,000 for the first one-mile circular flight by a British subject in an all British aeroplane.

It was not long before Cody's flights were being acclaimed even by those who had derided him, and he had made flights before the Prince and Princess of Wales. His first flight was made on October 16th, 1908, and within a year he was able on August 15th, 1909, to take up not only his wife, who thus became the first woman passenger in Britain, the Empire and the United States - but also his former chief, Colonel Capper. Later he made the world's record cross country flight, and the world height record at Rheims in August, 1909.

Cody and his family were living in Patrick Alexander's house "Pinehurst" at Mytchett, and Cody would fly over the house waving to the group on the lawn.

H.G. Wells made a significant comment on Bleriot's flight:

"What does it mean for us? One meaning, I think, stands out plainly enough, unpalatable enough to our national pride. This thing from first to last was made abroad. . . Gliding began abroad when our young men of muscle and courage were braving the dangers of the cricket ball. The motor car and its engine was being worked out "over there", . . . Over there, where the prosperous classes have some regard for education, . . . where people discuss all sorts of things fearlessly and have a respect for science, this has been achieved . . .It means, I take it, first and foremost for us, that the world cannot wait for the English. It is not the first warning we have had. "It has been raining warnings on us - never was a slacking, dull people so liberally served with warnings of what was in store for them . . .In the men of means and leisure in this island there was neither enterprise enough, imagination enough, knowledge, nor skill enough, to lead in this matter. . . Either we are a people essentially and incurably inferior, or there is something wrong in our training, something benumbing in our atmosphere and circumstances. That is the first and gravest intimation in M. Bleriot's feat. The second is that, in spite of our fleet, this is no longer, from the military point of view, an inaccessible island.''

Patrick Alexander pasted the cutting prominently in his current volume.

Chapter 32

Patrick Alexander and his involvement in Exhibitions, Colleges, Societies and Clubs

On July 6th, 1909, Lieut. Shackleton, the South Pole explorer, opened 'The Travel, Sports and Pastimes Exhibition' at Olympia. There was an aeronautics section to the exhibition, but this was more a museum of past achievements than a view of the future of aeronautics. Within two weeks of the opening, Bleriot was to fly the Channel, but the items in the exhibition were far from a prologue for progress in aviation.

The Aeronautical Society had Stall No. 64, where they displayed the principal exhibits on show. Minor displays were made by the Aeroplane Club, and the Aero Club League etc. The Kite Flying Association and "Aeronautics" had displays.

The Society showed an 1893 glider constructed by the late Otto Lilienthal, also Perry Pilcher's 1899 "Hawk", and contemporary Voisin, Wright, and Bleriot machines. The display included a collection of prints, photographs and posters, rare books, and specimen medals including the Silver Medal awarded to the Society at the Milan Exhibition of 1906.

The President, E.P. Frost, showed a working model of wing propellers, also two huge artificial feathers from his steam-driven flying machine of 1877. Major Baden-Powell showed the original model for his flying machine, which was at the Society's flying ground at Dagenham, also his "Balloon Camera" which automatically took photographs, complete with compass ring, aneroid and compass needles, so that the route of a balloon could subsequently be plotted on ordnance sheets. Sir Hiram Maxim showed one of the two engines built for his flying machine of 1894, also one of the 18ft. diameter propellers. J.R. Porter showed his Experimental Direct-Lift Flying Machine and A.V. Roe displayed his full-sized Triplane, "Twice the size of that used for short flights on Leighton Marshes."

Patrick Alexander displayed the experimental propellers used in the Henson-Stringfellow flying machine model of 1842-7; and the starting-rail used by Stringfellow in experiments with his models, which were run along a fixed wire. At the end was an arrangement to release the machine. He showed the hull steam engine, boiler and superheating chamber (weight 15lbs) of a flying machine constructed by F. Stringfellow about 1886. This boiler was the same design as that used by J. Stringfellow in his model aeroplane, which flew in 1848. The display included two wings and tail made by F. Stringfellow, circa 1875, copied from the 1848 model. Some of the above were presented to the Victoria and Albert Museum by Patrick Alexander, and are now in the Science Museum. He virtually commenced the museum Industrial Archaeology of Aeronautics collection.

The Aeronautical Society dated from 1866, the Aeronautical Club from 1901. The former was the society of scientists and theorists, (some critics added "semi moribund" to the description), while the Aeronautical Club was more concerned with the social side of the sport, and races. As aeronautics developed, the English passion for forming clubs caused some enthusiasts to promote their own. There was the Aeroplane Club, which ridiculed balloonists, the Aeronautical Club established the Aero Club League, an associate group, then came the Flying Club, The Aerial League of the British Empire was formed to rival the Navy League. The was rivalry between the three main organisations, and in May, 1909, the Aeronautical Society, the Aero Club and the Aerial League entered into an agreement that defined their spheres of action. When the latter was started, Patrick Alexander warned that the multiplicity of societies was likely to hinder rather than help progress. Within two months there was the Aeroplane Society formed in connection with the Aero Club, then another - the Aeroplane Club, was started by Captain Windham. Soon Patrick Alexander was pointing out that these new societies had not begun any practical work, and he thought that this was the last thing they would accomplish. But the Aeroplane Club had been launched at Claridges, supported by a large number of gentlemen in evening dress, including the Private Secretary of King Edward, Lieut. Colonel Ponsonby. It had a glossy new magazine with contributions from the Hon. C.S. Rolls, the pioneer woman balloonist Mrs Assheton Harbord and other leading aeronauts. The Aeronautical Society was not pleased when Major Baden-Powell joined the new club. There was confusion between Major General Baden-Powell, busy in Yorkshire on his military duties, and Major Baden-Powell, his aeronaut brother.

The storm in a tea cup persisted, and eventually in January, 1912, the two older societies - now honoured with the prefix "Royal" - were notified by the Aerial League that it was withdrawing from the agreement of May, 1909.

Alexander's fear had been that the cause of aeronautics in Great Britain would be jeopardised by getting too much into the hands of individuals with private rather than public ends to serve, and unsuccessful societies would only add to the conflict of interests. The prestigious Aeronautical Society had only been kept solvent by his financial assistance.

Eventually the patriotic stand by the Aerial League of the British Empire seems to have overcome Patrick Alexander's objections, and at a meeting of the League, held at the Carlton Hotel on 30th September, 1909, he gave a cheque for £1,000 to be devoted particularly to colonial propaganda, and offered a prize of £1,000 for a British built motor for aerial navigation, capable of running 24 hours non stop. The Daily News interviewed Alexander, and reported his opinion that the greatest difficulty facing British aviation was the lack of such a motor for aeroplanes.

The donation of £1,000 for colonial propaganda was soon seen to be bearing fruit:

Evening Standard 25.11.09
AERIAL LEAGUE ENTERPRISE

With a view to the development of aviation throughout the Empire, Colonel H.S. Massy will leave London to-day for India on a special mission from the Aerial League. In India he will visit the chief centres and lecture on aviation, at the same time assisting in the formation of branches of the league. Later on, as the opportunities and funds of the league increase, it is the intention of the committee to extend their sphere of utility to all the Oversea States and Colonies, and it is expected that before the close of the coming year branches of the League will be formed in every important military and commercial centre throughout the Empire, linked up and working hand in hand with the parent association in London.

A few days later Alexander contributed to the cost of an Aerodynamic Laboratory at the East London College, now the University of London. He also financially assisted the Governors to arrange a special course of lectures by Mr. A.P. Thurston B.Sc., a member of the Aeronautical Society, and draughtsman and engineer to Sir Hiram Maxim. Thurston was the first to obtain a Doctorate in Aeronautics. He helped Patrick Alexander with his educational material for use at Windsor.

The syllabus comprised:

1. The Normal and Inclined Plane.
2. Streamline surfaces, the Centre of Pressure, Resistance of bodies.
3. The Propeller and Helicopter.
4. Calculations applied to a Flying Machine.
5. The Biplane.
6. The Monoplane.
7. Aeronautical Engines.
8. Automatic Stability.
9. Dirigible Balloons.

The Army and Navy Gazette stated on October 9th, 1909, that "Mr. Patrick Alexander has earned the gratitude of all students of aeronautical matters by his generous offer of a prize of £1,000 for an aeroplane engine of British make. The primary conditions of the award to be that the engine of 20 h.p. should run without stopping for 24 hours. A committee of the Aerial League was to draw up rules for the competition."

The Womens Aerial League was also established, and got busy all over England.

On 18th March, 1910, he wrote again to the Secretary of the Aeronautical Society, this time bleakly. In the interval between the letters he had given two donations of £1,000 each, one for colonial propaganda of aviation to the Aerial League, and the other the prize for his engine competition. As will be seen, at Windsor he had completed one laboratory and was embarking on another. In 1909 there had been his contribution to the cost of an Aerodynamic Laboratory for the East London College, and to the cost of lectures on Aeronautics.

"2, Whitehall Court, London, S.W. Friday 18/3/10.
Tel; Victoria 3169, Windsor 195, Portsmouth 658.

Sir,
Will you please be good enough to cross my name off the list of members of the Aeronautical Society of Great Britain. I have instructed my solicitors to cancel my donation of 1911."

"2, Whitehall Court, London, S.W. Friday 18 3/10.

My Dear Col. Fullerton,
I have sent in my resignation of the Aero Society of Great Britain as I must not support you any further financially. The £1,000 I have given you during the last ten years has enabled the Society to take its position in the whole world as the pioneer of Scientific Aeronautics, and the recent appointment of Committees will enable individual members to fully promote the objects of the Society."

(Superscribed "I have replied asking this" 20/3/1910)

Copy letter to Patrick Alexander from the Aeronautical Society:

Undated.

"Dear Sir,
At the meeting held yesterday the Council passed a unanimous vote of thanks to you for your generosity to the A.S.G.B. during the past 10 years. They have directed me to convey the sense of the resolution to you, and at the same time express the sincere hope that you will reconsider your resignation from the Society, which can ill afford to lose so distinguished a member.

Fullerton

P.S. Do you know anything about Billing, Farnbridge (?) in this week's 'Flight'? What superb weather. . . ."

It seems that Patrick Alexander may have become more than a little financially embarrassed by his generosity.

The Aeronautical Society had been carried on by a self-elected Council of members since 1866. Despite it being the senior society, and regarded as the most scientific society engaged in the scientific approach to the subject, it had a small membership and but for Patrick Alexander's financial assistance, would have become bankrupt years before 1910, when it was decided that a new constitution was needed so that ordinary members could be attracted in greater numbers, and take part in the committee work.

An article in 'Country Life' (Dec. 24th, 1910), describes the proposed reconstitution of the Society, adding that "One of the most extraordinary things about the situation was that Patrick Alexander . . . who had been its Fairy Godfather, greatly objected to the proposals put forward. ." These were intended to get more active (and probably) more competent men to take an interest in controlling its affairs.

The problem was that recently formed bodies were leaping to large memberships right away. Patrick Alexander had not been on any Committees of the Society and before his resignation in March, 1910, refused to be considered as a candidate. Possibly he was opposed to the Society nominating a selection of candidates, and considered that the membership should nominate its own, but the "Old Guard" had weathered the dreary years of waiting for practical achievements in aeronautics, and kept the Society together in the dark days, and must have been reluctant to be superceded by the sort of energetic business men who were running the new groups, despite being relatively uneducated in the theory and practice of aeronautics and aviation.

In the long run, only the Royal Aeronautical Society has survived.

Patrick Alexander was never certified as an aeronaut or aviator, yet his experience rendered him as qualified for the former as, say, Griffith Brewer, who was accepted as an aeronaut by the Aeronautical Club in September, 1906, by which time Alexander had been ballooning for a decade, and had been accepted in Germany and America as a practical expert.

Possibly he spoke out of turn, and was somewhat eccentric, but his eccentricities had been greatly to the benefit of aviation, the societies and clubs in England.

In France, the Aero Club de France commenced granting pilots' certificates in 1909, and within a year "brevets" were being granted at a rate of 3 a day - an eloquent proof of the development of aviation. In England the local clubs were busy granting certificates, but these did not have the prestige of the Aero Club de France certificates and those of the Aeronautical Club, which issued their first Aviation Pilot certificate on March 8th, 1910. A few days later His Majesty George V granted permission for the club to use the prefix "Royal".

Chapter 33

"Solvitor Volando" — "The Problem is solved by Flying

Patrick Alexander became actively concerned with the teaching of aeronautics in schools in 1908, when Mr. Nagel the headmaster of United Services College, St. Marks, Windsor, came to his laboratory in London.

The United Services College Chronicle, dated November, 1909, printed on the College Press mentions Patrick Alexander in the Editorial:-

"Last term Mr. P.Y. Alexander brought his time of residence amongst us to a temporary close. We are glad, however, to know that visits will be frequent and his return not long delayed. Although we have known him for only a comparatively short time, he has earned our genuine regard and respect. His interest in the Coll. and his many generous gifts, not the least of which is his latest - the laboratory - have inspired in us an appreciation of aeronautics. Consequently, we have been among the first of the Public Schools to recognise the new science of aerial navigation. We wish him all success in the future."

He added that:

"The new Aeronautical Laboratory is now equipped completely and awaits your inspection. The old one has been converted for temporary use as a Museum and Reading Room."

During Founders Day speeches at the College in 1910, Patrick Alexander gave a speech welcoming the Prince and Princess Alexander of Teck to the new Aeronautical Laboratory he had presented. His speech of welcome explained how it had come about:

"Just over two years ago Mr. Nagel came to my laboratory in London, and I took the opportunity of asking if I might come to the United Services College, to try and foster an interest in aeronautics. At first in the smaller laboratory much interesting work was accomplished, careful demonstrations with kites and gliders were made, and lectures dealing with the theory of aerodynamics were given, supplemented by cinematograph exhibitions showing dirigible balloons and flying machines in actual flight. Last March, Sir Reginald Hennell, C.V.O., gave me an opportunity of extending this base, and it is proposed next session that practical flights shall take place in the grounds, of course under the instruction of competent and responsible advisers. In the Aeronautical Society of Great Britain, the oldest society of aeronautics in the world, much knowledge and help has been propagated during nearly 50 years, and during the last 20 years that I have had the means to help this learned and venerable institution, the British have extended the helping hand to those who study aeronautics for itself and not themselves. During the last two years we have seen the American brothers Wright make demonstrations in Europe; the French have crossed the Channel, and the Germans have sailed for hundreds of miles in the air. Be all this as it may, the problem is not yet solved, but awaits a discovery that will give us practical machines to navigate the air at our pleasure.

There never was a time when England held a more dominant sway of mankind, and whether we have to fight on the seas, on land, or in the air, British brains and British boys are as good as ever they were, and the boys going through their training at this College will prove that Old England means to have and keep the supremacy of the air" applause. Mr. Alexander afterwards explained the various machines etc., to the Prince and Princess, who expressed their delight at all they had seen, and entered their names in the Visitor's book.

He presented the college with a series of gifts, commencing with a naval flagstaff in 1908, a small laboratory fully equipped for the study of aeronautics in 1908/9, a hundred guineas (£105) to the Foundation Fund in June, 1909, and then the second laboratory opened by Princess Alexander on Founders Day 1910.

There were local misunderstandings when one of the five school houses was named "Alexander House" after Prince Alexander, the Chairman of the Governors of the College, because Patrick Alexander once astonished Mr. Beckwith, the first headmaster of Imperial Service College, (which became the title of the College in 1912), by including a cheque for £10,000 in some papers handed to him in class, "to be devoted to educational purposes". Patrick Alexander was known as a respected resident of Windsor, while Prince Alexander was known mainly in the College.

In 1909, his work at United Services College attracted the attention of the press. In February, the Aerial League had formed junior branches, and lectures were being given at Wellington College, Felstead, Haileybury, Bromsgrove and Charterhouse. The League offered a silver medal to the boy whose kite flew highest, and who made the best working model of an aeroplane. By this date the matter was already well advanced by Patrick Alexander at Windsor.

Illustrated reports in 'Motor Illustrated London News', and the 'Daily Graphic' referred in April 1909 to the growing interest in aeronautics, and credited United Services College at Windsor as having the first special laboratory for instruction in the science. Patrick Alexander—who had taken to wearing a cap or "flat hat" instead of his usual bowler - gave blackboard lessons on the theory of aviation, and provided a wind machine to test the boys' model aeroplanes. Perhaps the cap withstood the hurricane of wind better than his winter bowler or summer straw hat.

On the playing fields they could test gliders, and wing sections for pressure and lift.

Patrick Alexander was an enthusiast for bringing aviation within the reach of all schools. This article "Airmanship in our Schools" was published by the Aeronautical Society, (page 117, 'The Aeronautical Journal', July, 1910), after his resignation from the Society:-

206

AIRMANSHIP IN OUR SCHOOLS
By Patrick Y. Alexander

At a time when demonstrations of flight are daily taking place all the world over it surely cannot be out of place in the Journal of the Aeronautical Society of Great Britain to encourage attention to airmanship in our schools.

There are 15,000 boys at this moment in the British Isles competent to participate in the great development that has occupied the attention of the Society for the last fifty years, and at slight cost the aid of the Board of Education might be asked to advise the authorities of schools and colleges and technical institutions as to the importance of, as well as of the value that may be derived from, theoretical and practical demonstrations.

Scholarships have already been awarded by South Kensington for particular evidence of practical ability to those who have shown talent and resource to continue their work as a practical means of earning their living. Theoretical and practical instruction is quite within the capacity of nearly all our schools and colleges. Short lectures assisted by simple models costing but a few shillings supplemented by lantern slides or actual machines do much to help the imagination of the boys, and if this is continued by outdoor work with summer camps, models, gliders, and visits to aviation meetings the ground will be prepared for a very excellent appreciation of the elements of aerial navigation.

Farmers and landowners generally could do much to assist and at the same time benefit themselves financially by allowing camps for short periods on their property, and of course, under the authority of competent and responsible instructors.

Materials for models, even large ones, are easily procurable and not expensive, and such vast funds of enjoyment and instruction can be derived from flying models or even if funds can be arranged for the construction of a glider that every boy could have the experience of power flight.

It has been patent to experts for many years that 100 sq. ft. suitably disposed is sufficient to carry a boy when travelling at 20 miles an hour, and this can be achieved by a tractive pull of 30 lbs., which can be obtained from an adaptation of cycle motors. Such an aeroplane and motor would probably cost about £30.

There is a great deal being published in many excellent weekly and monthly periodicals containing a vast fund of information, and this is being done at an unremunerative return which could be made to pay by the support of our young budding aeronauts. The weekly papers especially contain practical and valuable reports of aviation meetings not only in the country but abroad, and many boys abroad would be glad to correspond with their fellow workers in this country.

It is premature to arrange a curriculum for schools, but the advent of aerial machines has been so rapid that many parents are really wondering whether boys may become practical aviators or constructors as a profession. Certainly, the prospects of all boys will be materially improved by a sound knowledge of the science and practice of airmanship.

At first he resided periodically near the College, which became one of his business addresses, and later he took up residence permanently in the College, becoming a familiar and popular figure at all school occasions. It gave him great pleasure to perform little acts of kindness, and Mr. Beckwith noted in his obituary that they would remember his chuckle of enjoyment when he had perpetuated a quiet leg-pull.

On 22nd December, 1909, the Pall Mall Gazette reported that "Patrick Alexander, one of the chief aeronautical authorities in this country, and President of the Hampshire Aero Club, has gone to New York on a visit to the Aero Club of the United States. An interesting announcement, as the result of the visit, is expected to be made on his return early next month."

The Pall Mall Gazette also revealed that the London Balloon Company of the Royal Engineers was without technical equipment after 18 months, during which period no practical work has been possible. Their rifles were the wrong pattern for the regulation waggons, and their bandoliers were unable to hold the cartridges which the rifles were supposed to fire.

In Australia, the government was offering a prize of £5,000 to be supplemented by a similar sum publicly subscribed, for the invention of a flying machine which could be put to practical military use. Restricted to residents of Australia, models and designs had to be ready by the end of March 1910. Alexander noted the offer, and there is some evidence in later cuttings that he "went to the Antipodes", possibly in this connection.

The New York Herald dated 11/6/1910, had two pages with illustrations "How Boys are Learning to Fly". Apart from minor mistakes - Alexander was not an "old boy" - the article is comprehensive:

HOW BOYS ARE LEARNING TO FLY

"The United Services College, Windsor, is the first public school in England to adopt airmanship as a serious study, and to give its boys an opportunity of learning to fly. This has been made possible by the generosity of an old boy, Mr. Patrick Y. Alexander, who has built and given to his old school a special workshop for the close study of aerial dynamics and the construction of aeroplanes.

The United Services College workshop, which cost over £600 to build and fit out, stands in a corner of the fine playing-fields of the college, and during the play hours is always full of keen youngsters eager to learn and experiment. Indeed, so great is their interest - deepened by recent brilliant flights - that many of them often bolt in for a few minutes during the changing of classes.

The work is not compulsory in any way - there is no necessity to make it so - and the boys simply study the principles of airmanship and practise flying whenever they feel inclined to do so."

IN THE WORKSHOP

"Mr. Alexander, who personally instructs the boys, feels that it would be somewhat premature at this stage to include a course of study in airmanship in the school curriculum, although he believes that before long all the leading public schools will imitate the enterprise of the United Services College and seriously take up airmanship.

The workshop, a substantial building measuring 60ft. × 25ft. is fitted with every convenience for the construction of model aeroplanes, and here the enthusiastic young airmen plan and construct according to their own particular ideas and fancies.

When an aeroplane model is finished, it is taken by the proud and anxious designer and parent to Mr. Alexander for examination, and he in a few terse sentences gives judgements as to its merits, and offers helpful criticism and advice."

THE CAPTIVE GLIDER

"At the far end of the splendid workshop there is a white screen, on which, by means

208

of lantern slides (made by the boys themselves), various types of aeroplanes are shown, and the different methods of construction are pointed out; also diagrams illustrating and explaining many of the principles and difficulties of flight are displayed by the same means.

Right in the centre of the workshop, there stands, on a fixed pedestal, a direct current motor propeller, with blades measuring 30 inches each, which is driven by a 20h.p. National gas engine.

This propeller creates a wind varying at the will of the operator from twenty to forty miles an hour, which lifts a captive double-decked glider, with a boy passenger, from the ground and keeps it in the air until the engine is shut off, when it glides softly to earth.

This teaches the pupil to balance, lift, drift, and plane down at different currents.

It is interesting to note the manner to which the propeller is aided in its artificial wind-making. The propeller, as previously stated, stands right in the centre of the shed, and facing it on both sides are large, open doors in the side walls. When these doors are open there is a direct passage through the shed from side to side, with the propeller set up half-way.

When the engine is working the propeller sucks in the air from the rear opening and drives it through the front opening at whatever rate, up to forty miles an hour, the operator wishes. The flying machine is pegged down a few yards outside the latter door.

This is Mr. Alexander's own idea, and it has worked with splendid results.

Another interesting appliance, which derives its power from electricity, is the machine that is used for testing the pressure of air on a given surface. This knowledge is very important and necessary for the thoughtful student of the airmanship problem.

After the boys have learnt to balance and control the glider in the artificial current and have passed other tests they are allowed, under proper supervision, to make short flights (the machine being raised on the principle of a large kite and held captive) of 1,000 to 1,200 yards at a height of about 15ft. to 20ft. from the ground.

All the latest literature of all countries dealing with the construction and science of aeroplanes is procured by the boys, and they read the various works with great attention.

The workshop, which was built by the school clerk of the works, who completed the whole work in the wonderfully short time of eight weeks, is the first one built for any school for purely instructional purposes in airmanship.

"I am often surprised," said Mr. Alexander to the writer, "at the rate of progress made by the boys.

"They are exceptionally keen, and are always ready for a 'talk', and further, ask a great many intelligent and searching questions.

"Though all the boys are good and show promise, three are quite original, and look at the problem of the air in a new light altogether. This fact alone shows what real good will result from the adoption of airmanship by the school.

The boys here come in whenever they like - and they like pretty often - and work as they choose. I give lectures dealing with the subject from various aspects, and the boys not only take in all the information that I give, but retain it to a marked degree. "Prior to the building of this shed we used a small one on the other side of the college, but it did not meet with requirements, and so I had the present one erected."

"It will be a great day when all the public schools have their own classes for airmanship, and that is bound to come at no very distant date.

"I have been in communication with headmasters of the leading public schools, and in all cases, have received favourable replies.

"When all the schoolboys of England are studying this problem of the air, I shall be satisfied, but not till then."

"Mr. Alexander founded and is the president of the Hampshire Aero Club, the members of which now number over a hundred. He is the author of "Alexander's Aeronautics," which Major Baden-Powell edited."

Instruction with wings to show resistance and direction of pressure.   Instruction in the science of aviation.

TEACHING THE YOUNG IDEA TO FLY IN THE SCHOOL OF AERONAUTICS AT THE UNITED SERVICES COLLEGE.

(i) "The Rising Generation".
Top right: The Great Hall, schoolroom and gym.
Top left: Alexander House.
Bottom right: Blackboard instruction in the science of aviation.
Bottom left: Instruction with wings to show resistance and direction of pressure.

210

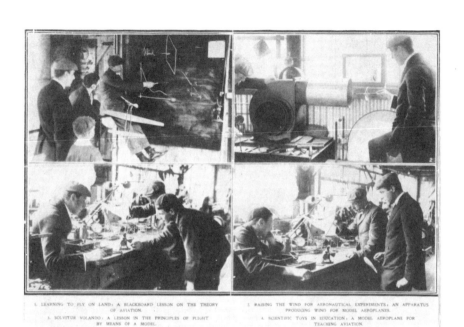

1. LEARNING TO FLY ON LAND: A BLACKBOARD LESSON ON THE THEORY
OF AVIATION.

2. RAISING THE WIND FOR AERONAUTICAL EXPERIMENTS: AN APPARATUS
PRODUCING WIND FOR MODEL AEROPLANES.

3. SOLVITUR VOLANDO: A LESSON IN THE PRINCIPLES OF FLIGHT
BY MEANS OF A MODEL.

4. SCIENTIFIC TOYS IN EDUCATION: A MODEL AEROPLANE FOR
TEACHING AVIATION.

AERONAUTICS AS A SCHOOL SUBJECT: TEACHING THE THEORY OF FLIGHT AT THE UNITED SERVICE COLLEGE, WINDSOR.

So much interest is now taken in the science of aeronautics, and its future importance especially in war, is so fully realised, that some of the public schools are forming special laboratories for instruction in this subject.' The first to do so was the United Service College at Windsor, where, as our Illustrations show, pupils learn the theory of flight partly by means of diagrams on a blackboard, and partly by experiments with model aeroplanes and a special apparatus for producing artificial wind. This apparatus is worked by a motor, and the wind produced can be so regulated in pressure and direction as to test its exact effect upon the aeroplane.—

(ii) "Man Passes : The World Goes On"

Top right: Patrick Alexander demonstrating the apparatus producing wind for testing model aeroplanes.

Bottom right: Scientific toys in education - Patrick Alexander using a model aeroplane.

Bottom left: "Solvitor Volando" — a lesson by Patrick Alexander in the principles of flight using a model.

211

*(iii) Experimental work in progress in the grounds of United Services College,
Windsor. ('Motor', 20th April, 1909)*

*(iv) Assembling a wing outside the Great Hall,
United Services College*

(v) A group of photographs showing the features of
United Services College, Windsor, in 1910.
This postcard was sold to the boys

213

Imperial Service College, Windsor. – Engineering Laboratory

*(vi) The 2nd Engineering Laboratory provided to the school
- now Imperial Service College*

Chapter 34

The United Service College Glider of 1909/10 and the Hampshire Aero Clubs

Kites and model aeroplanes were all very well, but the construction of a man carrying glider would be much more interesting both for the boys and for Alexander. The workshop had similar resources to those of his Experimental Works at Bath, which he had used until 1903, including a lathe, wind tunnel, forge and electric power.

He had long experience of the work involved, from the time he prepared for the 1902 Centenary at Batheaston with S.F. Cody, also from what he had seen of the 1902 Wright brothers' glider at Dayton in 1902/3. He had built gliders at Iveley Farm, Farnborough in 1905, and his experience of the building of 'Nulli Secundus' at Farnborough in preparation for its flights in 1907 had involved the solving of many problems. The finished glider was described in the 'New York Herald' in June, 1910.

He had become President of the Hampshire Aero Club, where his old friend Captain Mariott - Assistant Secretary of the Royal Meteorological Society - was secretary. Marriott was also Vice-President of the Aerial League of the British Empire.

Captain Marriott was involved in the planning of the Bournemouth Aviation Meeting of 1910, when C.S. Rolls was killed in a flying accident on 12th July.

In 1909, Patrick Alexander had started the Portsmouth Aero Club, becoming chairman and its first president. The subscription was kept very low - half a crown (12.5 pence) per annum - with a view to attracting the technical workers at the dockyard and building up a large membership.

It was hoped to arrange an International Aviation Week during Cowes week, and to promote the first flight from their flying ground at Grange Field, Gosport to the Isle of Wight. Grange Field was just west of Gosport, adjoining the railway to Lee-on-the-Solent, on part of Fort Grange, one of the Palmerstonian outer fortifications of Portsmouth, now H.M.S. Sultan and War Department housing.

The Hampshire Aero Club arranged a smoking concert at the Fratton Hotel on the Friday of Christmas week, 1909. Patrick Alexander as unable to be present, as he had gone to New York again on a visit to the Aero Club of the United States. This was probably the occasion when the book of cartoons and verse mostly about

American aeronauts was published, in which Patrick Alexander is the only British aeronaut included. The press added to the announcement of his departure that "an interesting announcement, as the result of his visit, is expected to be made on his return to England early in January 1910." In Alexander's absence, Lieut. Shaw R.N. took the chair, and Mr. Powell gave a lantern lecture on aviation. He anticipated that some gliding experiments would be arranged in the near future.

Patrick Alexander brought the United Services College, Windsor glider to Gosport, and this was flown in April, 1910, and again in 1911. It had been partly dismantled, placed on a trailer, and towed behind a motor car.

The Hampshire Telegraph report includes the following:

AVIATION IN GRANGE FIELD

The members of the Hampshire Aero Club were disappointed by inclement weather on Saturday, and the experiments which it was hoped to carry out in Grange Field had to be abandoned. Press representatives were, however, given some interesting information as to the objects of the club, and the programme which will be carried through during the summer months by the courtesy of the Secretary, Capt. F.W. Marriott.

There already exists an aero camp in Grange Field, the necessary ground having been granted by the War Office, and Mr. Patrick Alexander (the President), Captain Marriott, and other members of the club, frequently make the camp their permanent quarters while experimenting.

Already good results have been obtained by gliders, which, pulled with ropes by members of the club, have risen some feet in the air, carrying an embryo aviator. Simple as this part of the work may appear, it has the very useful purpose of accustoming members to flight and being in the air, so that they may have increased confidence when indulging in more serious trials.

Lieut. Porte, of the submarine depot at Blo' house, was to have tried his monoplane on Saturday, but the weather rendered this impossible. He will attempt a flight at the earliest suitable opportunity, however. Other members of the club are constructing machines, and Mr. Day, of the Warrington Woven Wire Company, has a neatly constructed monoplane almost ready for experiments, and this is housed in a large shed in Grange Field.

There will be some determined experiments during the summer, and it is probable that in the early stages the public will be permitted to view the trials.

The following Saturday the club was more fortunate:

HAMPSHIRE AERO CLUB
Field Day at Fort Grange

On Saturday the Hampshire Aero Club had a field day at the Aeronautical Camp, Fort Grange, Gosport. In the absence of the President (Mr. Patrick Alexander) the Secretary (Capt. Marriott) superintended the operations, in which task he was ably assisted by members of the Club. Officers and men of the garrisons of Fort Grange and Fort Rowner gave very welcome assistance.

In a breeze of about 20 knots an hour the large glider was very successfully manipulated. There was general improvement in the management, but some pilots were more skilful than others in keeping their balance. After half-a-dozen successful glides had been made, a spar broke, which prevented further experiments.

Mr. Day's monoplane attracted a large concourse of spectators, and the skill evinced in its construction met with very favourable criticism from those able to judge. A limited company is in course of formation to exploit the machine at the Bournemouth centenary and other meetings. Weather permitting, the Club will meet at Fort Grange today for further experiments.

For each flight, the glider was placed on a launching rail formed by a length of rolled steel angle with one end on the ground, the other on a trestle. The "pilot" stood centrally on the main biplane, clutching a strut on either side. At the word of command, the towing crew of some six men started to gallop with the tow rope across the field into a stiff 20 knot breeze, the glider slid up the launching rail, and became airborne.

A photographer took a series of snapshots showing the glider taking off, and bearing down upon him, then passing and continuing into the distance. The launch was repeated several times, to everyone's satisfaction.

Patrick Alexander had his own caravan - a horse drawn affair, with a glazed area at one end to increase the head room. The others lived in army bell tents and marquees.

Hampshire Telegraph 16/9/1910 p.4.

ENCOURAGEMENT OF AVIATION
FORWARD WORK IN PORTSMOUTH

A general meeting of the members of the Hampshire Aero Club was held at the Admiral's Head, Kingston Crescent, on Monday evening, the President (Mr. Alexander) in the chair. The principal business was the discussion of the annual report and arrangements for the first annual meeting which is to be held on October 3rd.

It was stated that the past year had been a very satisfactory one, the membership being 105, and there was a substantial balance in hand. In the course of the twelve months eight papers had been read on subjects relating to aeronautics, and there had also been lectures. The competitions had included those for members who had constructed models, as well as gliding competitions. For five months there had been a camp in Grange Field, Gosport, the arrangements for which were well in hand. For the coming year a full programme had been prepared. During the winter months papers would be read, and some of the best lecturers from London were to address the meetings, in addition to which there would be cinematograph views of flying machine displays. A new feature would be competitions for juveniles.

A special appeal for new members was made, and it was announced that at the annual meeting Mr. Alexander was to give an address.

Hampshire Telegraph 7/10/1910 p.5.

Mr. Patrick Alexander, President of the Hampshire Aero Club, took the chair at a meeting at the Crown Hotel, Northstreet, on Wednesday evening, when a Gosport branch of the club was formed. A Committee was formed consisting of Messrs. Andrews, Wills, King and Weatherby, and Mr. E. King undertook the duties of Hon. Secretary pro tem. A question was asked as to the best means of furthering the science of aviation, and Mr. Alexander expressed the view that the construction of models and the holding of lectures, demonstrations, and cinematograph exhibitions would do much to further the object. On the table were a number of of periodicals dealing

217

with the science, and these together with experimental apparatus, were provided by Mr. Alexander, who is himself defraying the expenses of meetings, etc., until March, by which time it is hoped the branch will be firmly established. The subscription is 5s. per annum (25p).

9 photographs from the Hampshire Aero Club Meeting, 1910

(i) An aeroplane on its trailer

*(ii) The Hampshire Aero Camp at Gosport, 1910,
with Alexander's caravan in the background*

*(iii) Lieut. Kennedy and Patrick Alexander
experimenting with a model aircraft*

219

(iv) Patrick Alexander's caravan

(v) Bringing out the Windsor glider

(vi) Discussion before a flight
Alexander is seated on the launching ramp
Capt. Marriott in bowler

(vii) The Hampshire Aero Club and the Windsor glider
(Note launch ramp)

(viii) The first "take-off"

(ix) Getting up speed

222

(x) The "pilot" changes his grip

Chapter 35

Teacher Alexander's Notes and Aids

From the end of 1910, Patrick Alexander's cuttings collection include a number of examples of articles to assist teachers to keep their classes informed regarding balloons and aircraft, their history and practical application. A typical paragraph reads:-

"Thus, balloons filled with coal gas are lighter than the same volume of air, and for example 1,000 cubic feet of gas is lighter by 40 pounds than the same volume of air, so a balloon of 45,000 cubic feet could lift (40 × 45) pounds, or 1,800 pounds. If the basket and ropes etc., weigh 1,000 pounds, the balloon could lift 800 pounds of aeronauts and ballast, the ballast being discharged as the balloon ascended into rarer air if a continued ascent was desired. Gas would be released by a valve when the aeronaut desired to descend."

The difficulty of propelling the balloons by reason of their size and wind resistance precluded rapid motion by engine power using propellers, and cigar shaped airships while giving less air resistance, were very liable to damage, being bulky and liable to destruction in high winds.

The theory of the wind acting on the surface of a kite pulled by its string causing flight was also explained, with the part played by the engine and vertical control surfaces used by the aviator to steer upwards, downwards or sideways.

It was elementary, but speeds of 100 miles an hour, and transatlantic flights taking no more than 24 hours, were confidentially anticipated by Alexander.

Chronologies were published showing how the occasional and intermittent progress of aeronautics from earliest times had been followed since the last decade of the 19th century with an increasing rate of invention and progress, until the number in the list of one year greatly exceeded the total for the previous century.

Inventions rarely brought monetary rewards, and it was the prize money - especially from the Daily Mail - that rewarded successful flights such as the first cross Channel flight by Bleriot, after which his aeroplanes benefited from the advertisement arising from such a success, whether or not the element of chance was responsible. Better designs could be dogged by bad luck or bad weather.

The 'Hobbies' edition dated February 11th, 1911, described the Dring-Sayers model Bi-plane, winner of Class V at the Crystal Palace meeting of the Aero Models

Association open flying meeting, held in August, 1910. The illustrations and details indicate that this was a popular design among model makers with its 36 inch span.

'Cassell's Magazine', June, 1911, had a four page article "The Building of an Aeroplane" by Atherton Fleming which Alexander kept in his books of cuttings. The cost of materials and an engine was estimated by the writer at £200. (''Less than the price charged by a well known maker'') plus £80 for a hangar. The latter was reduced to £18, on the understanding that the carpenter concerned could subsequently watch the aeroplane fly.

Patrick Alexander annotated a copy of the 'New York Herald' dated 5th September, 1910, "How men learn to fly at Monsieur Maurice Farman's new school 5 miles south from Versailles." The learner sat in the aeroplane behind Monsieur Farman, with his arms under those of the latter, and just touching the "steering-gear wheel" . . etc.

The Daily Express described Monsieur Bleriot's school at Hendon (Learn to Fly in Six Hours), and The Field listed schools and fees.

The books of cuttings contain several about Model Aeroplane construction from September 22nd, 1910 (Model Engineer and Electrician Vol 103, p181 & 180).

In 1911 the Union rate of wages for a skilled mechanic was between £1.92 and £2.25 per week - the higher rate for a man able to keep aeroplane and engine ready for instant use, like a motor car. At this time Patrick Alexander employed an engineer, Mr. Fugler, for duties including aeroplane club metings.

*Three of the original models made by Dr. A.P. Thurston in 1912
for Patrick Alexander's science of aviation classes at Windsor now in the Windsor collection*

He recorded Winston Churchill's Aircraft Prohibition Order for the City of Norwich on 28th June, 1911, prohibiting any aircraft flying within 4 miles of the city on that date, and a similar Order that applied to Windsor Castle on 1st July, 1911, both arising from Coronation celebrations.

The 'Boys Own Paper', collected by Patrick Alexander, no doubt for United Services College use, included long articles on kite flying, model aircraft and a man-carrrying glider, relating the incidents that accompanied these pursuits without giving construction details. Apparently kites were anathema to game keepers, as the pheasants regarded them as giant hawks. A giant kite 10 feet high proved controllable on Esher Common, until the line broke, while ability to climb trees to recover model aircraft became almost a condition of membership. A man carrying glider was invariably obstructed by pedestrians who stood in the way as it descended from the top of a hill. One of the young members went on to win a competition at the Crystal Palace with his own long distance design. No doubt the experiences related were more common to most such clubs, including the United Services College, Windsor, and Sydney Camm's Windsor Model Aero Club which was founded in 1911.

Another paper in 'Arena', in his collection, dealt with "The Study of Flight Problems by Means of Models", by "R.P.G." - probably Percy R. Gurr of the Balloon Factory, Aldershot, who Patrick Alexander would know well.

When Alexander went to New York in 1911 he found that the Aero Club of America was moving to new, luxurious accomodation. One member said "It is very different from the old shop where we used to meet to listen to Octave Chanute and the Wright brothers discourse on flight, while we sat on a school form borrowed from next door. . . "

Chapter 36

The United Services College becomes Imperial Service College - 1911/1912

1911 was a time of increasing financial worry for the School Governers and when the headmaster Rev. Nagel died suddenly in November, 1911, they decided to approach the Imperial Service College Trust for additional assistance.

The College was maintained at Windsor by the Imperial Service College Trust, which had been incorporated in 1903. The aim of the Trust was to "promote the extension of educational facilities for the sons and descendants of Officers of the Navy, Army and territorial forces of the British Isles, Dominions and Crown Colonies beyond the seas, and of the Higher Branches of the Civil Services at home and abroad."

To consider the problem, there was a Public Meeting at the Mansion House attended and supported by royalty, nobility, and the services. Funds were raised, and as a result, financial help was given to the governors who, in gratitude changed the name to Imperial Service College. They also appointed a new Headmaster, E.G.A. Beckwith M.A. He arrived after the change of name to be met with, as he wryly said, "lurid letters of personal abuse for having changed the name of the college on my own".

In April, 1913, the ISC Chronicle included the following:-

THE ELECTRICAL LABORATORY

Mr. Patrick Alexander, who erected the building previously known as the Aero Laboratory, has suggested that in view of altered conditions in the pusuit of the study of Aeronautics his gift to the College should be utilised in future as an Electrical Laboratory and Workshop, and be re-named accordingly. Now that a resident Mechanic has been engaged it is hoped to offer facilities for giving instruction in Electrical Engineering.

The following machines are available for that purpose:-

An 18 H.P. gas engine, which drives a 100-volt dynamo capable of feeding about 400 lamps, if necessary, at the cost of one penny (circa) per unit.

Two large motors taking 100 volts, and a couple of smaller ones suitable for spinning ventilation fans.

A charging board, from which accumulators can be changed, has been fitted up this term, and should be of great use in the future.

A small blacksmith's forge is available in an adjacent room.

It is unnecessary to add that such an equipment is far beyond that possessed by practically any other school.

Mr. Beckwith did not know Patrick Alexander except as the name of the donor of the Aero Laboratory, and as one of the leading pioneers of aeronautics at the end of the nineteenth and at the beginning of the twentieth century. He wrote in his "Short History of the First Twenty-One Years of the Imperial Services College": . . .

"Then what happened on 9th December, 1914, must be almost if not quite a unique happening in the annuals of any Public School one morning when, in the period after the break, the Headmaster was in his classroom taking a class in Latin, a stranger appeared, placed in his hand some papers relating to the College, and left."

"On cursorily looking through the papers, the recipient came across a cheque made out to him, which at first sight seemed to contain a meaningless sequence of noughts, but which was in fact for £10,000 to be devoted to educational purposes! The donor of this magnificent gift was Mr Patrick Young Alexander."

"To perpetuate the remembrance of Mr Alexander's munifence, "Alexander Day" was "inscribed in the School Calendar as near as conveniently possible to December 12th (the date when the cheque was passed), this date being reserved for the Final of the Inter-House Rugby Competition. . . ."

I.S.C. CHRONICLE (December 1915, page 57)

"We venture to think that December 9th will always remain a red letter day in the annuals of the College, for it was on that day that Mr. Patrick Alexander knocked at the door of the Headmaster's class-room and presented to him a cheque for £10,000 to be used "for the furtherance of the education of boys of the Imperial Service College, Windsor. I.e., for the training of character and the development of knowledge".

Although the donor of this magnificent gift is personally well-known to all the present boys but expecially to those who work in the engineering laboratory, many are probably ignorant, owing to their having been so short a time in the College, that Mr. Alexander is a very old friend of the I.S.C., and we think it well to bring to their notice the fact that he not only gave both the engineering laboratory (originally fitted for aero work) and the apparatus, but in addition recently bore the expense of "doing it up" again. But extraordinary as this generosity is, we are not sure that we ought not to reserve some of our thanks to him for having by his presence and kindly suggestions and help given such a stimulus to the inventive and engineering spirit in the school, which we understand by no means absent, but only dormant. We tender him our most sincere and hearty thanks.

E.G.A. Beckwith"

Patrick Alexander became one of the first Trustees for a Berkshire Scholarship.

Chapter 37

The Alexander
Engine Competition 1910/1912

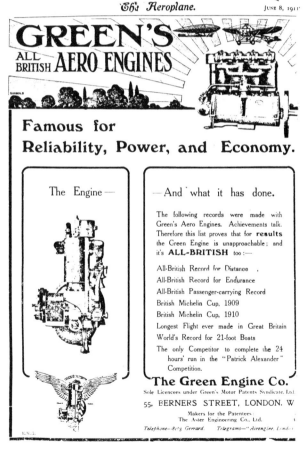

The "Green" All British Aero Engine advertisement of June, 1911

One of the matters for which Patrick Alexander's name is remembered is the competition for which he gave a prize of £1,000.

At Olympia in March, 1909, the first Exhibition of practical flying machines was attracting large crowds. One of the best and most improved aero engines was that of the Aster Company, Green's patent, a British engine of which more was to be heard.

The need for such an engine was illustrated by the news that orders for £100,000 worth of aeroplanes were being sent abroad, and English firms were having to refuse orders because they were unable to obtain British engines.

Aerial navigation had developed at such a rate during 1908/09 that making do with motor car engines, which had developed little over more than 10 years, had disadvantages from an aeronautical point of view. Designers wanted an engine that was light, efficient and reliable, and did not require attention while working. This was less important in a road vehicle, which could be stopped for attention as necessary. In an airship it might also be possible to give the necessary attention. In an aeroplane there were difficulties!

In France the building of aeroplanes and special engines had attracted capital and the attention of celebrated motor firms. In England a comparatively small amount of capital had been invested, and the few moderately successful aero engines were being produced by a few small firms.

Alexander expressed the opinion - which was widely held among aeronauts - that just as the motor car of 1911 made those of 1900 look as antiquated as Stevenson's Rocket alongside an express locomotive, so would the flying machine of, say 1921, be equally in advance of the Wright aeroplanes, or the 3 cylinder machine in which Bleriot made the first crossing of the Channel. He hoped that the early pioneers' names and work would be treasured for all time.

The future would bring improved engines that would work for days with the ease and precision of marine engines. Fuel consumption would be lessened and the stability attained would enable flying machines to defy any wind less than a hurricane.

Prizes for spectacular flights were increasing, and success was largely a matter of luck and organisation, but failure was often due to engine failure. This was the crux of the situation, and Patrick Alexander decided that his prize would give incentive to designers and result in concentration upon reliablity. The competition would need to be properly organised and run, and he made his offer to the Aerial League of the British Empire in September, 1909. There had been previous schemes promoted by the Aeronautical Society and Aero Club but without the incentive of a substantial prize.

The Aerial League approached the Government Advisory Committee in October, 1909, inviting them to draw up conditions for the competition, and to appoint judges. A sub-committee was formed to co-operate with Alexander, and three gentlemen were nominated by the Aerial League, including, as he desired, representatives of the Aeronautical Society, Aero Club, and the Royal Automobile Club. The test would be carried out at the National Physics Laboratory, and the results reported to the Aerial League.

In the event, the competition was held under the auspices of only the Aerial

League. The Times Engineering Supplement set out the agreed regulations for the competition on 24th November, 1909:-

> The regulations governing the Alexander aerial motor competition, £1,000 prize for the best 35h.p. aerial engine of British manufacture were drawn up by the advisory committee for aeronautics in conjunction with Mr. Patrick Alexander and the representatives of the Aerial League of the British Empire. The tests were to be carried out at the National Physics Laboratory with the following regulations:- (1) The machine to be of British manufacture; (2) The motor to be designed to give 35 b.h.p. The machine being required to reach this brake horse-power during a preliminary run; (3) the maker to supply a detailed description and drawings, together with a statement of the principal features of the machine. The drawings to show the engine, radiator, tanks, etc., fixed to a known type of aeroplane, so that the length of the connecting pipes can be determined, and impossible combinations for trial purposes guarded against: (4) motors weighing more than 245lbs., that is, 7lb. per b.h.p. will not be admitted for competition. For the purpose of this clause the weight shall be taken to include the weight of the motor itself with crank-case and supporting arms, and all parts necessary for ordinary running, also the cooling apparatus with all accessories (clauses 18, 19). It will not include the supply of cooling water, petrol, and lubricating oil, or the containing tanks and vessels for these. The main points which will be considered in the comparison of motors admitted for competition will be:- (A) Weight and consumption of petrol per brake horse-power; (B) reliability and steadiness of running; (C) wear of working parts; (D) security against fire; (E) air resistance offered by the motor and accessories.

The report upon the tests carried out for the Patrick Alexander prize was published in a Blue Book by Eyre and Spottiswoode, "Interim Report of the Advisory Committee for Aeronautics on the work for the year 1910-11." This was the subject of many articles, including 'Engineering', January 13th, 1911, pages 56, 57, and 58 complete with some illustrations. The conditions which each entry had to satisfy included that the engine should run for twenty-four hours with not more than three stoppages, and these not to total more than half an hour.

Six engines were entered, but only three arrived by the date specified:
(1)   The Wolsey Tool and Motor Car Company;
(2)   Messrs. Humber Ltd., Coventry;
(3)   The Aster Engineering Co. Ltd., Wembley Park (entered by Green's Motor Patents Syndicate Ltd.)

Not one of these was able to satisfy all the conditions of the tests.

The Wolsey was pulled up first by an oil leak, then a connecting rod big end melted, after the engine had run irregularly and finally stopped. This stop disqualified the engine, but it was repaired and restarted - then ran irregularly and after 11 hours it had to be stopped to replace two sparking plugs. After another six hours (total 17 hours 41 minutes) it failed again, due to water getting in the cylinders.

The Humber ran steadily for 11 hours, with only a short stop for a new sparking plug, then stopped suddenly with one of the cylinders broken off and two connecting rods buckled.

The Green engine completed the 24 hour test with only one short, 10 minute stop for a new sparking plug, making 31.5 brake horse-power at 1,213 revolutions. Then for 7 minutes the machine was run at 1,390 revolutions, making 36.4 b.h.p.

There was some criticism at the alleged failure of the Green engine, as it had met the brake horse power criteria of 35, but not throughout the test, although the subsequent test showed that it was capable of the required output. The Aerial League were pedantic in their decision, but awarded Mr. Green their silver medal. Patrick Alexander felt that he had to accept the National Physics Laboratory's decision, but with his usual characteristic generosity, paid the designer Mr. Gustavus Green an ex gratia £200.

Patrick Alexander renewed his offer of a prize of £1,000 with varied conditions. Foreign and Colonial engines could compete, and two runs of 12 hours each would replace the 24 hour test. The first test had shown the value of running engines under test for more than the usual 2 hours, and proved that longer tests were more likely to show up any weaknesses in the engines. All the engines would have passed the shorter test. The Green engine was shown to be best, and needing only to be increased slightly in size to meet the conditions of power required. There was some criticism of the high oil consumption of the engines - up to half the weight of fuel used - and residents in the Bushy Park, Teddington area of the Laboratories were not amused, by reason of the unsilenced engine noise over twenty four hours.

Colonel Cody had already decided that the Green engine would help him to win the Michelin competition of 1910. On the last day of 1910, Cody at Farnborough, and Sopwith at Brooklands both struggled to remain airborne in closed circuits in conditions of intense cold, mist and blustering wind. Sopwith gave up, faint and stiff with cold after 150 miles. Cody's Green engine kept going and he won his first great prize on the last day that the competition conditions permitted, for a flight of over 185 miles.

The Alexander Engine Competition attracted much attention. The 'Court Journal', 24th August, 1911, commented: "One of the most interesting and useful prizes that have yet been offered in connection with aviation, is that given by Mr. Patrick Alexander who has himself been a student of aeronautics for a number of years - for the best Aeroplane engine."

Comparisons were made between the popular French Gnome rotary engine and the British Green engine.

During the next great competition, the Circuit of Britain in 1911, 12 Gnome engine users started, only 3 finished. One Green engine user started - Colonel Cody - and this finished in perfect condition.

The 7 cylinder Gnome rotary engine developed 50 h.p. at 1,200 revolutions or slightly more than 3lbs. per horse power. Its centrifugal effects were reputed to cause problems on some turns, and it was extravagant of fuel and oil. It was very noisy, and could not be fitted with a silencer. The Green engine weighed 13.71lbs. per h.p. gross or 6.96 lbs. per h.p. nett, with similar speed and power.

The rules for the new Alexander Aero Engine Competition differed from the first contest, as it was opened to engines of from 40 to 75 h.p instead of 35 h.p., and the 24 hours run was divided into two periods of 12 hours each, throughout which the engine must average at least 40 b.h.p. The weight must not exceed 8 and a half pounds per horse power. Three main points would determine the winner:

(A) Gross weight per measured B.H.P.; (B) Reliability and steadiness of running; (C) Wear of working parts. Engines had to be delivered for test by September 30th, 1911. Seven firms entered engines, but only two delivered their engines for trial:- E.N.V. Motor Syndicate Ltd., Willesden, N.W.; and Green Engine Company, Berners Street, London, W.

The eight cylinder "V" engine entered by E.N.V. completed the first 12 hour run, but the competition had to be terminated when a cylinder cracked 28 minutes after the start of the second 12 hour run. Although it was no longer eligible, the E.N.V Syndicate was permitted to replace the defective cylinder, but when the engine was being run tilted about its longitudinal axis, another cylinder broke and lifted several inches, leaving the piston free. Considerable damage was done before the engine could be stopped, and this brought the trial to an end.

The Green engine completed both periods of test satisfactorily, and was awarded the £1,000 prize. The result was acclaimed as a world's record for any type of internal combustion engine.

The aeronautical writer Charles C. Turner wrote an article for The Observer on 18th February, 1912:-

AERONAUTICS
BRITISH ENGINES AND THE WAR OFFICE COMPETITION
(By Charles C. Turner, C.Av.)

"It will not surprise anyone who is closely watching matters aeronautical if the coming military aeroplane trials prove the occasion for a triumphant vindication of the British-made engine. More than one circumstance points that way, but the most important indication at the moment is the performance - a world's record for any type of internal-combustion engine - of the Green motor in the Alexander Aero Motor Competiton. This was an international contest, from which, however, most of the foreign makers kept aloof, whilst none of those who entered submitted an engine to the tests. The tests were so severe, indeed, that it is not surprising that many motor makers regarded the case as hopeless.

Let me sum up the performance of the Green motor as briefly as possible:- It was an engine of the standard type, of 50 to 60 horse-power. The trial was made at the Government Aircraft Factory, under the control of the engineers of the National Physics Laboratory. The engine was started in the morning at 10.12 o'clock. It ran without the slightest attention until 10.12 p.m. It was at rest throughout the night, but was not allowed to be touched; and in the morning it was again started, when it ran for another twelve hours without attention.

The engine was then run for one hour in a position 15 degrees declined from the vertical, and it was then tilted 15 degrees to one side, when it ran equally well. All this without a misfire or hitch of any description, and with variations from uniform power that were scarcely measurable.

The total length of the run was 25 hours 7 minutes, during which time the number of revolutions was nearly 2,000,000. At one period of four hours the revolutions did not vary by more than four. Throughout the trial the engine was giving out power in excess of the nominal 60 horse-power - the average was 61.6 horse-power - and the maximum power at 1,210 revolutions per minute was 67.8 horse-power. The test was the most severe because of the breaks in the runs. An uninterrupted test would not, of course, prove so exacting. And there is little doubt that it is at least as great a strain upon the engine to run a dynamo, as in this test, as it would be to drive an aeroplane propeller. A propeller has a certain fly-wheel effect; on the other hand, in actual flight, there are sudden variations, due to gusts and lulls, and there is the phenomenon of screw-racing. At the conclusion of the tests the Green engine was examined and there were no visible signs of wear.

But an exceedingly important fact to aviators is that the rate of petrol consumption made by the engine, while it was, moreover, giving out power above the nominal, constituted a record in the economy. The amount used was 429 lbs. in the first twelve hours and 441 lbs. in the second twelve hours. It works out at .590 lbs. of petrol per brake horse-power per hour, or slightly more than half as much the rate of consumption with the Gnome engine, which is, however, exceptionally extravagant. Now, the weight of the Green engine is about five and a half pounds per horse-power.

The Green engine has, by winning this £1,000 prize, confirmed the hopes entertained when it won the two British Michelin prizes in the hands of Mr. Cody, who, be it said, pins his faith to this engine, which carried him round the 1,000 mile circuit of Britain last year, without trouble. So that it is not surprising to hear that the French and Germans are beginning to make inquiries for it with a view to coming trials. That it will be represented goes without saying, but upon how many machines depends largely upon the rate at which it can be delivered. Probably some makers would certainly require the six-cylinder size which the Green Engine Company are turning out.

Gustavus Green and the 50-60h.p. 4-cylinder engine
which won the Alexander £1,000 prize.

234

Gustavus Green and the 100h.p. 6-cylinder engine used by Samuel Franklin Cody
when winning the Michelin Trophy No. 2 in 1912

Fred May - later Commodore - was the chairman of the Aster Engine Company that made the Green engines, and he and Gustavus Green would do anything to help Cody. But when he crashed on 7th August, 1913, Cody was beyond all help.

The Green Engine Company's wreath at Cody's funeral was in the form of a huge four-bladed propeller ten feet across.

Two Green engines, both a six cylinder and the four which won the prize are to be seen in the Science Museum. The engines were found to be too heavy for the 1914-1918 war planes, and the production was transferred to coastal motor boats.''

One advantage of the Green is that, like all other fixed-cylinder engines, it can be silenced. It is heavier than the Gnome, which, however, can certainly not be effectually silenced. The Gnome has proved a very excellent engine, and has done and is doing much for aviation; but in no point of reliability it is easy to see that it has now by no means easy honours. It is most improbable that any rotary type of engine could run for 24 hours without wear and attention. The British military trials demand reliability above all things, and in view of the fact that special encouragement is to be given to all-British productions it is matter for rejoicing to all who have at heart the interest of a new national industry that a British motor should have achieved so fine a performance.''

The Green engine was selected by Colonel Cody so that he could compete for the all-British prizes. J.T.C. Moore-Brabazon had, on 30th October, 1909, won the first of the Daily Mail £1,000 prizes for a circular flight by a British subject on an all-British machine.

Colonel Cody planned to use two 60h.p. Green engines driving one propeller by chain drives, but when he could only obtain one engine, he tested his machine with that one only.

He was a great "fan" for the Green engine, saying "If you supply the Green engine with petrol and oil from without, the engine will do the rest from within." In return, the engine made Cody internationally famous, and at the head of his contemporaries.

Cody's machine was the only British machine to finish in the Circuit of Britain race which commenced on Saturday, 22nd July, 1911, and The Aeroplane stated "In the triumph of Cody's pluck, perserverance and ability as a designer and constructor, the British built and designed Green engine must share, for it is the only thing about the machine which is not all-Cody. The engine came through with all its 'marked parts' as did the machine itself. It behaved splendidly throughout, and, be it also remembered, propelled the biggest and heaviest machine in the race. Mr. Fred May and Mr. Green have every reason to be proud of this fine proof their engine has given of its reliability and power when handled by a man who understands it and treats it as it should be treated."

Chapter 38

Patrick Alexander returns to Bath

Patrick Alexander was remembered in Bath from the time of his earliest experiments in the 1890's, which culminated in his celebration in 1902 of the 1802 balloon ascent by James Garnerin. The Bath Herald in a gossip paragraph dated 27th September, 1907, "I believe I am right in saying that a distinguished gentleman aeronaut who formerly resided on the outskirts of Bath is the mysterious amateur who is believed to have solved the problem of a practical aeroplane. It is now being built for the Government under strict secrecy at Aldershot, and if it proves successful the British Army will be well ahead of any other in the mastery of the air." The writer went on to recall a parachute descent from a balloon at a fete in Kensington Meadows some 12 or 15 years earlier and descended at a point to the eastwards near St. Saviour's Church or the Horse Show Ground. "I can remember that there was a strong wind that caused the balloon to sway a good deal, and he had a somewhat rough experience, but was driven back to Kensington Meadows quite safely."

Colonel Samuel Cody gave a lecture at Bath in the Tea Room at the Assembly Rooms on 28th February, 1910. He related how he had visited Bath at the invitation of Patrick Alexander for the 1902 centenary celebrations, and how he had carried out experiments in Alexander's private workshops at The Mount, Batheaston. He covered the entire history of his aviation work, from the man-lifting kites he developed during the Boer War when the War Office were having problems with the "lift" of small gas filled captive balloons.

Subsequently, Cody had been the first man to fly in Great Britain, and his accidents - inevitable with experimental machines - increased his knowledge of the problems to be overcome. He described his man carrying glider, which led to his "Power Kite", and the British Army dirigible, Nulli Secundus, also his last aeroplane which he said was based upon a seagull that he took as a model. He showed a 1 inch to the foot scale model of his aeroplane made by his son.

Colonel Cody returned to Bath at the end of February, 1913, under the auspices of the Bath and Somerset Aero Club, to give a lecture at the Palace Theatre upon "The National Aspect of Aviation." Mr. Roland C. Cross M.I. Mech. E. related what a romantic and inspiring character he was, and how he talked about his aeroplanes.

His previous visits to Bath - including the great celebrations at the Sydney Gardens in 1902 at the invitation of Patrick Alexander were recalled.

Five months later, Cody crashed at Aldershot on 7th August, 1913, and was killed.

Patrick Alexander appears to have collected every report in the Bath newspapers relating to aviation and aeronautics. One such appeared in the Bath Chronicle dated 30th March, 1911, about the lecture of Mr. Sydney Walker R.N. to the Bath Selbourne Society, the subject being the "Conquest of the Air". The science of flying was a phenomena of such recent realisation that, as the Chairman said, they regarded it with additional amazement. The speaker confidentially stated that the speeds then attained of up to 66 miles an hour would soon be increased to 100 m.p.h., while flights of 30 hours to cross the Atlantic were expected, but he recognised the endurance required of the aviator, the unsolved problems of engines, and of national safety.

The South-West of England had seen both balloons and aircraft experimented with around the turn of the century, but the first event of importance regarding aviation was the formation of the British and Colonial Aeroplane Company at Filton, Bristol in February, 1910. They had built over 120 machines by the end of 1911, and the Bristol Boxkite was in service with several flying schools. So, things were moving, but the average citizen had seen nothing that demonstrated progress until Salmet and his Bleriot aeroplane toured the West Country in 1912 under the auspices of the Daily Mail. His visits to towns both large and small caught the public imagination, and his machine something that had to be seen.

Monsieur Henri Salmet, "the intrepid Daily Mail airman", was engaged on a 13 week tour of England and Wales "to prove the practicability and reliability of the modern aeroplane". A crowd of many thousands watched him make a fine descent in Parker's Mead, a large field near Newton St. Lo. He had been delayed 2 or 3 hours by a late start and wind troubles, and was due to leave for Bristol the next day.

FLYING AROUND THE CITY OF BATH IN 1912
Some Press Cuttings from Alexander's Collection

BATH HERALD 18.5.1912:

Places of vantage were taken up on the railway bridges, and elsewhere, while many paid for admission to the field where the aviator was to bring his machine to earth. Five o'clock came, and still no sign of machine or man. Six o'clock came, by which time the road for fully half a mile was one mass of people, and still the trams and buses brought more.

Six-thirty! And still waiting. People began to grow tired; of false alarms there were plenty, but these only served to increase the tedium than otherwise. One's hopes, on the other hand rather decreased, for the wind appeared to have gained in velocity, and became more gusty, for evidence of which, one only needed to glance up at the box kites (sent up to act as a guide to M. Salmet) which were tossed about by the high wind that was blowing.

Just before 7.20 a speck was espied in the heavens over Kingswood School. "There it is" shouted the crowd. Larger and larger the speck grew, heading straight for the field. The faint hum of the propeller came to the ear, but it was soon drowned in the cheer upon cheer that went up from the spectators. A second more, and the aeroplane came to ground as graceful in its movements as a bird, ran along the grass for a short distance, and then stopped. The moment the little, unassuming Frenchman stepped out, he was surrounded by a large, excited crowd. He was almost pulled off his feet by the many handshakers.

Seen by a Herald representative, M. Salmet remarked that the wind had given him considerable trouble. He added that once he was nearly flung out of his seat by the force of it. He also said he started from Reading at 4.20, and from Marlborough, where he remained half-an-hour, at 6.25.p.m.

The passage over Bath of M. Salmet, created widespread interest and it was quite surprising to see how for hours every coign of vantage in and around the city was occupied. The grand parade and other open spaces were excellent places from which to see the airman pass, but the favourite place, excepting the neighbourhood of Newton, was Beechen Cliff. Children gathered in Alexandra Park and all down the cliff path early in the afternoon, and shortly before the aeroplane was sighted it was difficult to walk up the path for the press of people. Camden Crescent was another prominent position much favoured.

BATH HERALD 18.5.1912:
TO-DAY'S FLIGHT TO BRISTOL
Yesterday's Difficulties

To-day the spectacle afforded by a Bleriot monoplane lying inactive exercised a peculiar fascination over a large section of the general public. All roads led to Newton St. Lo this morning. Some spectators arrived in motor cars, others by tramcar, but all bent on viewing at close quarters the machine which had borne M. Salmet to Bath. The only disappointment expressed was that the flying man himself was not to be seen. Autograph-hunters went away unsatisfied, for the intrepid air-man, who spent the night at the Castle Hotel, early set out for Bristol, where he proposed to inspect the Gloucestershire County Cricket ground, with a view to securing a satisfactory descent. Airmen have a perfect dread of buildings, and the fact that there is numerous property surrounding the site of this evening's descent, influenced the aviator in preparing for any possible risk. Meanwhile, Salmet's mechanic was engaged at Newton in delivering lectures to groups of interested listeners of both sexes. He had scores of questions to answer, the most important being as to the likelihood of a flight. Up to mid-day the conditions were by no means favourable, but an improvement in the elements in the latter portion of the day, which has proved the airman's salvation on many occasions before, was hoped to permit of an ascent shortly after 4 o'clock. Should the plans laid down not be followed, Salmet will break his usual practice and fly to-morrow morning, unless the strong westerly wind which is blowing today again prevents.

Salmet, it appears, experienced the greatest difficulty in covering the distance between Marlborough and Bath, and retired to rest very fatigued. He had a trying experience in crossing the city. The cross-currents caused by the heights circling the city tended to suck him down, yet he managed to maintain a speed of upwards of 60 miles an hour.

BATH AVIATION MEETING
MR. HUCK'S ACHIEVEMENT.
Early Morning Papers by Aeroplane.

Bath to-day came into line with most of the other leading centres by having an aviation meeting inaugurated on Combe Down. Attempts at flying have, of course, been made as long ago as there is any record of human endeavour, and ballooning is a very old sport - there was an ascent from Bath early in the 19th century - but aviation by means of motor-driven aeroplanes is a modern innovation. Although there were experiments in 1879, the first to really bring the matter to a head were the Wright machines in 1900, and it was not until M. Bleriot did his dash across the Channel on Sunday morning, July 25, 1909, that the world really awoke to the fact that flying was no longer a dream. Gazing at the monoplane which did this record, as it lay in the big Exhibition building off the Champs Elysees, Paris, the writer could hardly credit that the little weather-torn machine had accomplished the stupendous task of carrying a fairly heavy man across the green waters of the Channel.

Mr. Grahame-White's greatest feat was, of course, the winning of the Gordon Bennett Cup which was offered for competition at the Belmont Park (New York) aviation meeting. The trophy was to be allotted to the aviator who succeeded in covering 100 kilometres (62 and a half miles) in the shortest time. Several others of the world's finest aeroplane pilots had entered for the race, among them M. Le Blanc and Messrs. Latham, Brookins and Moisant, and the international rivalry was very keen. Mr Grahame- White covered the sixty-two and a half miles in 1 hour, 4 and three fifths seconds, and thereby set the seal of fame on his career for all time. The company with which he is associated, and which includes Mr. H.W. Matthews, of Bath, among the directorate, is doing consistently good work in bringing on aviators of English nationality, and in arousing the attention of their countrymen to the fact that the flying machine has come to stay and has long since passed the experimental stage.

The first meeting the writer ever attended was in October, 1909, during the great Paris Flying Fortnight at the Aerodrome of Port Aviation, on a fine site between Juvisy and Savigny-sur-Orge, some 15 miles from the French metropolis. Among the airmen were Robert Nau, Busson, and Desvaillieres, and they all flew just overhead, and one of the machines wobbled dangerously. The accomodation for the French and foreign journalists was excellent, 16 expert telegraphists were present, and three special telephone bureaus with several lines switched direct on Paris. The course was very wet from heavy rains, and sand was liberally sprinkled on the soil to facilitate the running of the wheels of the aeroplanes. Ambulance men were there in strong force, for it was never known when they might be wanted.

Since that time flying meetings have fallen into some disrepute, and that is why Bath is to be congratulated on the fact that its meeting is educative, the idea being to let Bathonians learn all about the elements of flying, and the possibilities of the machines. Besides the Juvisy meeting, the Rheims, Doncaster, Blackpool, and Bournemouth meetings all attracted much attention. Like all other new outlets of activity the pioneers have had many fatalities in their ranks, and the many brave British and French pilots who have lost their lives have not died in vain, and their memory is enshrined in the annals of flying. Aviation has brought a new zest into the world, and the airman is becoming quite a distinctive type of good, honest, plucky manhood, while there are also one or two lady aviators to introduce the needed variety.

The newspapers have played a big part in the development of flying, among those giving the best prizes being The Mail, The Matin, The Standard, and the Paris Journal. Recent developments have convinced most people that for good or evil the future of aviation will lie much in its use as an effective war arm, and despite the outcry being raised by the Peace Society, it is absolutely certain that the leading nations will not agree to any restrictions in its use, hence England must continue its efforts to form a formidable aerial fleet in sheer self-defence.

BATH HERALD 21.5.1912
MR. HUCK'S ARRIVAL

The uncertainty surrounding the movements of the quartette of famous flyers who are to demonstrate the high standard of efficiency to which the more modern type of aeroplane has been brought, was to some extent relieved by the reception late last night by Mr. Geo. H. Mansfield (secretary and Aerodrome manager) of a telegram from the the London Aerodrome at Hendon, announcing Mr. B.C. Huck's determination to fly at daybreak. It was then too late to intimate the fact to the Bath public, but those early astir and residents of the Downs were fortunate enough to catch a glimpse of the aviator as he made the final stage of his journey. Out of the fog and mist of early morn came the throb-throb of his engine, and then without the slightest effort he swooped with all the gracefulness of a huge bird on to the aviation ground. Many first became aware of the intrepid aviator's appearance by the hum of the propellor of his machine. The officials of the aerodrome and mechanics were in attendance, anxiously awaiting his arrival, which was timed to be shortly before 8 o'clock. He left Hendon at 5.30 a.m. and accomplished the journey in 2 hours 5 minutes, representing an average speed of nearly 60 miles an hour, despite the fact that he was carrying a load of early morning papers depicting pictorially his latest flight. This is in itself a noteworthy achievement, setting up as it does a record for the carriage of newspapers over so great a distance. The flight was not marked by an incident. Heavy rain served to drench the airman, while cross-currents and eddies made negotiation difficult, but with that daring which has characterised his previous flights, he gamely set his machine for the Queen City, and landed safely preparatory to the exhibition flights which it is hoped will stir up interest in aviation in general.

Mr. Hucks was first sighted in the neighbourhood of Southstoke, and was assisted in locating his bearings by means of the buildings of the Bath and West and Southern Counties Show. He made a circuit, and then commencing a steep volplane he entered the ground just over the main entrance, and bringing his Bleriot to earth ran gracefully into the mouth of the hangar, which was supplied to the Government for use at Weymouth during the recent naval demonstration, and which will be used to house the several machines. It was then noticed that the aviator was suffering terrible discomfort from cold. His hands and feet were numbed, while he was drenched. A cup of hot tea was his first request. This was immediately supplied. He then reported rain at Reading, Swindon and Chippenham, and in the usual practice of things gave vent to his objection to the air pockets caused by the hills of Bath, which Salmet and other flying men have found so treacherous.

MESSAGE FOR THE MAYOR

With him Mr. Hucks carried a message for the Mayor (Alderman T.F. Plowman) from the Lord Mayor of London. He immediately jumped into a taxi-cab and accompanied by Mr. Mansfield, drove to the Mayor's residence in Pulteney Street, where he was warmly received by his worship, and congratulated him on his flight. Other formalities were then observed, and the Mayor, having extended a hearty welcome to Mr. Hucks and his brother aviators to the show ground, expressed his regret that pressure of civic duties consequent upon the show week, prevented his presence at the meeting.

The machine used by Mr. Hucks was a 50 h.p. Bleriot which, as he announced in yesterday's Herald, will be used in the flights, and which it is interesting to note, was used two years ago by Mr. Grahame-White in the Gordon-Bennett cup for speed, when the airman won the blue ribbon of the air at Belmont Park in the States in 1910, and in other speed flights.

MR. HUCKS ON HIS EXPERIENCES

Mr. Hucks was none the worse for his experience to-day. He returned at an early hour to the aviation ground, where everything is now complete in every detail, and there superintended various matters. "It was a very smooth flight, with the exception of rain by Reading, Swindon and Chippenham", he told a Herald representative. "The average height at which I travelled was about 4,000 feet. I found Bath a very bad place to get at by air owing to its lying in a hollow. I was so frightfully cold that I could only place the machine on land."

"No, I have never been to Bath before," he continued, but I am well acquainted with the West, having flown around Minehead, Weston, Newport, Cheltenham - the speaker naming a number of places in the West Country. In view of M. Salmet's complaint of suction, Mr. Hucks was asked as to Bath's features as a flying centre. "It is a very bad position for climbing," said the airman, "for it is very hilly, and the wind sweeps up the valley in gusts and goes down the hills until it becomes dreadful. When there is so much wind it blocks the machines a bit."

"Oh, the Mayor's reception. Well, his Worship was pleased to see me, and congratulated me on my flight. I also brought down, together with the letter, a special edition of the Daily Mirror. This is the first instance, I believe of a newspaper being carried over a distance of 100 miles non-stop." Even with this load Mr. Hucks got above the clouds.

"I got above the clouds on several occasions" he said. "What is it like? - like a sea of cotton wool. No, I didn't get lost. The only means, however, I had of finding my way was simply with a map which I took out of my railway timetable, which is no bigger than a postcard. I took my bearings by the railway. Not once during my flight was I uncertain as to my bearings."

"Yes, the show ground looked like a yellow village. I also saw the Box Tunnel and that place above - Chippenham, that's it. Could I see Bath? No, not very well. You see, it lies in the valley."

A word as to the capabilities of his machines, and Mr. Hucks then proceeded to meet the many calls for his autograph. He was steadily signing portraits of himself when the interviewer withdrew.

THE LORD MAYOR'S MESSAGE

The letter from the Lord Mayor of London, which was delivered by Mr. Hucks, contained the following message:-

"The Lord Mayor sends his warmest salutations to the Mayor of Bath by aeroplane, and his sincere good wishes for the prosperity of his famous city."

Benjamin C. Hucks (Benny), Blackburn's one-time pilot
Later, he flew a Bleriot

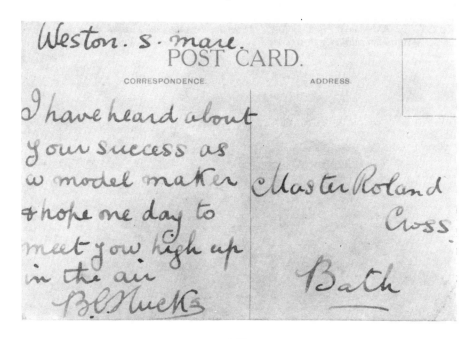

Monsieur Henri Salmet, the intrepid Daily Mail airman
- standard publicity postcards from his 1912 tour of the West country

B.C. Hucks had become Chief Pilot to the de Havilland Company after being connected with the Blackburn workshop and their "Mercury" monoplanes. He started as a smart young recruit with Grahame-White with the latters Farman which Benny Hucks maintained in return for flying lessons. Benny Hucks had some engineering training with Thornycrofts and became a test and demonstration pilot who could put an aeroplane into evolutions never seen before. On one occasion an engineer who asked for a flight was put through some spectacular manoeuvres, and who appeared to be waving his enjoyment from the passenger's cockpit. When Hucks landed, the passenger was found to be in a state of collapse; having a weak heart he thought he was going to "pass out".

TIME OF ARRIVAL OF OTHER AVIATORS

Mr. Ewen was expected to-day by train. His Caudron biplane had arrived this morning by rail, and he will fly this, in the event of his other machine, which as announced yesterday is undergoing repair in Paris, is not delivered.

Mr. Ewen had decided not to fly the little 35 h.p. Caudron biplane at Hendon, as the wind was too strong. His Caudron monplane had a wing smashed through some cattle grazing on the aerodrome using it as a scratching post. ("Car", 15.5.1912).

The Daily Mail airman Henri Salmet continued to encounter rain and mist which delayed his progress from Bath and Bristol to Newport and Cardiff. The rain poured with dreary steadiness, and the hills were veiled with a soaking mist. His monoplane was consequently repeatedly earthbound.

Bad weather had also ruined the Bath Flying meeting organised by the Grahame-White Aviation Company Ltd.

BATH AND WILTS DAILY CHRONICLE 12.6.1912
AVIATION UNDER DIFFICULTIES.
RAIN AND WIND

Once again the general public lured by the fascination of flight through space returned home yesterday with its appetite unappeased. The flying meeting held by the Grahame-White Aviation Company Ltd. was again unproductive of any startling aerial feats, not that the promoters were not prepared to satisfy the public taste in this direction, but that the meteorological conditions were against them. A heavy rain in conjunction with fierce gusts of wind put flight out of the question, although early in the afternoon, a short 'stunt' by both Messrs. Hucks and Ewen served to stimulate interest in the meeting.

The fortunate few who witnessed the circuit of the ground must have noticed, as reported yesterday, the difficulties with which the airmen had to contend. "Ghastly", said one, when asked for his impressions, but despite this, both fliers were prepared to make a second ascent. Rain, however, damped their ardour, and instead aviation in theory occupied the attention of the crowd. Popular lectures on flying, followed by question time, served to pass the time spent between brief speculations as to whether the sky would clear. A heavy mist, however, obscured the horizon and rain-laden clouds hung ominously overhead. It was certainly not flying weather.

MORE AVIATION AT BATH
Aeroplane Flights to be made on Claverton Down

Aeroplane flights will soon be witnessed on Claverton Down. The experiments will be conducted under the direction of Mr. Patrick Alexander, formerly of "The Mount", Batheaston, who has for years taken a great interest in aerial navigation and its possibilities. Mr. Alexander is at present abroad, but is expected home in about a fortnight's time. The experiments will take place at Copseland, between Claverton Down and the village of Claverton. We understand that Mr. Alexander has been in communication with the Bath Aero Club, and will be prepared to give them the benefit of his experiments. Mr. Fugler, Mr. Alexander's engineer, since Wednesday has been down on the ground making the necessary arrangements. His quarters are in a caravan. A meeting of the Bath Aero Club will be held later in the week and some interesting developments may be expected at an early date.

BATH CHRONICLE - 14.6.12

I hear that some flying experiments will be made to-morrow (Saturday) afternoon by members of the Bath and Somerset Aero Club at Mr. Patrick Alexander's camp, the situation of which was described in the "Bath and Wilts Chronicle" on Wednesday. The camp is officially described as adjoing "Norwood Farm", Bathwick Hill, and the apparatus includes a full-size glider and an excellent tent workshop, equipped with aeronautical tools, which, through the kindness of Mr. Alexander, every member of the club is privileged to use. The club is chiefly indebted to Messrs. R. Young and G.F. Rawlings for arranging with Mr. Alexander to visit Bath for his camp this season. In addition to the experiments with the glider, some model aeroplane flying will also take place, and the work to be witnessed should be very interesting. Mr. F.B. Bartelt is the president of this club. The joint honorary secretaries are Messrs. G.E. Page and S.H. Baker, and Mr. G.E. Powell is the honorary treasurer.

BATH HERALD - 17.6.12
AERO CAMP AT CLAVERTON
Gliding Exhibition Postponed

The inclemency of the weather of Saturday was the cause of the postponment of the gliding exhibition with which it had been proposed to inaugurate the aero camp on Claverton Down.

The camp had been erected by Mr. Patrick Alexander, who is a well-known enthusiast in aviation matters, not only in Bath, but in other places farther afield, and the Bath and Somerset Aero Club are to be congratulated on securing such a hearty worker in aerial navigation. Mr. Alexander has had erected five tents for visitors, and members of the club will be allowed to encamp there if they so wish.

In addition there is a mechanics' tent in which there is a workshop fitted up for the convenience of the club with a lathe and forge and a large selection of requisite tools and materials used in the construction or repair of aeroplanes. There are also a stores and provisions tent, and a camp kitchen presided over by a chef who looks after the campers in first-class style, and at the other end of the encampment is fixed Mr. Alexander's private caravan, which is furnished in a plain but comfortable style.

An ideal position has been chosen for the site of the camp, for it stands at the corner of a large field adjoining Norwood Farm, about half a mile from the top of Bathwick Hill. Mr. Alexander, who is expected to arrive in about a fortnight, will probably make Bath his headquarters for the summer, so that the members of the club should have many opportunities of learning even more of the technicalities of aviation and the principles of flight. The chief praise for inducing Mr. Alexander to make Bath his camping centre is due to Mr. R. Young and Mr. G.F. Rawlings, while valuable assistance was also rendered by Mr. S.H. Baker, the secretary of the club.

As already mentioned, the rough weather of Saturday prevented the use of the glider, which is a simple-looking structure, made of spruce, with iron sockets, and is 40 feet in length, with a span of six feet. The members had also intended to bring with them some of the models they possess, but for the same reason this was impracticable, and the only thing in the way of flying which could be attempted was to send up a bird kite.

At present, the members are constructing a glider of their own, the material for which were given by Mr. E. White, of Green Park, Bath. This will be completed on the ground and trials of its capabilities will take place there. It will be 20 feet in length and powerful enough to carry a man.

It is interesting to note that Mr. Alexander has consented to become a vice-president of the club.

FLIGHT - 20/7/1912
Bath and Somerset Aero Club
(11 Elm Place, Bath)

A model contest and glider exhibition will be held on August 10th, at 3.30 p.m., at Claverton aero camp, adjoining Norwood Farm, Bathwick Hill, by permission of Mr. Patrick Y. Alexander. Admission free. Events (prizes in cash and goods for each competition): 1. Direction control. 2. Distance. 3. Gliding angle (after propeller stopped). 4. Speed (100 yard's course). 5. Duration. 6. Stability. 7. Best all-round model (club members only). For full particulars apply (enclosing stamped addressed envelope) to hon. sec.

BATH AND WILTS DAILY CHRONICLE - 12/8/12
Successes of R.C. Cross

MODEL AEROPLANE FLIGHTS
Exhibition at Claverton

The Bath and Somerset Aero Club, which with model aeroplanes, is doing much for advancement of the art of flying, is rapidly becoming a very live concern, and some of its members are gaining the notice of prominent flying men. On Saturday afternoon the club held a contest and display with models at the aero camp at Claverton, adjoining Norwood Farm, Bathwick Hill, kindly put at the disposal of members of the club by Mr. P.Y. Alexander himself a noted experimenter in aerial matters. The weather was rather boisterous, but not withstanding this some excellent flights were seen in the different contests. It was expected that a goodly number of people would be present to witness the flights, and this indeed was the case until the weather became so stormy that it sent them away again, there being no shelter in the field. Apart from the short delays, caused by the showers, everything went off well, and the club is to be congratulated on the success of the event.

Those who were competing were Messrs. L.S. White, R.C. Cross, C. Wilcox, and S.H. Baker (Bath Aero Club), F.L. Smith, A.E. Pearse, N.W.G. Edgar, J. Keyte, R.T. Howse, W.A. Smallcombe, J.H. Read (Bristol Aero Club), and G. Haddon

The Bath and Somerset Aero Club in 1913
(S.H. Baker, secretary, back row, second from left; R.C. Cross, front row on left)

Wood (Birmingham Aero Club), and among those present were Dr. E. White (vice-president of the club), Messrs. Scott White, H.W. Frampton, G.F. Rawlings, Miss White, and Major L.M. Boilean.

Mr. Frampton, hon. secretary of the Bath Cycling Club together with Mr. Rawlings, acted as judge, the decisions giving universal satisfaction. The arrangements for the event were ably carried out by Messrs. S.H. Baker and G.E. Page. The latter gentleman had hoped to compete with a power driven model, but the engine had not arrived in time.

The results of the various contests were as follows:-

Direction control. - 1, R.C. Cross; 2, L.S. White.

Distance. - 1, R.C. Cross (201 yards); 2, W.A. Smallcombe (197 yards).

Speed (100 yards course). - 1, R.C. Cross (9 secs.); 2, J.H. Read (15 secs.).

Duration. - 1, R.T. Howse (36 secs.); 2, W.A. Smallcombe (30 secs.).

Stability. - 1, W.G. Edgar; 2, L.S. White.

Best all-round machine. - 1, L.S. White; 2, R.C. Cross.

At the conclusion of the flights Major Boilean presented the prizes to the successful competitors, and to him a vote of thanks was accorded on the proposition of Mr. G.F. Rawlings.

The donors of prizes were Messrs. G.E. Powell, H. Harris, Dr. E. White, F.W. Bascombe, T.W.K. Clarke and Co., F.L. Bartelt, E. Pitman, and Bonn and Co., Ltd.

The interest of the young Roland C. Cross in aviation and aeronautics possibly stem from his being taken by his father to see Alexander's balloons being inflated, and also the actual ascents. It is likely that Patrick Alexander would have given them prior notice of these events as R.C. Cross' father and Patrick Alexander were quite closely acquainted.

In later years R.C. Cross became the founder of the Cross Manufacturing Co. Ltd. and acquired one of the sheds which Patrick Alexander had originally used for his ballooning and aeronautical experiments. This shed still exists and is preserved at the Midford Road, Bath factory of the Cross Manufacturing Co. Ltd.

As well as supporting the model aeroplane club, Patrick Alexander advocated building an aeroplane large enough to make a crossing of the Atlantic. This was an idea that was generally ridiculed, except by Lord Northcliffe, who offered a prize of £10,000 in 1913 for a flight in either direction. Colonel Cody was another who thought it could be done, and designed a machine with a 400 h.p. engine, but neither was ever built.

Chapter 39

The Aeronautical Society in 1912/13 — Membership, Finances, and some Obituaries

The period was not a happy one for the Aeronautical Society; they had yet to receive the honour of the title "Royal" which had been given to the Royal Aero Club and some of their oldest supporters had died.

Wilbur Wright died of Typhoid fever in May, 1912, and Patrick Alexander would have been saddened by the news. The Wrights' achievements at Kill Devil Hill, North Carolina on December 17th, 1903, was the first to which "flight" could be applied. The brothers had made more than one hundred flights on a second aeroplane in 1904, including the first complete circular flight and the first flight of three miles.

On 26th September, 1905, they achieved eleven and a half miles, and by October 5th, 1905, the distance had been extended to twenty-four and a quarter miles.

During the greater part of the period covered by these flights, the world by and large heard little about them, and did not believe what it did hear by way of these reports such as Alexander's possibly because the American public appeared to give no credence to the statements of those who had witnessed flights. The Wrights were regarded as cranks, and despite their modest demeanor and quiet dignity, were considered to be self-advertising schemers. Any report by a person visiting the remote headquarters and finding nothing going on, or observing an unsuccessful attempt, was enough to confirm them as charlatons. Their repeated bad press resulted in the Wrights doing their best to keep reporters at a distance, until Wilbur's flights at Le Mans in 1908 proved that the Wrights were right and their critics wrong.

When the Aeronautical Society opened a Subscription list to found a Memorial to the late Mr. Wilbur Wright, Patrick Alexander's name led all the rest with £100. The total of 64 subscriptions was £500.

The Society Journal for 1913 recalled the financial help given over the years by their former member, Patrick Alexander:-

FINANCE

It will be within the recollection of Members that the finances of the Society have not been in a satisfactory position for many years. The yearly expenditure has considerably exceeded the income from Member's subscriptions, and the generosity of one Member, Mr. Patrick Alexander, has alone kept the Society from bankruptcy. His donations, which have amounted in all to over £1,200, ceased in 1910, since when the yearly excess of expenditure has been met from the accumulated balances of past donations, which are now exhausted.

Taking the eleven years ending December 31, 1911, the average excesss of expenditure over subscription income has been about £140 per annum and for the last three years of that period over £200 per annum.

Realising the above unsatisfactory financial position, the Council made an exhaustive inquiry last summer into the possibilities of reducing expenditure, with the result that considerable savings have been effected. On the other side of the Account the subscription income has been increased owing to the creation of the technical side, and to a large incease of Members in the autumn of 1911, whose subscriptions and entrance fees appear in the statement of accounts for 1912. In the past year, therefore, the subscription income exceeded the expenditure by about £100. Although it may be said that this satisfactory result·is due to abnormal causes, the improved financial state of the Society will be evident from the fact that without counting on any increase of Membership the expenditure for the present year will not, the Council consider, exceed the income exclusive of any donations.

Only by the most rigid economy, however, can this result be attained, and as yet no adequate salary can be given to a Secretary, nor can funds be allocated to Scientific Research, which it is so desirable to encourage.

The Council again urge the absolute necessity for increasing the membership, and appeal to each member personally to obtain at least one new member during this year.

Griffith Brewer was becoming increasingly important in the Society - he eventually became President - and in 1912 he was one of 20 elected as their first Associate Fellows.

Obituaries and tributes in the journals of the Aeronautical Society reflect to some extent the importance of the departed in the Society. Griffith Brewer was the most appropriate person to write these by reason of his long and active connection with aeronautics. Thus it was that he wrote the obituaries for their mutual friends. Patrick Alexander (1943), and earlier Wilbur Wright (1912), Lieut. Colonel F.C. Trollope and Percival Spencer (1913). The latter obituary is reproduced as it contains the story of the first ascent ever made by Patrick Alexander and Griffith Brewer with Percival Spencer, the pioneer of ballooning in the last decades of the Victorian era. (Acknowledgements to the Royal Aeronautical Society).

PERCIVAL SPENCER

"Percival Spencer died on Friday, 11th April, aged 49. His connection with the Aeronautical Society goes back to the year 1897.

He was a man of sound judgment and cool in the presence of danger. His sense of proportion and of justice were admirable also.

When I first met him, he had returned from a tour of India, China, and Japan, where he had been astounding the inhabitants by jumping into space from a balloon from a height of many thousand feet. In those days this feat appeared nothing short of miraculous, to be classed with walking on water or passing unburnt through a fiery furnace, and it is small wonder that those who saw the sight of a man coming down from the sky with nothing but an umbrella without its frame to hold to, attributed

251

to him divine powers. His coolness on several occasions brought him safely through many adventures, and in the spring of 1891 he arrived home in London and took charge of the balloon ascents at the Naval Exhibition at Chelsea. It was there that I first learnt to appreciate his many sterling qualities.''

"The first ascent I made with him stands out in my memory as illustrating much of his character. Mr. Patrick Y. Alexander was my fellow passenger on that occasion, and the day was rainy, with a rough westerly wind. The balloon, soaked with water and loaded with its three occupants, would lift but one spare bag of ballast in addition to a bag of valuable instruments. The clouds scudding to the eastward towards the mouth of the Thames were so low that the ground was lost sight of almost immediately on leaving the Exhibition. We passengers were raw novices then and Mr. Spencer had to judge the risks entirely alone, and when the roar of London faded into the distance he opened the valve and we came into sight of the ground bowling along at the rate of thirty or forty miles an hour. The solitary bag was poured out to avoid striking the spire of Bexley Heath Church, we crossed over High Street, threw the grapnel in the back garden of a shop, thus lightening the car sufficiently to enable it to clear the wall and demolish a pigsty on the other side. The balloon then rolled around, taking off tiles and chimney pots from the adjoining houses, and ultimately became piled up on the muddy ground. When we rolled it up we found a man lying beneath the balloon overcome with the gas, and I immediately drew a knife in order to release him by cutting the net.

Mr. Spencer stopped me doing this, and drawing back the net he released the man through the doubles without cutting it. The man revived in a few minutes and was none the worse for his experience of being gassed.

This is a typical example of Mr. Spencer's appreciation of proportion. He might have thrown Mr. Alexander's bag of instruments away as ballast and so secured a more suitable landing place, and by cutting the net the man could have been released a few seconds earlier. But after-events proved that neither of these sacrifices were necessary, and his cool judgement secured safety without unnecessary loss.

Percival Spencer possessed great patience and could bear misfortune with fortitude. Unfortunately, his business methods were not in harmony with many of his old ballooning friends, but although this caused him some pecuniary loss, he bore no resentment on that account. It is therefore with the greatest sense of loss that his old ballooning friends and pupils heard of the death of the pioneer of modern ballooning.''

GRIFFITH BREWER

The death of Samuel Franklin Cody on 7th August, 1913, was a great blow for British aeronautics. He crashed with his passenger at Ball Hill, South Farnborough while testing the giant aeroplane he had built specially to take part in the £5,000 prize air race round the coast of Great Britain.

He worked with Patrick Alexander at Batheaston including the centenary celebrations of 1902, and at Farnborough when Cody was engaged upon the mechanical part of Nulli Secundus for the engine of which he was largely responsible. Cody was ever able to obtain more from an engine than most others, as he was a natural motor mechanic of exceptional ability. His funeral was attended by thousands of servicemen and civilians who wished to show their respect for a brave and clever man.

In the first six months of 1911, thirty four fatal accidents, including two British aviators had taken place in Europe and America, attributed to inexperience, carelessness, recklessness, or faults in the flying machines. Air-pockets or "holes in the air" and similar irregularities were suspected of causing strains beyond the margins of strength given by designers. Fatalities to British aviators amounted to nine in the complete year.

About half of the number killed were French and the death toll was rising.

The importance of some events were hardly noticed, such as the introduction of the French armaments millionaire's Schneider Trophy race after the Gordon Bennett Cup race banquet in 1912. This, after many incidents, was to lead to the Spitfire with its fantastic Rolls Royce engine.

As Anthony Tucker stated in The Guardian recently, "There are some spirits in the aviation cupboard which from time to time, must be released for a day, lest the world withers without them."

Chapter 40

Aviation at Windsor

In 1911 and 1912, Patrick Alexander had been in both the Antipodes and the Far East. In the Field (July 15th, 1911), his friend Charles C. Turner reported meeting him during a very hurried visit to London on his return from the Antipodes on the eve of his departure for the Far East. They briefly discussed the Alexander Aero motor competition, and an erroneous report that there had been no entries, whereas actually there had been eight.

During 1911 there were several reports from Windsor of aviation incidents, all of which Patrick Alexander collected into his books of cuttings after his return, and no doubt received first hand stories from his aeronautics classes at Imperial Service College. The boys must have been excited to learn that King George V, who was deeply interested in flying machines, had "commanded" Mr. T.O.M. Sopwith to fly to Windsor from Brooklands in his all-British Howard Wright biplane with an E.N.V. engine.

Although a bank of fog barred Sopwith's way, he landed first at Datchet to lunch with his sister, then he circled the Round Tower and on to the royal golf links at the appointed time, the first aeroplane to land in Windsor. The King and Queen Mary and their family - Princes Henry, George and John - met Mr. Sopwith on the lawns near the castle, and his tactful compliment to the British aeroplane industry was greatly appreciated. The air-minded boys of Windsor and Eton College turned up in force to see the machine perform, which it did to great effect.

Sydney Camm hurried to see Sopwith's plane. It was announced that prizes would be given for the best models, and Sydney won 2nd prize, the first reward of so very many he was to receive during his life. He was to become Sopwith's chief designer in 1923 at the Hawker Engineering Co.

On the same day as Sopwith's flight, the War Office scoffed at the idea that aeroplanes could be of use for military work. The scoffer was Major Sir A. Bannerman, the new head of the War Office military aeronautical department, at a Royal Aero Club dinner, of all places.

If a number of newspaper cuttings in the Alexander collection from Australia and Shanghai around March/May, 1911, can be taken as evidence that Patrick Alexander visited these areas during that period - and there is corroborating

*T.O.M. Sopwith on the East Lawn at Windsor Castle,
1st February, 1911, a flight made at the request of King George V*

evidence in The Field, July 15th, 1911, and a contemporary Bath newspaper - the
contents of the cuttings is of doubtful value. The North China Herald referred in
detail to the collapse in mid air of an aeroplane flying before the Chinese
authorities, with the result that the aviator was killed and negotiations ceased
abruptly. The British Australasian referred to a lecture in which it was
authoritatively stated that a new discovery of "a means of making petrol solid
would result in a big step forward."

Probably of more interest to Patrick Alexander was the Dunlop Rubber
Company and Aeroplane League proposal dated 21st March, 1911, to raise £15,000
prize money for an aeroplane flight competition from Sydney to Melbourne.

Saturday, July 22nd, 1911, was announced as the start of the Round-Britain
flight for the prize of £10,000 offered by the Daily Mail. There were twenty-five
erstwhile "starters" but some machines were unfinished or barely tested, and little
time remained for tuning-up. The Field referred to some very public-spirited
actions in connection with aviation, naming Patrick Alexander, G.C. Cockburn
and H. Barber, adding that while success in trade and liberality to party funds
resulted in public honours, services to science were not sufficiently recognised.
While the pursuit of science and any form of arm might contain its own reward,

it was a mean spirited nation that rested satisfied with this reflection, and bestowed its benefactions upon smart tradesmen. H. Barber was giving up the commercial pursuit of aviation, and Patrick Alexander was examining the aviation situation in the Far East and the Antipodes.

During September, 1911, the press was full of anticipatory news concerning the Aerial Post experiment for certain mail to be carried from Hendon to Windsor by aeroplane. King George V had given permission for the aeroplanes to alight in the grounds of Windsor Castle, while he was at Balmoral.

The Windsor, Eton and Slough Express reported (from Patrick Alexander's collection):-

WINDSOR, ETON AND SLOUGH EXPRESS - Saturday, September 16th, 1911

The Aerial Post has been the chief topic of the week. Success attended its inauguration but it is not likely to become a permanent institution yet awhile. "Weather permitting" must accompany any announcement of a proposed aerial flight. On Saturday afternoon Mr. Gustav Hamel conveyed a bag of mail a distance of about twenty miles in fifteen minutes, but he was the only aviator of four who reached Windsor, the other three not venturing out with their machines owing to the gusty wind. During the week we have had many interesting experiments, and the scenes in Windsor Great Park have been remarkable. Some splendid flights have been made to and from Windsor, and it is conceivable that one day there will be a flying department of our Post Office. The views of Mr. Rushton, the representative of the Postmaster General, on the subject, which he gave us on Saturday, appear in another column, and will undoubtably be read with interest. An aerial post is not a new idea, and the special article elsewhere on attempts to fly in the past will probably interest our readers. The Postmaster General may be commended for lending his sanction to the first authorised demonstration in England of the utility of the aeroplane for postal work; and it is easy to imagine circumstances in which it might prove invaluable for the national service. Recent events remind us that even in times of peace ordinary postal communications may suddenly be in danger of interruption. The service is too costly yet for regular use, and it is also too risky. It is hoped, however, that something more than passing interest will be taken in this latest endeavour to keep abreast of the times.

Flying is very fascinating, and the skilful way in which the aviators ascend and descend is certainly marvellous. Huge strides have been made in aviation, and, as has been pointed out, it will indeed be a pity in many ways if, when the novelty of the idea is over-shadowed by the next new sensation, the mail-carrying aeroplane is allowed, metaphorically, to drop.

The Windsor Postmaster (Mr. A.A.T. A'Vard) and his staff are to be heartily congratulated upon the way in which they have got through the extra work this week. Aerial letters and post cards have been pouring into the Windsor office in thousands, but the earliest mails have been caught. Every available man has been employed, and it is a feather in the cap of the local postal staff that they have been able to cope with the tremendous amount of extra work in such a satisfactory way. It shows that the staff is thoroughly well organised and most efficient, and we are sure the Postmaster General has recognised the splendid manner in which the Windsor Post Office officials have carried out their part in the aerial service. Very few staffs of the size of Windsor's could have equalled their record this week.

"The novelty of the aero-post is soon over, and were such a service permanently introduced tomorrow it would create no undue notice. The fact is there is not time to give due appreciation to any great innovation. Trips to the sky would be a nine-days wonder - or even less.''

In East London, ''owing to the generosity of Patrick Alexander and the Governors of the East London College, the aero-dynamic laboratory will again be open for experimental research during the winter. The Council of the Aero Research Society would gladly welcome a few gentlemen desirous of experimenting.'' Applications to Hon. Secretary R.H. Walters. 'Engineering' 22/9/1911

Defence - A Start at Last

In December, 1911, the War Office published the conditions and particulars of the prizes for the military aeroplane competition to be held about the middle of 1912. The first prize for an aeroplane made in any country was £4,000, the second prize was £2,000. Prizes open to British subjects only for aeroplanes manufactured wholly in Great Britain (except the engine) were 1st - £1,500, two 2nd prizes of £1,000 each, and three 3rd prizes of £500.

In May, 1912, the Government authorised the purchase of 60 aeroplanes, and by the end of the year it was expected that 60 pilots would have been trained at the Central Flying School, Upavon, Salisbury Plain. The years of pressure from Patrick Alexander and those who shared his views were at last having some success, added to which the German build up of arms was increasing in menace.

British expenditure on aviation in 1912 was estimated at £308,000, including purchase of land. The French figure was £1,250,000 while the German figure was secret.

ARMY AIRSHIP "GAMMA 11"   CIRCA 1910
Hampshire County Library ©

Army Airship "Gamma 11" flew over Windsor Castle during the Eton College 4th June celebrations, 1912

257

There were other incidents at Windsor - the Army airship 'Gamma' flew over Windsor and Eton on the occasion of the 4th of June celebrations at Eton College in 1912. It arrived at 8 o'clock and circled the Castle for about 10 minutes. Thousands of people including the Eton crews and their guests hurriedly left their dinners to watch the airship with intense interest. It was the first to pass over the Castle. To add to the excitement, an Army monoplane "going at a great speed" accompanied the airship from the Castle back to Farnborough, the airship taking 1 hour and 15 minutes for the double journey. The Gamma had been built in 1911, and was the first British Army airship to have swivelling propellers for her two engines. Rebuilt in 1912 with a larger envelope, the airship was used until July, 1914, for training purposes.

On February 2nd, 1914, Gustav Hamel demonstrated "Looping the Loop" 14 consecutive times above Windsor Castle for the King and Queen.

THE INSTITUTION OF MUNICIPAL ENGINEERS,
PATRICK ALEXANDER
AND AVIATION IN 1912

The President of the Institution of Municipal Engineers in 1912 was E.A. Strickland, Borough Engineer of Windsor. His offices and depot were in Alma Road, Windsor, a short distance from Imperial Service College - and Patrick Alexander—and an even shorter distance from the Alma Road home of Sydney Camm, whose club premises in Arthur Road backed on to the Borough Surveyor's office. On June 12th, 1912, the Institution of Municipal Engineers met at the London Aerodrome, Hendon, by courtesy of Mr. C. Grahame-White and his directors.

Patrick Alexander included the eight large pages containing the report of the meeting in his books of cuttings. It is the only technical paper of its kind in the collection, and was probably supplied to him by Mr. Strickland. The report shows that the municipal engineers were giving consideration to the impact of aviation upon matters for which they were responsible. The matter was without precedent and the engineers theorised regarding things to come. There would be special buildings, the possibility of a "London Aerobus Company" for public services, and aeroplane sheds at houses, together with take-off spaces - as it was undesirable for private flying machines to take off in an ordinary street. There was the problem of landing in town centres. Why not have a large and lofty building from the flat roofs of which aeroplanes could arrive and depart? A landing stage 80 to 90 feet wide and 200 foot long could, it was thought, accomodate both arrival and departure platforms side by side for the machines of 1912, but in the future an area about the size of Selfridges, 200 feet square might be required at least 20 feet higher than existing buildings, and therefore 120 or 130 feet above street level. Workshops to store and service the machines would be on the outskirts of the towns, but workshops for urgent repairs would need to be at the central landing spaces. Commutor traffic to principal landing stages on the Oxford Street and Holborn

*Gustav Hamel 'looping the loop' before the King and Queen at Windsor,
on February 2nd, 1914*

route and from Marble Arch to Aldgate and the Bank of England were envisaged, with another area along the Strand. The congestion and danger that would arise from such a scheme pointed to the need for a central zone in which flying was prohibited. The writer admitted that he had been theorising as would everyone until the problems were solved.

Other speakers touched upon the problems of boundaries being aerially projected upward and this was a practical impossibility. The ownership of the air above land had been lost for ever, and even the sacred rights of game preservation would not permit the shooting of aviators.

Aerial advertising should be prohibited, with other nuisances. To drop liquid or solid matter from a height would be a nuisance, as was spitting. The disposal of waste matters and materials, low flying, careless landing, and the control of passenger services would need consideration also construction, qualifications, capacity and speed, "rule of the road", flying heights, lights, storage of fuel, precautions in fog and bad weather, means of escape, compulsory parachutes in place of lifebelts - the list was a long one. The urgency was exemplified by the fact that the French Minister of War had been killed in an accident at Paris, and other spectators seriously injured.

The representative of the Aerial League of the British Empire suggested that rules were required for the public rather than the aviator. He thought that in a short time aeroplanes would be collapsible, and needing less space for storage.

Reputed to be Patrick Alexander in a Wright aeroplane,
but more likely Mrs. Griffith Brewer
in the passenger seat at Dayton in 1911

Another speaker referred to the legislation that Parliament in its wisdom had not much earlier enacted for the motor car. The unfortunate Locomotives on Highways Act of 1865 - which has been misnamed the "Red Flag Act" - required drivers of mechanical vehicles to be preceded by a man on foot, and the speed not to exceed 4 miles per hour. This had caused England to follow in the wake of continental nations, and anything similar for aviation would be a national misfortune. It was generally agreed that all tall chimneys and overhead wires would have to be done away with, and that a large number of aircraft accidents could have been prevented by duplicate engines, so that when one failed the other prevented the aviator from being dashed to death.

After tea, and touring the hangars and extensive workshops, Mr. Strickland was taken up for his first flight in an aeroplane piloted by Mr. Turner, and the Institution Secretary Mr. Wygand by Mr. Grahame-White. On landing, they noticed the pile of wreckage that was all that remained of of one of the aeroplanes that had been engaged a few months before in the Hendon-Windsor aerial post. Some aircraft were more collapsible than others.

Patrick Alexander very occasionally annotated cuttings, but unfortunately not this unique report of an event that took place the same day as the Bath Chronicle reported his absence abroad until the end of June, 1912.

Did Patrick Alexander fly in an aeropane in 1911/12? No conclusive evidence has been found, but there is one unannotated photograph among his collection that might be a clue. It is reputed to show Patrick Alexander in a Wright aeroplane. The aeroplane is a Wright of c. 1911 - it has wheels, and these were not fitted in place of skids before 1910. It is similar to the famous "Gin Fizz" used for the flight from Long Island to California in 1911. The figure on the left appears to be female, in which case the photograph could be Mrs. Griffith Brewer in the passenger seat at Huffman Prairie, Dayton in August 1911, when Orville Wright took Mrs. Griffith Brewer for a flight. She was also photographed before take-off, with her skirts tied tightly round her ankles to avoid aerodynamic and moral hazards. This was insisted upon by Wilbur Wright ever since he had Mrs. Hart O'Berg as the first lady passenger on October 7th, 1908. Mrs. Griffith Brewer's flight is well recorded, and it seems probable that the photograph was presented to Patrick Alexander by his friends the Griffith Brewers.

Chapter 41

The 1914-1918 War

The outbreak of war brought one problem to Patrick Alexander, what could he do to aid his country? At age 47, with a bad leg, he found that his services were not in demand. He decided to go to Cornwall, there had been reports of submarines being seen, some of these reports might have been correct, but he would go to see for himself.

He was fond of going to the Lands End Hotel, which had recently been reconstructed, redecorated and refurnished. Now fitted with electric light, and with a garage for motor vehicles, guests arriving at Penzance railway station could be met, and saved the slow horse drawn carriage journey of previous years. The hotel proprietor, Benjamin Trehare welcomed him, and on the outbreak of war in August, 1914, he was seen there, patrolling the cliffs with his binoculars at the ready, looking out for German submarines, still in his usual black jacket, sponge bag trousers, and black bowler hat, although his friend from Imperial Service College, E.A.S. Beckwith, who told me the story, is not so sure about the hat as he sometimes wore a straw "boater" on sunny days. In 1915, when Mr. Beckwith was there on holiday, Patrick Alexander was still keeping watch out to sea.

The view from Lands End is incomparable on a clear day. Far to the south-west can be seen the Isles of Scilly, and many ships could be seen rounding Lands End in what was once a never ending stream. These came quite close to land in fine weather, and at night the procession of ships to and from all parts of the world showed their green, red and white lights.

It seemed to Patrick Alexander that if the German U-boats were to be active anywhere, the area off Lands End was more likely than anywhere else that was accessible to him and his binoculars. There were plenty of ships to observe, but no submarines, but keeping a look-out for them was better than doing nothing.

He also made several journeys for unpublished purposes to New York. In 1914/15 some aircraft factories had anticipated the need for aeroplanes, but generally finance was an obstacle to building in anticipation of orders. It was a young man's business to a considerable extent. Tom Sopwith was 26, Robert Blackburn and Frederick Handley Page were 29. Alexander was older than Horace Short and Mervyn O'Gorman both of whom were 45. Griffith Brewer had become

Ben Trehare, standing in the porch of the Lands End Hotel
He is said to still haunt the hotel
and was Patrick Alexander's host in 1914/15

honorary adviser to the R.N.A.S. on Airships and Kite balloons, and as he held Ballooning Certificate No. 5 and U.S.A. Aviator's Certificate of a Wright aeroplane in 1914, besides being a pilot in balloon races such as the Gordon Bennett, he probably had the edge on his friend Patrick Alexander, who was the same age. Brewer's knowledge as a Patent Agent was also useful.

Patrick Alexander had many friends and acquaintances in America among manufacturers including Mr. Schwab, the steel millionaire, and by 1916, he had visited U.S.A five times, running the gauntlet of the German U-boats, who by 1916 were thought to have received instructions to operate against shipping without regard to any guarantees. The U-boat campaign had started on February 10th, 1915.

There were several services he could perform as a patriot in U.S.A. although he was no longer regarded as a leader in English aeronautical development. He could obtain quotations for munitions including engines and aircraft, besides reporting American progress to the British Government.

He could, and apparently did, aid British propaganda, by making statements to the American press, as the following column in a New York paper indicates. This is undated, but the evidence is that it was published towards the end of April, 1916, after he left Liverpool for New York on the 18th April, 1916, on the Cunard 'Orduna', travelling first class. He was well known to the New York newsmen, who reported his views at length:

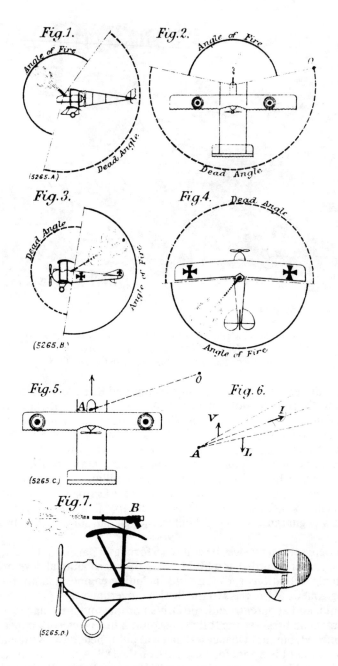

Fig.1.

Fig.2.

Fig.3.

Fig.4.

Fig.5.

Fig.6.

Fig.7.

"The Armament of Aeroplanes"
- Patrick Alexander's cutting from the 1914/18 war

264

PREDICTS AMERICA WILL BE DRAWN IN
P.Y. Alexander, Just From London, Says English
Think We Cannot Avoid Clash With Germany.

That the United States will face new danger of being drawn into the war before the end of six months was said to be the opinion in well-informed circles in England by Patrick Y. Alexander, who arrived yesterday on the Cunard steamship Orduna, on his fifth visit since the beginning of the war in Europe. Mr. Alexander, who formerly was a leader in English aeronautical development, further predicted that the war will last three years more.

"One of the absorbing topics abroad in connection with the war," he said last night, "is the position in which the United States is placed. The feeling in England is that the States have been forced into a position that will soon prove embarrassing. In fact, it is generally believed that the United States will be in the war within three to six months. The reason for this is that it is generally thought that the German submarines have received orders to start operating soon without regard to any guarantees.

"This is not all. There are underground influences at work which are dragging the United States into the conflict. It is my opinion, and that of many better informed than I, that this country is practically on the brink of war."

Speaking of the war in general, Mr. Alexander said:

"Every one in England and France feels that it will last three years longer. All preparations are being made with that idea in view. It is generally understood that England has at least 5,000,000 men under arms and munitions sufficient to supply them. The Allies will soon be in the position where they will have no fear about their ability to maintain their armies in the field.

"Probably the greatest development has been in aeronautics. Everything indicates that the war will be decided in the air. Aeroplanes by the thousands are being added to those in service, so it is safe to estimate that the Allies have nearly 100,000 machines. There are aeroplane bases of large sizes in the most unheard-of places.

"It is now proposed to name an Air Minister, who will be in charge of the Allied aeronautics. Under him would be the national heads who would manage this fighting arm in their own countries.

"In England aeroplanes are now flying that can carry tons of explosives, being driven by motors developing more than 1,000 horse power. In addition, there are new fast machines which can climb faster and make greater speed (nearly 150 miles an hour) than any others yet built.

"It is safe to say that the Zeppelins will not cause much more trouble. They will not move so fast and the danger of destruction will be so great that they are not likely to do much damage. If England had had 10,000 aeroplanes at the beginning of the war there never would have been any destructive Zeppelin raids.

"I find Americans much interested in what English women are doing in connection with the war. Before the fighting started we had 1,0000,000 surplus women, and before it is over there will be at least 2,500,000. That is, the men, who normally support these women, will be killed or incapacitated by wounds, so that they will be practically non-productive and have to be taken care of. Women are at work everywhere, not alone in the war industries, but in every other industry where they can supplant men. Thousands of men have been released to the army by the women being willing to do their bit. After the war they will have to be reckoned with, and it is likely that many thousands will emigrate to this country and the colonies."

Mr. Alexander believes that this year will see the first transatlantic aeroplane flight.

265

He also thinks it is likely that a Zeppelin may fly across as this will be quite possible under the conditions usually found in the summer.

Mr. Alexander will return to England on the Orduna, which will sail Monday. According to him the vessel has been ordered to return as soon as possible and will be taken over by the Government.

Patrick Alexander seems to have been back in New York in May 1916, and within a few days, 'Aerial Age Weekly' published his further statements:

PATRICK Y. ALEXANDER IN NEW YORK

In the course of his ceaseless journeying around the world, Mr. Patrick Y. Alexander, one of the fathers of aviation in Great Britain, the first man to offer a substantial prize for an aeronautical motor, visited New York for two days last week. Mr. Alexander has devoted a large part of his fortune to the development of aeronautics.

Mr. Alexander's father, Andrew Alexander, was one of the founders of the Aeronautical Society of Great Britain in 1866. Patrick inherited a large fortune and his father's hobby. In 1878 he built his first glider model. As geographer and explorer he has trotted the globe in every direction. He was the official British observer of a Zeppelin's first ascent. He reported the Wrights' first flight, and was a close friend of Professor Langley.

So when Patrick Alexander talks about aviation, those who really know the history of its development give attention.

"The science of aeronautics is in its infancy," said Mr. Alexander. "No man can foretell its possibilities. Twenty years ago I was thought crazy for predicting what now has happened. But I do not see the end short of the neutralization of the force of gravity. Then we shall be able to launch a craft as bulky as the Aquitania and travel will be generally through the air. Don't tell me it is impossible! Some one yet will find the secret and unlock it. Some one will discover how to make Newton's apple fly back to the tree - perhaps a Chinaman, perhaps a Peruvian, perhaps some American genius will do it. It is no more incredible than flying seemed to be twenty years ago.

"There are three great new factors in this war that make it different from any other war that was ever fought," says Mr. Alexander. "They are aircraft, the wireless telegraph and the internal combustion engine. They have compelled such rapid readjustment that the older fighting men have been retired, and only the young men, abreast of these modern scientific developments, are generally being thrust into the positions of responsibilty. We are now equipping aeroplanes with a wireless apparatus having a sending radius of 150 miles. I was astonished to be told that in this side your navy's aeronautical equipment so far has provided only ten or fifteen miles of wireless communication.

"It is true that England," Mr. Alexander declares, "has not attained yet her stride in aeronautics. We have 1,000 factories turning out aeroplanes or parts. Women are proving very faithful workers in the aeroplane factories as well as in other munition plants. What we need - and you need it, too - is aeronautical leadership. We have in Great Britain no less than fourteen unofficial 'Ministers of Aviation'. We need a head for the service. We need a man or men who can apply aeronautical science in offense as well as defense. You must remember that the man who can do this must know naval as well as military tactics. He should be an admiral and a general and a geographer, and a statesman, all in one. The day is coming for England, and for America, when the aeronautical branch will be more important than either the army or the navy.

"Your movement to take account of your industrial possibilities and provide for their mobilisation is the most important step you have taken toward preparedness,'' he says. ''Had we been thus prepared ourselves, the chances are that this war would be over by now. We have been able to buy aeroplanes in America. Fortunately they are good aeroplanes. You are turning out now some of the best aeroplane motors in the world. What you need now is some Henry Ford to standardize aeroplane construction so that a serviceable machine can be bought for $500 or $1,000. Aviation is not going to be forever the sport of wealthy men. The air is going to be the great, open highway over land and sea. We are going to travel through it because it is the quick, direct delightful route. We are going to transport our wares that way, too. In another ten years we shall be thinking in terms of taking the Aquitanias and Mauretanias out of the water.''

Back in England, 'The Aeroplane' published in June, 1916, extracts from the 'New York World', which had copied the 'Aerial Age Weekly' article.

England was buying aeroplanes in America, and Alexander praised the best American aeroplane engines, saying ''You are now turning out some of the best aeroplane motors in the world.'' As an entrepreneur, with many years experience of the American aeroplane industry, it seems likely that he was engaged in some way in connection with the purchase of aeroplanes in America, and possibly reporting improvements in design. It seems unlikely that he would make so many transatlantic crossings in war time without particular objectives.

At the Summer 1916 meeting of the Royal Aeronautical Society, reference was made to the letter from Orville Wright that Patrick Alexander had read to their meeting on 15th December, 1905. This was the letter dated November 17th, 1905, which related the Wrights' experiments for the preceding season, including the unheard of success in remaining airborne for half an hour. The letter was repeated verbatim in the journal dated July-September, 1916.

There was a possibility of his getting employment as a Meteorological Officer, and he applied to be re-elected a Fellow of the Royal Meteorological Society from which he had resigned in December 1908. His application was accepted, and he signed the forms in which he again accepted the duties of Fellowship on 26th June, 1917.

Early in 1917, he was given a job by the Air Ministry, at the Meteorological Office at Falmouth. The Ministry had been paying the Royal Cornwall Polytechnic Society for the use of the Observatory at Falmouth, together with the cost of maintenance of the Observatory garden. The accomodation was spartan, and Patrick Alexander obtained the use of the Society's sitting room from 28th February, 1917. In August he took 18 days leave, and his Professional Assistant, Lieut. T. Harris, M.A., A.R.C.Sc., R.E., was ''in residence'' with his wife and child - then Alexander reoccupied the sitting room until 12th June, 1918.

In May, 1918, Falmouth was a ''protected harbour'' and all records seem to have been veiled in secrecy. Alexander kept some cuttings from 1918 that although he had stopped filling his series of press cuttings volumes five years earlier, he must have thought were prophetic. When the two sides were diverting every known device of science and ingenuity, of learning and enterprise, of capital and industry to the one supreme purpose of destroying life and wealth, Horatio Bottomley, Editor of ''John Bull'', wrote in May, 1918, ''After this struggle is over, war must be made so terrible and appalling that in years to come no nation dare embark upon it. In other words the cynic will say, Might will be Right, and Force the only remedy . . . sooner or later a means of wholesale extermination will be discovered which will put an end to war. . .''

The work at Falmouth continued until the war ended, and after the armistice on November 11th, 1918, his address was once again the Lands End Hotel.

One of his colleagues at Imperial Service College, Windsor, sent him a greetings postcard bearing a photograph of his laboratory at the school, and this was redirected on 23rd December, 1918, from the Lands End Hotel to 12, Queen Anne's Gate, London where he was staying for the Christmas holidays.

Chapter 42

The Benefactor of Imperial Service College, Windsor

From the time when Patrick Alexander placed the cheque for £10,000 in the hands of Mr. Beckwith Senior, he had a special status at Imperial Service College. He was invited to take his place on the platform on special days in the college year where he sat with the Governors or staff, and to make speeches as the occasion required.

With no relations, and unable to keep up with the incredible rate of progress in aviation under wartime conditions, he could still interest the boys in what might be regarded as elementary aeronautics and science.

With his exceptionally wide travel experience, he could give lectures of great interest, which he illustrated with slides. Reports of two of his lectures are in the I.S.C. Chronicle for April, 1916:

LECTURES

Mr. Patrick Y. Alexander, on 12th February, gave an interesting lecture on New York, which he knows like the palm of his hand. Among the slides were some of sky scrapers, a birds-eye view of the streets and harbour, and the private palace of Mr. Schwab, the man of steel. After depressing us by saying that, with a population of seven and a quarter millions, New York was now bigger than London, and that with bank clearings of 20,000 millions sterling it had distanced our poor metropolis in still another respect, he raised our spirits again by the declaration that in twenty years the United States would be all British.

On Saturday, 1st April, Mr. Alexander was kind enough to give us another lecture, and in an hour or so took us all around the world. We were shown the lion-shaped rock of Gibraltar, and with regard to the covetousness of certain enemies towards that key of positions which we have held for two centuries, he told us grimly that "we were ready for 'em." The Mediterranean as a sea is little better than a bottle; the Straits are no more than 14 miles in width - a mere neck of which Gibraltar is tantamount to a cork. But if the westerly entrance is nothing more than a neck, the exit at the other end is by comparison a crack. The ditch called the Suez Canal, made at a cost of twenty-four millions, is forty yards wide, and navigation therein is conducted by arrangement. We saw India kaleidoscopically, and then had a glimpse of the Celestial Empire. Even here, where one had supposed sleep and opium to be the staples of a man's life, speed has arrived. The officers in the Chinese Army actually fly; a journey

269

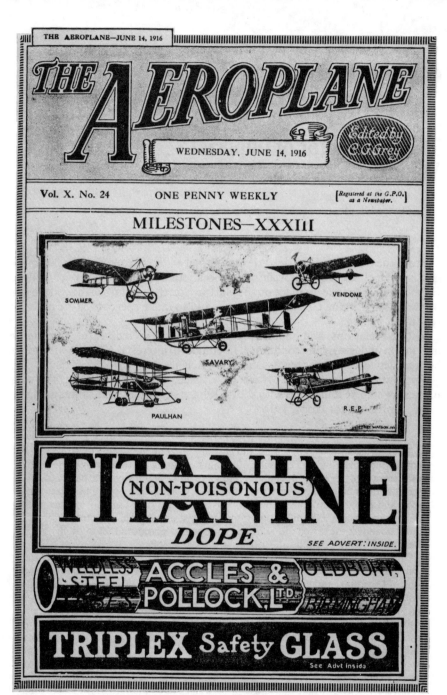

THE Aeroplane

Edited by C.G. Grey

WEDNESDAY, JUNE 14, 1916

Vol. X. No. 24   ONE PENNY WEEKLY   [Registered at the G.P.O. as a Newspaper.]

MILESTONES—XXXIII

SOMMER

VENDOME

SAVARY

PAULHAN

R.E.P.

TITANINE
NON-POISONOUS
DOPE
SEE ADVERT: INSIDE.

WELDLESS STEEL ACCLES & POLLOCK, L.TD OLDBURY, BIRMINGHAM

TRIPLEX Safety GLASS
See Advt inside

"The Aeroplane" front cover, June 14th, 1916

270

which some years ago took six weeks is now accomplished in seventeen hours. We passed on. Like a bird we beheld Australia, and then Africa. We saw the Victoria Falls, with twenty million horse-power running to waste. We wasted no time, but fled on the wings of the lantern to America. Finally, dazed and giddy, we returned to that comfortable grey and black which only London can provide. At the end of a most illuminating tour, Mr. Alexander said that he hoped next term to give a terrestial globe, to be awarded on the result of an examination in geography - another proof of his practical encouragement which aroused much enthusiasm.

He was now fifty years old, the age by which he had said he expected he would be dead, but he seemed to be as fit as ever. It was 30 years since he had fallen from the rigging of the 'Minero'' and broken his leg, and there is no record of his having spoken to the boys of the voyage to Australia in 1885 which changed his life.

His enthusiasm for travel - and aeronautics - was unabated, as was his patriotism.

Alexander's old aeronautics laboratory with its belt-driven ''aero engine'' was still an attraction; boys would persuade the Corporal in charge to switch it on to see the propeller whizzing round and round and to smell the engine oil. ''It's funny how evocative smells can be'', said my informant.

According to Mr. E.A.S. Beckwith, later to become the Headmaster of I.S.C. Junior School, Patrick Alexander came to be regarded as a benevolent elderly eccentric friend, his tall increasingly gaunt figure instantly recognisable in his short black morning coat, wing collar and black tie, plus striped sponge bag trousers, always with a walking stick to aid his lame leg, and usually wearing a black bowler hat, whatever the weather. The story of the £10,000 cheque was repeated to every newcomer to the school, and lost nothing in the telling. The sum was really something in those days.

Mr. E.A.S. Beckwith first met Patrick Alexander in 1912, and speaks of his being kindly, tall and lean, an individualist as well as an obstinate Scotsman, who might have put certain peoples' backs up - a reason advanced for his never being given the Royal Aero Club certificate as an aeronaut, adding that a prophet is not without honour except in his own country. Certainly he was known to be eccentric, and this was explained by his being something of a genius.

Nothing definite is known about Patrick Alexander's participation in commer- cial aviation projects, but his name has been associated with that of Horatio Barber who spent large sums on such projects, apparently with the Wright brothers' works at Battersea (H.T. and Warwick Wright, not the Dayton brothers). Barber worked alongside them in the railway arches they occupied at Battersea for a period, and Patrick Alexander's name has been linked with their financial backing. Barber retired to Bermuda after heavy financial losses from aircraft construction in 1913.

After the armistice in 1918, Patrick Alexander presented Mr. E.A.S. Beckwith with a barometer from a captured German submarine. He would sometimes talk about his pre-war adventures, when he ''met all the crowned heads in Europe.'' He continued to live in the school, and had his meals with the masters.

Eventually it was learnt that he had given all his money away, and Mr. E.A.S. Beckwith informs me that at his late father's instigation, Alexander lived on the income from the gift of £10,000 to the Imperial Service College. He would go to the old Headmaster's house, Clewer Lodge, for Sunday lunch, bearing a bundle

271

The memorial to Patrick Alexander's friend, E.G.A. Beckwith,
"Statue of Ambition" at Imperial Service College, Windsor

consisting of every Sunday newspaper. The Headmaster protested that never before had he been so well informed—or misinformed—on weekly doings.

Imperial Service College grew, and in addition to the old buildings of St Marks (a few of which survive having been converted into flats) new classrooms were erected, and in 1931, a Hall to the memory of the King Edward's Horse Regiment recruited from India, Australia, New Zealand and South Africa, the regiment that in a force only 400 strong withstood a German attack. The Headmaster wrote:

"In the most critical days of the War (1914-18) when the Germans were attacking with the greatest energy, due to a mistake somewhere the only troops between the Germans and the Channel ports in a particular point were 400 men of King Edward's Horse, who for eight mortal hours withstood the onslaught, and the Germans never got through . ."

272

In 1935, the much respected Headmaster, Mr. E.G.A. Beckwith, Patrick Alexander's very good friend, died in the middle of a service in the Chapel. The 'Statue of Ambition' was erected in his memory between the King Edward's Horse Hall and the new classrooms in the centre of what was planned to become a quadrangle. The unveiling ceremony was on Speech Day 1936, and was performed by H.R.H. Duke of Connaught who took the salute from the Guard of Honour. It was a wet day and Patrick Alexander changed his walking stick for an umbrella. A new Headmaster was appointed - Lyonulph Tollemache.

The Rudyard Kipling Memorial plaque at Imperial Service College, Windsor

Patrick Alexander continued to live in school, but times were changing. The Governors were worried by financial problems and came to the conclusion that the day of their sort of Public School was drawing to an end. They decided to accept an offer of amalgamation with Haileybury School. The senior boys and masters - with Patrick Alexander - are known to have paraded for a final photograph in 1942, then the school dispersed. The Army used the premises for the duration - and after. Patrick Alexander moved to 28, St. Marks Road, a few yards away.

The Imperial Service College Junior School was also amalgamated with Haileybury and remained in Windsor at Clewer Manor with Mr. E.A.S. Beckwith continuing as Headmaster as he had been from January, 1935.

The invitation to Sunday lunch - now at Clewer Manor - was extended by Mr. Beckwith, but the offer was only accepted spasmodically; previously he seems to have gone to Clewer Lodge because he was so fond of the late Mr. Beckwith.

In the Spring of 1943, Patrick Alexander was failing in health, but the gaunt, lame old man would still go to the newsagents to buy every newspaper he could, returning home with them rolled in a bundle.

Nearby lived Francis Burton, hairdresser and sometime Mayor of the Royal Borough of New Windsor who would call on Alexander in the evenings and at weekends to sit with him and hear tales of his travels and aeronautical work and about the personages he had met.

Miss Schofield was the daughter of Sergeant Major Schofield of Westward Ho! - Stalky and Co., in Rudyards Kipling's stories - and she had been secretary to Mr. Nagel, the first Headmaster of United Services College, Windsor, then secretary to Mr. E.G.A. Beckwith for 23 years, and then secretary to Mr. Lyonulph Tollemache, his successor, until the amalgamation of 1942. She was the epitome of loyalty to the Imperial Service College and its Headmasters.

Miss Schofield was also a loyal friend of Patrick Alexander and nursed him in his last illness. Dr. Malden would call daily, and so would Francis Burton who would bring him little delicacies from Mrs. Burton, which had to be hidden in the larder as Alexander was too proud to accept charity.

Towards the end he was unable to leave a sofa by the kitchen gas cooker, and there he died on July 7th, after a heart attack. It was war time, and the social services were unable to cope with every need. The funeral on 12th July, was attended by many old friends from Imperial Service College and Windsor.

Among the list of Old Boys of the College who in 1943 were reported in the Imperial Service College Old Boy's Journal as killed in action, missing or decorated for gallantry, is the obituary of Patrick Alexander:-

"The death of Mr. Patrick Alexander removes another landmark. The departure of the College from Windsor left him as one cast upon a desert island. His death occurred on July 7th, 1943 after a short illness.

Patrick Alexander came of an engineering stock and followed very keenly from his earliest days the development of aeronautics through all its stages. He made himself acquainted with most of the early experimenters from the Wright Brothers onward and, being a man of considerable means, he spared no expense in carrying out experiments on his own account, besides doing what he could to assist the efforts of others.

His connection with the College dates from 1907; he was very anxious that the boys should become air minded. He built and equipped an engineering laboratory for experimental purposes and resided periodically near the Coll. We all know of his famous gift of £10,000, which now forms the Alexander Trust. Later he took up his residence permanently at the Coll., becoming a familiar and popular figure at all school occasions. It gave him great pleasure to perform little acts of kindness and most of us will remember his chuckle of enjoyment when he had perpetuated a quiet leg-pull. His last days were made easier by the very great kindness of Miss Schofield.

The funeral service was held at Holy Trinity Church, Windsor, and was attended by Mr. S. Beckwith, Headmaster of the Junior School, Maj. G.B.T. Nicholls and Mr. T. Guthrie Morgan (representing Haileybury and I.S.C.), Mr. C.M. Woodbridge (Governor), Mr. E.C. Durant (Solicitor), Mr. and Mrs. T. Hughes, Miss V.H. Schofield, Miss Rhodes, Mr. E. Burton and a number of Windsor friends.

On 16th July, 1943, Patrick Alexander's life and work were summarised in the editorial of the Windsor, Slough and Eton Express, together with a full column of obituary:-

GAVE £10,000 TO THE IMPERIAL SERVICE COLLEGE
The Remarkable Career of Mr. P.Y. Alexander,
Scientist and Philanthropist

The death occurred in Windsor on Wednesday of last week of Mr. Patrick Y. Alexander. His tall spare figure was familiar to most people in Windsor and he was known, perhaps to most people, because of his generous gifts to and interest in the Imperial Service College. Few people, however, realised that this interest in the I.S.C. and education was but a small part of his life and that for half a century he pursued with unflagging zeal a knowledge of aeronautics and personally knew and often advised many men whose names are familiar to everybody who knew anything of the development of flight.

His father, manager of Cammells of Sheffield, was one of the founders of the Aeronautical Society and after he had been to school at Wesley College, Sheffield, he went into the mills managed by his father and there helping to roll iron plates. He then went for some years to sea, although little more than a boy, followed with very keen interest the great discussions then taking place on naval programmes and scientific development. It was in 1870 that his mind definitely turned to the air when he saw Giffard's balloon making ascents in Paris. Balloons had been used for observation in the Franco-German war in 1870 if not earlier, but very few people seriously thought of flying balloons and certainly hardly any man then dreamed that the future conquest of the air would be heavier-than-air machines.

Belief in Airships

Mr. Alexander early formed the belief that airships were practicable and he seemed to have lost no opportunity in getting into touch with the few people who held similar views. By 1896 he was known throughout Europe as an authority on practical and theoretical flight and he visited Count Zeppelin at Freiderichshaven in 1897. As early as 1894 he made a parachute descent from a balloon.

At the meeting of the Aeronautical Society in 1900 Mr. Alexander described Count Zeppelin's first journey in the air, which was one of three and a half miles. The development of airships, however, was not so rapid as enthusiasts then expected, but

275

Mr. Alexander never lost in those years his belief in their practicability.

It was not until the beginning of this century that heavier-than-air machines began seriously to be experimented with and here again Mr. Alexander, while not abandoning his faith in the future of the airship, lost no opportunity of getting into touch with people who were experimenting with what was then apparently an idle dream of conquering the air with aeroplanes.

The First Aeroplanes

It was in 1903 that Wilbur Wright first took off ground in an aeroplane and Mr. Alexander described the work of Wilbur and Orville Wright to the Aeronautical Society at their next meeting.

In 1906 he went with the Wright Brothers to New York and introduced them to the Hon. C.S. Rolls, who made the first double crossing of the Channel in a Wright biplane. In 1911 he offered £1,000 in an aeroplane motor competition which was won by the Green motor.

He was a tremendous traveller. He crossed the Atlantic no less than fifty times and visited Russia, Mexico, Siberia, Africa and lived at times in Germany and America. Wherever he was, it was scientific questions that dominated his mind and thoughts and his advice and knowledge was of immense value to scores of men whose names are more familiar perhaps to the general public.

He had a private laboratory at one time in Whitehall Court Buildings and whenever he was in London attended the meetings of many scientific bodies.

Generosity

His knowledge and experience and business ability brought him considerable financial rewards, but this seems to have been of hardly any interest to him for he gave away nearly all he earned. In fact there was one time in his life after he had given away many thousands of pounds, when he was in financial difficulties. Fortunately so many knew of his very valuable work that he was quickly relieved.

It was characteristic of the man that he should get into such difficulties. One of his gifts was a cheque for £10,000 to the Head Master of the Imperial Service College "for the training of character and development of knowledge" among the boys of the school. He had previously given the College an aeronautical laboratory fully equipped with wind tunnel and accessories and another of his gifts was an unequalled one of newspaper cuttings relating to aeronautics, forming a complete record of the progress up to the time of the gift, to the South Kensington Museum.

THE FUNERAL

The funeral was on Monday morning, the first part of the service being held in Holy Trinity Church, where the Rector (Canon Henry Tower) was assisted by Rev. E.A. McCarthy.

The mourners included: The Head Master of Haileybury and Imperial Service College Junior School at Windsor (Mr. S. Beckwith), Mr. T. Guthrie Morgan and Major G.B.T. Nicholls (representing Haileybury and the Imperial Service College), Mr. C.M. Woodbridge (a Governor of Haileybury and the I.S.C), Mr. E.C. Durant, Mr. T Hughes (formerly second master at the Imperial Service College) and Mrs. Hughes, Miss Schofield (formerly secretary) and Miss Rhodes (formerly a matron at Kipling House, I.S.C.), Mr. and Mrs. E.J. Brown, Mr. Edward Brown and Mrs. D. Winne and Mr. E. Burton.

Others present included Mr. A.H. Dyson, Mrs. Saunders, Mr. R.B. Walker, Mr. O.T. Fenner, Mr. F.H. Bellringer, Mr. J.H. Truglan, Mr. L.W. Cleave, Mr. E. Whitaker, Mr. F.J. Lane, Mr. Wilfrid Huggins, Miss Webb and Miss K. Webb, Mrs. W.H. Evans Langsford, Mr. G. Jefferies, Supt. F. Simmonds (Windsor Division St. John Ambulance Brigade), Miss Wilkinson, Mr. S. Hulls, Miss Tomlin, Mrs. Henry Luff (representing Mr. Henry Luff).

The 23rd Psalm was said, the lesson read by Rev. E.A. McCarthy and the Rector read the prayers.

The interment was at Windsor cemetary where Rev. E.A. McCarthy read the committal sentences.

The flowers included tributes from the Governors of Haileybury and the Imperial Service College; the boys of the Imperial Service College now at Haileybury and the Personnel at Windsor Fire Station.

The final words came from his aeronautic friend of over 50 years, Griffith Brewer, President of the Royal Aeronautical Society in 1943. His memory played him falsely on a few minor points.

PATRICK ALEXANDER FUND 1922

Patrick Young Alexander, who died on 7th July, 1943, deserves some memorial for his steadfast work in aeronautics, covering a period of more than fifty years.

He was born in 1867 and I first met him as a fellow passenger in the balloon taken up by Gaudron from the Naval Exhibition at Chelsea on 9th May, 1891. His father was A. Alexander, formerly a member of the Council of the Aeronautical Society. At the time I met Patrick, his father had died and left him his life's savings of about £60,000 earned in his engineering profession, which in the latter part of his life was devoted to the management of Cammell's Steel Works in Sheffield.

Patrick told me at that time that if his father had lived, instead of travelling by balloon as he and I had just done, we should no doubt be travelling in aeroplanes. This first ascent was the forerunner of several balloon ascents we made together in the early nineties, sometimes from the Crystal Palace and from Bath gasworks, where a special pipe was laid into a field and which I used in later years to inflate balloons as an alternative to inflating them at Battersea Park.

As stated in the Aeronautical Journal of August, 1943, Patrick Alexander collaborated with me in the publication of the abridgment of Aeronautic Specifications published by the Patent Office and dated from 1815 to 1891.

For many years Patrick Alexander assisted the Aeronautical Society with an annual subscription of £100, and during the 'nineties he spent a large amount of his time in Germany, where he came into contact with Lilienthal. He also travelled many times to America, where he got to know the Wright brothers. Afterwards he visited Peking.

He made experiments with balloons and even fitted them with oars in the 'nineties, but with little prospect of success. Then when the Wrights had flown he felt that his work in aviation had been achieved and aviation so far as he was concerned became a back number. He therefore advocated levitation, but no record has been left of any success he may have achieved in this field.

Alexander was renowned for his generosity and he spent far more in encouraging flying endeavours than was warranted by the income he received from the money left him by his father. He had a theory that few men could expect to live beyond the age of fifty and consequently this gave him freedom (seeing that he had no dependents) to spend his capital on prizes to encourage aviation and education with an aeronautical background.

The large last amount that he gave away was £10,000 to the United Services College at Windsor. Shortly after making that most generous gift, when about fifty years of age he found that his inheritance had been completely exhausted. He came in to me and told me how that morning he had paid a visit to the Bankruptcy Court and had signed all the forms required in order to become a bankrupt.

Knowing Patrick and understanding his generous nature, I was prompted then, in August, 1922, to see what I could do to raise a fund which would keep him from immediate want. With Patrick's permission I wrote to mutual friends and collected between £500 and £600. Then I was relieved to hear that the Trustees of the United Services College, at the instigation of the Duke of Atholl, who was one of the directors, had appointed him curator for life to the College at a salary of £250 per annum.

The money I had collected was administered by the Council of the Royal Aeronautical Society who decided to pay him at the rate of £1 per week until the total sum was exhausted which happened some years ago. In the meantime it was a welcome sight to see Patrick Alexander at the Royal Aero Club on the first day of each month after he had called at the Royal Aeronautical Society to receive his monthly instalment.

In his early life he had made a sea voyage round Cape Horn in a sailing ship. Alexander fell off a yard arm, fortunately on to the deck, but he broke his leg. I always remember his quiet observation that the second mate set his leg because his brother was a doctor. Most of his friends will have noticed that Patrick was somewhat lame and this first adventure at sea accounted for it.

Patrick at one time was interested in diving and on one occasion when I was with him and the opportunity occurred at the Antwerp Exhibition he put on the Siebe-Gorman diving dress and went down into the tank, so as to have some experience of diving and decide whether to undertake some wider diving adventures in the Greek Archipelago.

In his ballooning days he had a small engineering laboratory at Bath which was known as experimental works. There he had some engineering machinery and also an astronomical telescope by Grubb, rigged up on the roof. This telescope was afterwards given by him to the City of Bath.''

After Patrick Alexander's death, the Imperial Service College properties in Alma Road, Windsor were sold, the part including King Edwards Horse Hall, the Classroom Block, and Rudyard Kipling Memorial Building being purchased by the Royal Borough of New Windsor, the latter building being used as Council offices until the formation of the Royal Borough of Windsor and Maidenhead who sold the site to Rank Hovis McDougall. They cleared the site and built their headquarters on the area, and incorporated the Rudyard Kipling Memorial plaque in the new building. None of the buildings Patrick Alexander knew have survived, except some nearby Victorian buildings that once formed part of the original St. Marks School.

Miss Schofield, his sole Executrix and beneficiary collected up the few remaining photographs, papers, mementoes and relics of his life and these were placed in the Windsor Guildhall Exhibition (now closed by the Windsor and Maidenhead Council) and in the Borough archives. These are now in the Berkshire Record Office, Shire Hall, Reading.

278

Haileybury and Imperial Service College erected a granite headstone above his grave in Windsor cemetary with an inscription from Longfellow of the past of which he formed a part:

"Something Attempted Something Done"

Postscript

Sydney Camm 1893-1966 and Patrick Alexander 1867-1943

The Royal Windsor Gaslight Works adjoined the Central Station (GWR) just west of the Castle. The gasworks were originally equipped to fill the private balloons of the Guards officers, including the famous Captain Burnaby, the "True Blue" in the 1860s.

Ascending balloons would float above a nearby terrace of houses in Alma Road, one of which was occupied by the Camm family, including Sydney Camm, the eldest son, who became intensely interested in aviation. He was to become Sir Sydney Camm, designer of the "Hurricane" fighter aeroplane of 1939/1945. The records of balloon ascents from the Goswell Gasworks at Windsor have been lost, but Patrick Alexander and other members of the Aeronautical Society and Aeronautical Club would know of the facilities and use them.

What did these two have in common? When Patrick Alexander came to Windsor in 1907 Sydney was 14 and soon to be apprenticed as a carpenter. The boy attending the Royal Free School, Windsor used to spend his breaks whittling propellers instead of playing football. The propellers were tested in the model aeroplanes he built and flew in the Home Park, under the walls of Windsor Castle. The Eton College boys used to go to the Home Park to watch the town boys fly their aeroplanes, and would order copies of models that took their fancy. In 1911, Sydney Camm founded the Windsor Model Aircraft Club. Alexander used to talk to some of the boys. He once said that when Wilbur and Orville Wright first flew in 1903, he lost interest in his ambition of being the first man to fly.

Patrick Alexander may have been the anonymous benefactor of the Windsor Model Aero and Gliding Club. This club was run on a shoestring, and was sometimes unable to pay the rent of seven and a half pence (one shilling and six old pence) per week for their premises - a shed in Arthur Road, Windsor. When as a result, the landlord locked the members out, Sydney Camm's younger brother tunnelled through the outer wall, removed their precious engine and other valuables, and rebuilt the wall so that the landlord was nonplussed as to how they gained entry. Shortly afterwards the W.M.A. & G.C. records refer to an unexpected donation from a local resident. As Patrick Alexander was living at the Imperial Service College, Alma Road, Windsor, the same road as the Camm family, the Club's plight may have come to his attention.

There were at least three things upon which they would agree - the fascination and importance of aviation, the importance of propeller design - they both gave talks on the subject - and the importance of reliable engines.

Alexander would have heard about the Camm boys' engine - all Windsor knew one day in 1913, when Sydney Camm bought for £25 an engine complete with propeller from Lilian Bland, the Irish aviatrix. It was an air cooled 20 b.h.p. AVRO Cowley with two opposed cylinders which fired simultaneously, and was therefore claimed to be "perfectly balanced."

Sydney Camm
Designer of the Hurricane fighter of the 1939-45 war

As soon as possible after it arrived from Ireland, the club members bolted it to Sydney Camm's father's work bench, in a shed behind the Camm residence. Dressed in Sunday best, straw hats and all, they took turns at swinging the prop when suddenly it started with an earsplitting unsilenced roar that brought the police to see who was spoiling the peace of a Sunday afternoon in Windsor. The engine sprayed everyone with oil, and being unbalanced, the workbench "walked" around the workshop, propeller flailing, and woodshavings flying - with the straw hats. The problem was how to stop the thing, which seemed to have a life of its own. The only casualties were some straw hats and a stiff warning from the police, followed by caustic comments in the Windsor Express.

The war of 1914/18 intervened in time to stop the boys completing, and risking their lives, in their powered glider which was broken up in 1919.

Two "Mystery" photographs in the Alexander archives
What are they?

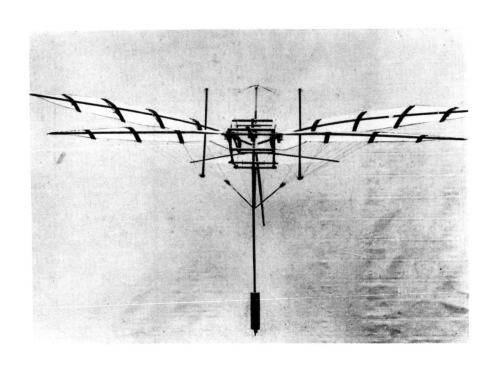

Model aeroplanes of 1910
- an advertisement from Alexander's files

Appendix

The Interests of Patrick Alexander

The Alexanders came from Gorbals, Lanarkshire, and his mother's family, the Youngs from Sansthorpe, Lincolnshire.

In 1912 Patrick Alexander had his "Family Tree" prepared back to the year 1618 for both the Alexander and Young families of his parents. There may have been the possiblity of an intestate inheritance, but some gaps made this unlikely to be proved. His address at the time was given as Whitehall Court in the City of Westminster.

He was elected a Fellow of the Royal Geographic Society in 1912, giving his address as The Writers Club, 2, Whitehall Court, London, and resigned in 1938. He only described himself once as F.R.G.S. when he was at Falmouth in 1917/18.

He was elected a member of the Royal Astronomical Society in 1921, but no records of active work have been found. He was, of course, active with his "Grubb" telescope at Bath and subsequently at Farnborough, where he donated the Army Observatory in 1906.

With the exception of a gap between 1909 and June 1917, he was a member of the Royal Meteorological Society from 1901 until 1938.

He was a member of the Aeronautical Society of Great Britain from 1901 until 1911, and their financial supporter to a most generous extent and for many years a member of the Aero Clubs of England (from April 1900), France, America Austria and Germany. He resigned from them all in 1907.

President of the Hampshire Aero Club in 1909.

Chairman and President of the Portsmouth Aero Club in 1909.

Vice President of the Bath Aero Club in 1912.

Member of the Aerial League of the British Empire during 1909/12.

BIBLIOGRAPHY

The Patrick Alexander Collection of Newspaper Cuttings on Aeronautics covering the period May 31st, 1892 to September 20th 1913. (Science Museum Library Archives: Shelf reference—B105, Callmark ALEX. Reader's Ticket required. The cuttings are fragile. Most have been microfilmed, and a microfilm copy, if available, will be provided for use in the library).

M.S. 380 *Alexander, Patrick;* A set of typewritten articles, 1889-1892.
Alexander, Patrick; "Alexander's Aeronautics". 1909.
Gibbs-Smith, C.H.; The Invention of the Aeroplane. 1966.
Gibbs-Smith, C.H.; Aviation; an Historical Survey. 1970.
Hobbs, Portia; Somerford Magna. 1982.
Hildebrandt, A.; Balloons and Airships. 1908 (Trans. 1973). (Berlin).
Penrose, Harald; British Aviation, The Pioneer Years. 1967.
Walker, Percy B.; Early Aviation at Farnborough. 1971.
Hurren, B.J.; Fellowship of the Air. 1951.
Gillispie, C.C.; The Montgolfier Brothers and the Invention of Aviation. 1983 (New Jersey).
Brewer, Griffith; Fifty Years of Flying. 1943.
White, Osmar; Under the Iron Rainbow. 1969. (Australia).
Broomfield, G.A.; Pioneer of the Air. 1953.
Lee, Arthur Gould; The Flying Cathedral. 1965.
Loobey, Patrick; Flights of Fancy. 1981.
Kelly, Fred C.; The Wright Brothers. 1943 (New York).
Renstrom, Arthur G.; Wilbur and Orville Wright, a Chronology. 1975 (Washington D.C.).
Brewer, Griffith and Alexander, Patrick; Aeronautics. 1893.
Rotch, A.L.; The St Petersburg Conference on the Exploration of the Atmosphere. 1904.
Beckwith, E.G.A.; A Short History of the First Twenty-One Years of the Imperial Service College. 1934.
Axten, J.W.; The Hon. Charles Stewart Rolls 1877-1910. 1977.

Edwards, Park; Celebrating the National Air and Space Smithsonian Museum. 1976 (Washington D.C.).
Aeronautics, Members of The Aero Clubs of America in Cartoon. 1908/09 (U.S.A.).
Hodgson, J.E.; The History of Aeronautics in Great Britain from the earliest times to the latter half of the nineteenth century. 1924.
The Harmsworth Encyclopedia. 1906.
Bacon, Rev. John M.; The Dominion of the Air.
Cole, Lieut. Col. Howard; The Story of Aldershot.

Periodicals:

Aeroplane Monthly; The Aeroplane; L'Aerophile; Bath Chronicle; Bath Herald; Bath and Wilts. Daily Chronicle; Bristol Industrial Archaeological Society Journal; The Car; Chronicle of the United Services College, St. Marks, Windsor; Daily Mail; Engineering; Flight; Gleanings in Bee Culture (Amos I. Root, Medina, Ohio); The Graphic; Illustrated London News; Journal of the Imperial Service College Old Boys Society; Journal of the Institution of Municipal Engineers 1912; Journal of the Royal Aeronautical Society; Journal of the Royal Cornwall Polytechnic Society; Reports of the Aeronautical Society; Scientific American; Sphere; Windsor Slough and Eton Express.

INDEX